MW00966703

SLAUGHTERHOUSE KID

SLAUGHTERHOUSE Kid

A Memoir

WENDELL W. CULTICE

ORANGE *frazer* PRESS
Wilmington, Ohio

ISBN 978-1939710-154

Copyright©2014 Wendell W. Cultice

No part of this publication may be reproduced in any material form (including photocopying or storing in any medium by electronic means and whether or not transiently or incidentally to some other use of this publication) without the written permission of the copyright holder except in accordance with the provisions of the Copyright, Designs and Patents Act 1988.

Published for Wendell Cultice by:
Orange Frazer Press
P.O. Box 214
Wilmington, OH 45177
Telephone: 800.852.9332 for price and shipping information.
Website: www.orangefrazer.com
www.orangefrazercustombooks.com

Book and cover design: Brittany Lament, Orange Frazer Press

Library of Congress Control Number 2014941037

To all the adult caregivers who patiently nurtured my youth,
imbuing me with the traditional values of respect for the
nobility of labor, moral accountability and patriotism,
and, as such, contoured my future.

—*WWC*

Cultice Meat Market, Cedarville, Ohio, 1915.

Acknowledgments

First and foremost, my love and thanks to my wife, Rebecca, who read each section as it was produced and assisted me—as she has done with previous publications—with sound advice. I acknowledge with genuine appreciation my obligation to Elizabeth Studebaker who shared with me her profound knowledge of journalism and publication savvy.

—*WWC*

Interior of Cultice Meat Market, 1918.

Contents

FOREWORD xiii
PREFACE xv
A BUMPY BEGINNING 2
BACKWARD HOGS 3
SUNDAY MORNING 4
HOME 6
MOVING TO THE COUNTRY 8
TREE HOUSE 10
ON TASK 11
FARM DOCTOR 13
SATURDAY NIGHT BATH 14
SUNDAY AFTERNOON 16
PIG TA(I)LES 18
OUR TIN LIZZIE 20
HAPPY WARRIORS 23
HOLY SUNSHINE 24
RECIPROCITY 26
THE BIG SCHOOL 27
THE SANCTUARY 32
SHAWNEE INDIANS 33
FOR THE LOVE OF REBECCA 35
EARLY DELIVERY 36
UNCLE REMUS 38
WORK, WORK, AND PLAY 41
GETTING TO THE "BIGS" 43
ON "SMITTY" 45
GRANDPA SANDY 46
SHOTGUN REVELRY 51
GLAD RAGS 52
HOLIDAY EVENTS 54
HOMEMADE GUNS 59
SETTING THE TABLE 60
MY HEROES 61
HOME ON THE RANGE 64
HOME GAMES 66
AWAY GAMES 67

EARLY HISTORY LESSON 69
A NEW ARRIVAL 71
ANIMAL SHELTER 71
HOLD ON 73
SPECIAL TREATS 74
BILL QUIRK 75
LOVING PIGS 76
FINDLAW FAMILY 78
GRANDMA'S LAMENT 79
SUPPER SLIPS 81
FAULTY EQUIPMENT 82
THE GREAT FLOOD 84
TRAINS CAN BE DANGEROUS! 85
JUNIOR CHEF 86
WHAT'S IN A NAME? 87
SPEEDWAY 88
THE BIG PARADE 89
THE DOCTOR IS OUT! 91
FIRST FUNERAL 93
TRY AGAIN 94
MY FRIEND FROGGY 96
SINGING FOR COOKIES 97
SASSAFRAS 99
MOTHER GOES TO HEAVEN 100
STRAIGHT TO HEAVEN 102
SPOTS ALSO GOES TO HEAVEN 103
ROYAL FLUSH 104
KING AND PRINCE 105
SPECIAL SUPPER 106
IS EVERYBODY GOING TO DIE? 108
SUMMER 109
HEAVENLY SOLES 110
CHARLIE SIMMS 112
USE YOUR NAPKIN 114
MORE PIG TA(I)LES 115
MRS. KNOCKA 117
THE SLAUGHTERHOUSE KID 118
A BUSHEL OF LOVE 119
NEVER ON SUNDAY 121
THE HOLIDAY CRISIS 123
WE BROTHERS LEND A HAND 124
SLEEPING LOVER 126
SIXTEEN 127
SPELLING BEE 128
THE NEW ERA 129
NATURE'S LABORATORY 132
THE FULL HOUSE 134
ECONOMIC TURN AROUND 137

LOOKING AHEAD 138
A TRUE FISH STORY 140
RECITATION 142
HILL TALK 142
"HAIR" TODAY, GONE TOMORROW 144
HOLY CHITTLIN'S 147
RITE OF PASSAGE 150
REYNARD 152
SLIM AND FRANK 153
RIDING SHOTGUN 155
MIDNIGHT LOVERS 157
BIG DISCOVERY 159
CHICAGO 161
A HEARTY BREAKFAST 162
ON THE PLATFORM 164
SPRING 166
STEP AND A HALF 167
SUMMER FUN 168
MY FAVORITE TEACHER 170
LEARNING EVERY DAY 171
HIDE AND SHOES 172
'TIS THE SEASON(ING) 173
A GOOD BREAK 175
CITIZENSHIP 176
KEEP 'EM SMILING 178
SPRING HAS SPRUNG 179
SHOW AND DON'T TELL 180
BIG BROTHER 181
LAUGH AND PLAY 183
BUTCHER BOY 185
POLITICS AND PRACTICE 186
SQUIRREL FEVER 188
HISTORIC WORDS 190
STANDING TALL 191
CHANGE 193
COUNTY FAIR 194
SCHOOL'S OPEN 195
THE WRONG LETTERS 197
GEORGIA PEACH 198
BONDING 199
STILL GROWING 200
HUMILIATION 201
MORE SQUIRREL FEVER 203
DIRECT COUNSELING 204
GIRLS 206
PEERS 207
A FAVORITE SUBJECT 209
BADGE OF INNOCENCE 210

DON'T ASK 213
HAPPY HOLIDAYS 214
CONSPIRACY? 217
ROOM FOR ONE MORE 218
HORSING AROUND 220
HE'S MY BROTHER 221
PRACTICE MAKES PERFECT 223
POINT OF PRAYER? 224
CAST IN BRONZE 227
REALITY 229
POTENTIAL? 231
HEAVEN, HOMINY, HISTORY, AND HIGHER LEARNING 233
THIRTY DAYS 238
POST HIGH SCHOOL 240
LOST INNOCENCE 241
A COVENANT WITH GOD 243
POST SCRIPT 245
GLOSSARY 248
ABOUT THE AUTHOR 253

Foreword

This memoir, written for his posterity, represents a "post-hole" approach to the author's young life and events between World War I and World War II.

It profiles his everyday life in a small, rural, Midwestern community.

The memoir reflects how he lived; where he attended school; what he ate and drank; how he worked; the way he spent his leisure time; and, finally, how he became aware of the local, national, and international events that were shaping his world.

The author acknowledges that he remembers events and individuals better than dates. However, every effort was made to record the events in this work in chronological order.

Out of respect some names have been altered.

Preface

After a courtship of nearly four years, my parents were married in a small church in Greene County, Ohio, in June of 1915. Family legend holds that my mother was pregnant within an hour after they recited their wedding vows. At the time, my father was twenty-three and my mother twenty-two years of age.

My father, of German ancestry and the son of a butcher, had served as an apprentice to a friend of his

Left page: Four generations, L to R: Fidelia Mullen; Hilda (Mullen) Cultice; Rachel (Hyitt) Peacock; James Winston Cultice, age 8 months—Winchester, Indiana, 1916.
Right page: My father graduated from Clifton Union School in 1909; William Walter Cultice, age 24, Cedarville, Ohio.

father's during the interim of his high school years. Within five years after graduation he owned a small slaughterhouse at the edge of the village of Cedarville with a retail outlet on the main street. He was, in the eyes of his siblings, peers, and local denizens, an enterprising young man whose future appeared to be manifest destiny.

Between her junior and senior high school years, my mother attended advanced classes at Antioch College in Yellow Springs, Ohio, in preparation for a career in teaching. It was here, while driving his older sister, Nellie, to and from the campus on weekends that my father was introduced to his future bride.

My mother, an only child, was a descendant of a very cultured Quaker family from Richmond, Indiana, with the surname of Peacock. She completed high school, passed the teacher's examination, and taught three years in Wayne Township, Indiana, prior to their marriage. While the courtship may have been too geographically unsuitable for some suitors, my father, according to my mother's diary, did not seem to waiver in his affections.

My mother graduated from Xenia Central High School in 1911; Hilda (Peacock) Mullen, Xenia, Ohio, 1913.

Following their marriage, they moved into a two-bedroom house within walking distance of my father's retail meat market. At that place, on March 5, 1916, exactly nine months and seven days after their wedding, their first child and my oldest brother, James Winston, was born. Two years and two months later, my brother Lowell was born.

Even though my father had registered for the military draft in World War I, he was never called into actual service.

By April of 1920, my mother was advised by our family doctor, Jim Harris, that she might anticipate giving birth to twins in the latter part of July. This revelation mandated at least one more bedroom. My twin sisters, Evelyn Belle and Rachel Nelle, were born on July 18, 1920, in a three-bedroom house directly across the street from my paternal grandparents in the same small village. My parents resided here until the fall of 1921, when they moved approximately eight miles south to the small town of Xenia, Ohio.

This property, located approximately one mile from my mother's parents, included a moderate-sized barn where my father could engage in seasonal custom butchering. In addition, in cooperation with his father-in-law, he could participate in construction work during the building season.

Shortly after closing his lunch box while working at a building site on the west side of town on May 22, 1922, my father was notified that his wife had gone into labor; Mrs. Sadie Hall was in attendance, and Dr. Jim Harris was on his way down from Clifton.

Thus, at sometime in the early afternoon, I interrupted the two-year, two- month birth interval that had prevailed for my older siblings. My parents, however, were soon able to reestablish the birth interim, and my youngest brother, Henry Dale, first saw the light of day on June 12, 1924.

My father's sisters, L to R: Susan Grace, Nellie Mae, Laura Elizabeth, and Dorothy Aline, 1915.

SLAUGHTERHOUSE KID

A BUMPY Beginning

Rachel "Runt" & Evelyn "Ev" Cultice, Xenia, Ohio, March 1922.

When my twin sisters, twenty months my senior, were informed that they had a baby brother, they were able to verbalize only two-thirds of the gender. Thus, within my family, relatives, neighbors, and playmates, I would carry the moniker of "Bo." According to my parents, my sisters were ecstatic to have a new doll in the house and quickly assumed the role of surrogate mothers. They were thrilled that their new doll, "Bo," always cried when he was hungry and sometimes after he had wet his "three-cornered pants." They were very disappointed, however, that he was too large to fit into their small doll cradles.

One morning, when I was nearly two weeks old, my mother sent my brother, Lowell, age four, to an upstairs bedroom to determine if I was still sleeping. Since I was awake, he took me out of my crib and carried me to the top of the stairs in the hallway. He then called to our mother indicating that I was awake and hungry. By this time, our mother, standing at the bottom of the stairs, shouted, "Lowell! Put him down right away!" My brother immediately dropped me at the edge of the hall landing, and I rolled, unassisted, the full fourteen steps into my mother's trembling arms. Years later, my father told me that each time my head thumped against a stair tread my mother screamed for me to stop rolling.

My twin sisters, Evelyn B. and Rachel N. were born in this house on July 18, 1920, Cedarville, Ohio.

My father also told me that about a month before my first birthday, my sister Evelyn was holding me in the front porch swing when one of the ceiling hooks pulled out and we were both dumped off the porch into the rose bushes.

Shortly before my second birthday, Mike Murray, who lived next door, took me for a ride in his brother's coaster wagon. Fortunately, for all concerned, it rolled over at the end of his driveway, near where his mother was standing at the mailbox.

The stork stopped at our home one month following my second birthday and my sisters, following two years of surrogate- motherhood experience, turned their attention to their new "doll" who also cried when he was hungry and sometimes when he wet his "three-cornered pants."

In retrospect, these were rather tranquil years in my life when contrasted with my older brothers' plans for my future.

Backward Hogs

On the north side of our house the driveway passed only a few feet from our kitchen window. As such, I was curious to learn what happened to the hogs in the back of my father's Model T Ford truck after he backed it into the barn. My queries to my mother about the disposition of the squealing animals received only cursory and/ or furtive responses.

The answer to my curiosity came at breakfast on a cold November day in 1925. My father, at my oldest brother's urging, agreed to allow me to accompany them to Coyle's farm to pick up two hogs to be custom butchered.

We returned with the hogs, backed up the driveway, and my father and I sat in the truck while my brother jumped out and quickly opened the barn doors. Once in the barn, the hogs were encouraged to scurry down a ramp into a very small, three-rail enclosure.

My father quickly checked the fire under a large cauldron of water and determined that the animals could be slaughtered before we were called into the house for our noon meal. Employing a large, long-handled dipper, he proceeded to empty the hot water from the cauldron into a recessed barrel in the floor of the barn. He then sat down on a wooden box, removed his shoes, and pulled on a pair of rubberized knee boots. Next, he removed a rubberized apron from a nail above the box and tied it securely behind his back. Walking a few steps toward a cabinet that was nailed to the wall, he removed a rifle and two .22-caliber shells and walked directly toward the hog enclosure. At short range, he aimed the rifle at an imaginary cross between the first hog's ears and eyes. At the explosion, the hog squealed, lunged forward, and rolled on its side with its body trembling and feet flailing off the pen floor. Without a hitch, the scene was repeated a second time.

Quickly, my father stepped over the low pen rail, grasped the first hog by one of its front legs, rolled it nearly on its back, pulled a long thin knife from his belt, and plunged it deep into the animal's girth. Even before the blade was completely withdrawn, a fountain of crimson blood gushed out upon his hand and bare arm. In very quick fashion, the second hog was also gasping its final breath in a crimson pool on the pen floor.

At this juncture of the process, my father sent me into the house to tell my mother that he and my brother would need to have their noon meal placed in the warming oven.

While it would be some time before I would witness the remainder of the slaughtering steps, it would never again be necessary for me to ask my mother about what happened to the hogs that rode backward into the barn.

SUNDAY Morning

Following completion of our chores and breakfast on Sunday morning, a typical day would consist of taking a "spit-bath" at the cistern pump in the kitchen, changing into our Sunday clothes, piling into the family Model T Ford touring machine, and riding about a mile to a small Methodist church located on a corner lot.

Upon arrival, my parents and little brother went directly up the front steps and into the sanctuary. The remaining five of us took a sidewalk past the left side of the church and entered the Sunday school building where a grown-up greeted us by our first names and directed us to a particular room. Mr. Wallace, our teacher, was a gentleman who appeared to be very adept at quoting scripture and keeping us from painting one another with our watercolor brushes. When class concluded, we raced back around the church, up the front steps, into the sanctuary, and filed quietly into the back right pew under the watchful eyes of our parents.

I don't recall that this pew had our name on it; however, it was occasionally referred to as "Walter's Pew." When the offertory plate was passed along our pew, we children would hold our hands as high above it as possible before releasing a few pennies into it. This practice seemed to embarrass our mother and amuse the folks sitting in this corner of the church.

When the ladies of our church smiled during the service, they generally attempted to conceal their amusement by holding those ever-present, hand fans with the funeral parlor advertisement on either side in front of their faces. On a rather warm Sunday morning, my brother Winston set all of the fans in our corner of the church in motion, embarrassed our entire family, and

Our family joined the Trinity Methodist Church in Xenia, Ohio, in 1922.

further added to Reverend Simpson's demise when he bounced a gigantic fart off the seat of that oak wood pew. If it had not been for the unmistakable sound, our mother's attempt at concealment might have saved the morning. She quickly sniffed the backside of my baby brother's diaper and took off for the restroom in the narthex. But when Joe Jacobs, a well-known and long-time fart offender in that corner of the church, got up out of his pew and pushed the window open another foot, there was no doubt in anyone's mind that the culprit was sitting in Walter's pew. On our ride home from church, Lowell pointed his finger at Winston and recited the following verse that was well-known to brothers and sisters alike:

Beans, beans the musical fruit
The more you eat, the more you toot.
The more you toot, the better you feel
So, let's have beans for every meal!

Aside from a few incidents such as the aforementioned, church was pretty conventional. After church, we quickly returned home, changed clothes, and awaited our Sunday afternoon instructions with regard to work assignments, a short family trip, or, hopefully, an extended period of playtime.

Cultice Family Portrait, December 1925. L to R: Lowell R., William Walter, Evelyn B., Wendell W., Rachel N., Hilda M., Henry D., and James Winston.

Home

The house where I was born was located on Columbus Street at the southeast corner of the city. The only houses were on the west side of the street. After you crossed a small creek, there were only three more houses before the street intersected a state route. The east side of the street was fenced and was the west line of Eavey's large farm.

Our house had a relatively small front lawn. However, Murray's house, which was between our house and the creek, had a very large lawn, and their driveway ran alongside our south fence. The Murrays had two older daughters and two sons, Spike and Mike, who were the same age as my little brother Hank and me. All four of us spent a lot of time playing in Murray's front yard which was visible from the kitchen windows of our respective houses. Our activities would sometimes cause us to migrate toward the dump near the creek in search of hidden treasure. These were very short searches since they always seemed to activate one or two voices calling for an immediate return to the lawn. One time, when our mother had given my sister Rachel and me

several cans to carry to the dump, I became angry and threw a can at her which left a small cut on her forehead.

When we four boys had parlayed a few days of extra good behavior, all four of us would be permitted to go in a group across the bridge and past Mr. Walker's house to play with Victor and Don Brown who lived in the last house. Mr. Walker, even to us, seemed strange, and we guessed that's why we could only go to Brown's in a group.

Spike and Mike were instrumental in our parent's lecturing Hank and me on the dangers of our Maytag washer. One day Mike had been missing for more than an hour when his mother found him sleeping soundly, curled up around the agitator in their Maytag on the back porch. I guess the message I received was, "If the washtub has wheels on it, you don't wash kids in it."

Approximately a half-mile southwest of our home was the four hundred acre state orphanage which served the children of soldiers and sailors. These children were shaken out of their beds, marched to duty and school, and put to bed with the loud sound from the steam whistle located at the orphanage's power plant. Except for meals, our home appeared to be on the same schedule as the orphanage.

Murrays had a small bulldog, Tippy, who would occasionally run away from home. According to Mr. Murray, Tippy went "to visit his slut girlfriend at the orphanage." Shortly after one of Tippy's visits, he was reticent to frolic with us in the yard. When we asked why, Mr. Murray explained to us that he had had an accident at the orphanage, and that Tippy would probably not be going back to the orphanage to visit his girlfriend, Slut. My brother Winston, however, was more to the point, when he said that some of the older boys at the orphanage had caught Tippy and castrated him. When I asked my mother what the word "castrated" meant, she told me to wait until my father arrived home and ask him. My father, in language that he thought my inquisitive mind would understand, told me that it meant that Tippy wouldn't ever be married or a daddy. I guessed he was saying that, if you have a girlfriend and intend to get married and be a daddy someday, you ought to make sure that she doesn't live in an orphanage.

MOVING TO THE Country

In 1925, my two older brothers were attending a four-year elementary school that was within walking distance of our home. Sometime during early winter, my father announced that in the spring we would be moving to a farm nearly two miles from our present location. My mother explained to me that my grandparents' home was about halfway between where we lived and where we were going. She also informed me that in addition to the dog and few chickens that we now had, we would probably have ducks, cows, and horses.

With my older siblings away at school and my brother sleeping late and too small to travel, these were special days for me because I had my mother and father all to myself. Sometimes, my mother would bundle me up so that I could ride with my father during pickups and deliveries. Of course, when my brothers and sisters returned from school, I was somewhat "lost" in the maze of domestic activites.

The gravel road leading out of the city to our new house passed the north fence line of my grandparents' orchard and continued past our place for a half-mile to another county road. The homes on the west end of this road that were within the city limits had electric power and telephones. My father planned to have the farm equipped with these utilities during an addition to the house and construction of several sheds and a small slaughterhouse.

The city of Xenia had grown very much in the shape of a horseshoe, and our farm was geographically located at the open end. Directionally, our world growing up on the farm was four-dimensional. On the south side of our road was a large farm which was always occupied by large, itinerate families. These playmates would invariably be a well-spring of new "cuss words" and highly vulnerable to our practical jokes and innovative games.

Back to the west was the city where, following an early Saturday evening bath before an open oven door, we would sometimes take the horse and wagon to see a silent western movie at the Orpheum Theater.

Four major railroad lines passed a few yards beyond our entire north fence line. The coal cargo from these trains, unbeknownst to our parents, would be a major source of fuel at our house for several years. Beyond this, the freight line consistently accommodated a plethora of hobos who walked a short distance to our house seeking work, food, water, and sleeping accommodations in the hayloft.

We children frequently gathered at the pump house and listened attentively as they spun their individual and collective tales of adventure. In fact, I'm sure that we knew their hieroglyphical sign language before we knew the alphabet.

On the other side of our entire east fence line was a large swamp surrounded by a densely wooded area.

This area was a haven for lovers, bootleggers, Model T Ford thieves, and roving bands of gypsies. Our parents quickly issued a "do-not-climb-over" edict with regard to this end of our farm. We children worked diligently to convince our parents that the turtles and frogs in the swamp and the blackberries and raspberries in the thicket were bigger and tasted better than those in our own Shawnee Creek area.

Within the confines of this "rural world," I enjoyed the affection and approbation of my parents, the camaraderie of my siblings, and vocational training important to our family's everyday life.

Tree House

"Now, little brother, when you drive the nails back out of these boards, you need to place a short piece of wood like this on the underside of the board. Then, after you pull them out with these pliers, you put them in this empty coffee can. If the nails are bent, you place them on this rock, watching out for your fingers, and straighten them with the hammer." Thus began my vocational training under the tutelage of my oldest brother who was all of ten years of age.

Our family had just relocated to a small farm on the edge of the city, and my two older brothers had taken on the ambitious project of building a tree house in a large elm tree which was located approximately one hundred yards northeast of our barn. The tree stood on the bank of a small tributary which emptied into Shawnee Creek at the northern edge of our farm.

Shortly after relocating to this farm, my father razed the standing 6' x 8' poultry coop and replaced it with a modern, two-room poultry building. Given access to the salvaged lumber, it was moved a few boards at a time to the base of the elm tree.

The major fork in the tree where the tree house was to be located was nearly twenty feet above the ground. Therefore, ably assisted by two older boys from an adjacent farm, it became necessary to build a staging platform on the front horizontal limb level which was about nine feet above the ground.

The building plan called for the poultry coop to be reconstructed in its original form, i.e. it was to be 6 x 8 feet in size. This, of course, would reduce the need to saw most of the boards. However, this could only happen if the foundation planks were plumbed to accommodate them. Again, ably assisted by the two brothers from across the road, a series of guy wires were employed to strengthen smaller branches, and a solid 6' x 8' floor frame, consisting of 2" x 6" boards, was nailed and/or suspended twenty feet above the ground.

After many days of anticipation, the box frame of the original coop was in place and work was begun on the tree house roof. The roof was to serve as a lookout for intruders. Therefore, it would need to be of flat design. In addition, it would be necessary to build a trap door in order to gain access to the roof from inside the tree house. The vertical siding was quickly installed, and the original window and door, including hinges, were secured, and a small, two-by-three stoop was constructed beneath the door.

When the tree house was nearly complete, my brother Winston, in the absence of our father, nearly convinced the utility workers electrifying the farm buildings to install a line pole between the barn and the large elm tree in order to have an electric light in the tree house. Unfortunately for my brothers, our father returned home while the workers were digging the post hole.

So there it was, every boy's dream—a large tree house, high off the ground with supporting limbs passing through it, an escape door to the roof, a glass window, and a walk-through entrance. In addition, it was visible from any place on the farm, including the east-west road that bordered our property. Later, a small hole was cut into the roof to accommodate the pipe for a miniature cast-iron stove, and a small table was hinged to an interior wall.

While I was not old enough to fully appreciate my brothers' sense of accomplishment, I'm reasonably sure that they felt confident that they had sent a cogent message to the surrounding neighbor boys that they were true Huck-Finn-type lads looking for a place to express themselves.

ON Task

In the tradition of his German ancestors, my father wasted little time in establishing an apprenticeship program for his children. If his rural enterprise was to enjoy a measure of success, it was essential that we children, individually and collectively, shoulder a dimension of the work. He was so very convincing in his theory that we children

My father and an older playmate, Clifton, Ohio, circa 1896.

earned our playtime only after successfully completing our assigned tasks.

About a year after our relocation, with the addition of the slaughterhouse, woodshed, poultry house, and three-hole privy, the work assignments were well established.

My sisters would serve a routine, domestic apprenticeship under the watchful eye and talented hand of our mother. Outside the house they had a choice, which they frequently exercised, of where they would spend their time and talents. My father preferred that his daughters be spared the masculine task of mucking-out the stables, driving the manure spreader, etc. In fact, my sisters were only required to bring the bedroom thunder mugs to the inside of the back porch door. The emptying and rinsing of these essential items was the responsibility of his sons.

We boys, under the watchful eye and work-hewn hands of our father, would serve a five-point apprenticeship that began at the pump house and passed through the poultry house, woodshed, livestock barn, and culminated in the many and varied basic labor tasks of the slaughterhouse. We, too, in times of seasonal demands or emergencies would broaden our responsibilities to one, or more, of the other four stations.

The pump house responsibility mandated a full pail of water be brought into the kitchen each morning before leaving for school and a repeat performance after the evening meal.

The poultry house assignment embraced the chores of feeding, watering, gathering eggs, and attending to newly-hatched baby chicks in a cardboard box behind the kitchen stove. I, however, did not look forward to the onerous task of removing the manure from the roosting room.

My brother Lowell, at age nine, reigned over the woodshed, and my eleven-year-old brother Winston assumed responsibility for the livestock barn.

The woodshed apprenticeship involved splitting wood and kindling, filling the wood boxes in the living room and kitchen, emptying the ashes from the respective stoves, and advising my father of the need to re-supply. P.S. My brother had already learned that my father would get you out of your bed late at night if he entered the kitchen and discovered that there was an insufficient supply of kindling or wood to make breakfast.

While the livestock barn assignment, by its very nature, had a few unpleasant details, it was varied and fun. The idea of serenading a reluctant milk cow on a cold winter morning would not be appealing for even the most adventurous lad, but the possibility that one might impale a sleeping hobo on a pitchfork while tossing hay down from the dark loft certainly gave the assignment a rural mystique.

In the winter, during these apprenticeships, we boys would be expected to work several hours each week in the slaughterhouse. In my father's local "guild system" of "each one, teach one" we learned a specific skill(s), a solid work ethic, the ability to take instruction, and most of all, to dignify the slaughtering of animals.

FARM Doctor

Shortly after we settled in on the farm, my father purchased our first cow. Almost at the same time, my grandparents and Mr. Bell, who lived near them, offered a kind of "loan-a-cow" program to my father. These parties would each purchase a cow for my father to range and maintain on the farm in exchange for a quart of milk every other day. I learned of this agreement when my brother Winston exclaimed to our father that he could not milk Bell's cow because she could not stand on her feet. When my father responded that he would call Dr. Ayers, a respected area veterinarian, I felt the need for more information. Since I had always associated sickness with our family doctor, Dr. Harris, why couldn't he come and make Mr. Bell's cow better? My brother explained to me that a farm doctor only treated animals and was not allowed to use those tools in his bag on people.

From a designated position in the box stall manger, I was permitted to observe my first animal husbandry laboratory experiment. Dr. Ayers had my father and brother retrieve and secure a pulley and rope above the cow, tie one end of the rope to a used automobile tire, slip the tire up over her legs and rear-end, and methodically pull the cow to a standing position. He then took a long sticklike-object from his large black satchel, placed a big white pill in the end, and forced the pill down the cow's throat. Even though I was not deemed old enough to participate, it was a most exciting event which would surely hold my city friends in awe. Besides this, I had learned several new "barnyard" words that might further impress them.

Subsequently, Dr. Ayers would be called to our farm to cure livestock, dehorn cattle, or ring young pigs. However, my observation of the doctor's castration of boar pigs probably made the most lasting impression on my young mind. My brother Hank and I watched this event through the horizontal rails of the sty. My older brothers, Winston and Lowell, would seize a pig by its hind legs, turn it backwards, pull it up, and render it immobile by tightly squeezing it between their legs. At this juncture of the surgical procedure, with the pigs squealing and Dr. Ayers cursing above their objection, he would cut a vertical incision on each side of the pig's scrotum and remove the boar's "batteries."

I do not remember discussing the experience with my little brother. It seemed to me that at least this aspect of it ought to be learned. One, someday we would be holding those pigs where our brothers had been holding them. Two, someday a farm doctor would be cutting about as close to our privates as those of the pigs. Finally, and maybe more importantly, that if the doctor's about to remove your testicles, don't try to get away and yell because, if you do, he will probably call you a bad name.

SATURDAY NIGHT Bath

At our house, not unlike the homes of practically all the people we knew, the week, by necessity, was divided into days designed for designated chores. No activity was more religiously adhered to than the "ritual" of the Saturday night bath. It was probably referred to as a ritual at our house because it was almost impossible to discuss any facet of the event without mentioning that one was going to Sunday school and church the next day.

In retrospect, I guess the ritualistic view was closely allied with the clean underwear-hospital parable that was employed at other times. In this case, of course, it was not necessary because the clean underwear, when one had them, conventionally followed a bath.

The ritual generally began at about four-thirty in the afternoon when we boys would set up a "bucket brigade" from the pump house, across the back porch, and into the kitchen. After filling the reservoir on the right side of the stove, we would fill two or three additional vessels. Before we sat down to our evening meal, my brothers, ably assisted by my father, would lift these vessels onto the stove.

Then about seven o'clock, the culinary utilization of the kitchen was quickly converted to bathing. The table and chairs were pushed to the north end of the kitchen. A splash blanket was spread on the floor before the stove and a large, galvanized tub was placed on the blanket and filled about one-third with hot water. A small bucket of "temper" or cold water was placed near the tub. Nearby was a kitchen chair with several towels draped over the top slat. On the seat of the chair were a large bar of Fels Naptha soap and a well-worn washrag.

Short of special circumstances, my sisters would bathe first, put on their nightgowns, retreat to their upstairs bedroom, and do whatever girls do after bathing until their ten-o'clock bedtime. After our mother had added a couple of ladles of hot water to the tub, my baby brother and I would follow. When we were finished and had responded to our mother's standard question, "Have you washed behind your ears and under your foreskin?," we would pull on our clean long-johns, were sent upstairs to our two double-bed bedroom, and did whatever little brothers do while their older brothers are bathing downstairs.

My brothers also bathed in reverse chronological order. However, they were authorized, subject to the viscosity of the tub contents, to empty the tub and pour in fresh water before they bathed, if they thought it necessary.

Since we children were always upstairs behind closed bedroom doors, we could only speculate relative to the ritualistic bathing of our parents. We always assumed since the vessels were empty the following morning that my father emptied the tub, refilled it, and while my mother bathed, stood sentry at the foot of the stairs near the kitchen door. Then, as my father bathed, our mother assumed the sentry post at the foot of the stairs. This was the conclusion we drew since brothers and sisters alike, we had already established that the bathtub would not simultaneously accommodate two persons. Several aspects of this Saturday night ritual perplexed my young mind. Firstly, are girls cleaner than boys because they always bathe in clean water? Secondly, while I could understand that on Sunday morning my teacher or preacher might possibly look behind my ears, it never occurred to me that they would be looking under my foreskin.

SUNDAY Afternoon

At our noon meal on Sunday there would sometimes be a round-table discussion about what we would like to do in the afternoon. As children, it took us quite a while to understand that this "discussion" was a rather circuitous method of telling us what we were really going to do on that particular afternoon. When the discussion concluded that there was nothing of interest for the whole family, it signaled, for all of us brothers anyway, that we would be engaged in a non-daily or non-weekly chore of some type. We boys would readily draw this conclusion because we knew that, at home or away, we were prohibited from engaging in any type of athletic activities on Sunday.

It appeared to be permissible, however, as our parents relaxed on the porch swing for brothers and sisters to engage in assorted games of tag on the lawn. Sometimes our mother would have us pick flowers. After wrapping the stems in wet newspaper, we would all pile into our Model T-Ford open touring machine and visit a cemetery where relatives and friends were interred. On site, we would attempt to elicit funny stories from our parents about the individuals resting there. I recall that my mother, noting that a designated military grave did not have a flower on it, would gently place a flower on the grave, then clasp her hands before her, close her eyes, and silently move her lips. In response to our queries about what our mother was saying, our father said he did not know what our mother was saying; however, she was being very patriotic. Thereafter, our Sunday afternoon visits to the cemeteries would be proposed at the noonday meal as "patriotic rides." In fact, we learned that being patriotic was a good way to avoid undesirable work assignments on Sunday afternoon.

A favorite Sunday afternoon form of family excitement would involve a picnic and fishing. Immediately after church, our mother would pack a large picnic basket that included cold, fried chicken and potato salad, and we'd drive to the edge of the Little Miami River and spend the afternoon fishing, playing games with new playmates, and enjoying "fish tales" told by grown-ups. These "fish tales" always seemed to be bigger and better when the other grown-ups laughed the loudest.

Another Sunday afternoon pastime would have us all travel in our "machine" to an air base about ten miles from our home to watch those "air machines" take off and land. Grandpa Sandy would later warn us that if we didn't stop staring up at those new contraptions with our mouths wide open, we might just get sunburn on the roofs of our mouths.

Sometimes Uncle Joel, Grandpa Jim's brother, and his wife Louisa would visit our house on Sunday afternoon.

Henry Ford produced the ten-millionth Model T the same year I was born, 1922.

Uncle Joel had a hearing impediment so our mother would remind us to speak loudly during their visit. When they departed, Uncle Joel would crank up their touring machine and wait patiently for Aunt Louisa to come out of the house. Before too long she would come out of the house. As she approached the "machine," she would cup her hands to her mouth and yell, "Joel, did you piss yet?" At that moment, we children, boys and girls alike, would roll on the ground in convulsive laughter. We couldn't help ourselves. We soon understood that Uncle Joel's hearing problem was not as serious as his water problem.

Pork parts demystified.

PIG Ta(i)les

During the summer of 1927 my father's small slaughterhouse was constructed at the edge of our road. By the first frost, it would be filled with the squeals of pigs. It was a very modest building, approximately 40 x 60 feet in area. Adjacent to the building were several small livestock pens and a ramp at the rear, which led to a slotted deck above a tankage waste pit. Basically, the floor plan included four rooms. The largest room, located in the southeast corner, was the butchering room. The animals were killed, scalded, cleaned, eviscerated, and split into halves in this room. The carcasses, suspended from an overhead track, were then pushed into a slightly smaller "cut up room" where they were reduced to fresh pork hams, shoulders, loins, side, etc. This room also accommodated the sausage-making equipment, including the seasonings and recipes, which were securely locked in a corner cabinet. The excess fat and skin that was trimmed from the carcasses in this room was further reduced into small squares or pieces known as lard cutting to be cooked or rendered.

The smallest of the four rooms, the curing room, partially covered a cool basement. The curing process took place at the floor level, and then the pork parts were lowered by hand into the basement and tightly packed into heavy wooden barrels.

The fourth room, located in the northeast section of the building contained the lard-rendering kettle and the smokehouse. Just a few steps outside the north door there was a large pile of assorted wood that fueled the lard-rendering kettle. Also near the north door was a small shed that contained only apple, hickory, and maple woods, which were all pivotal to the proper smoking of cured meats.

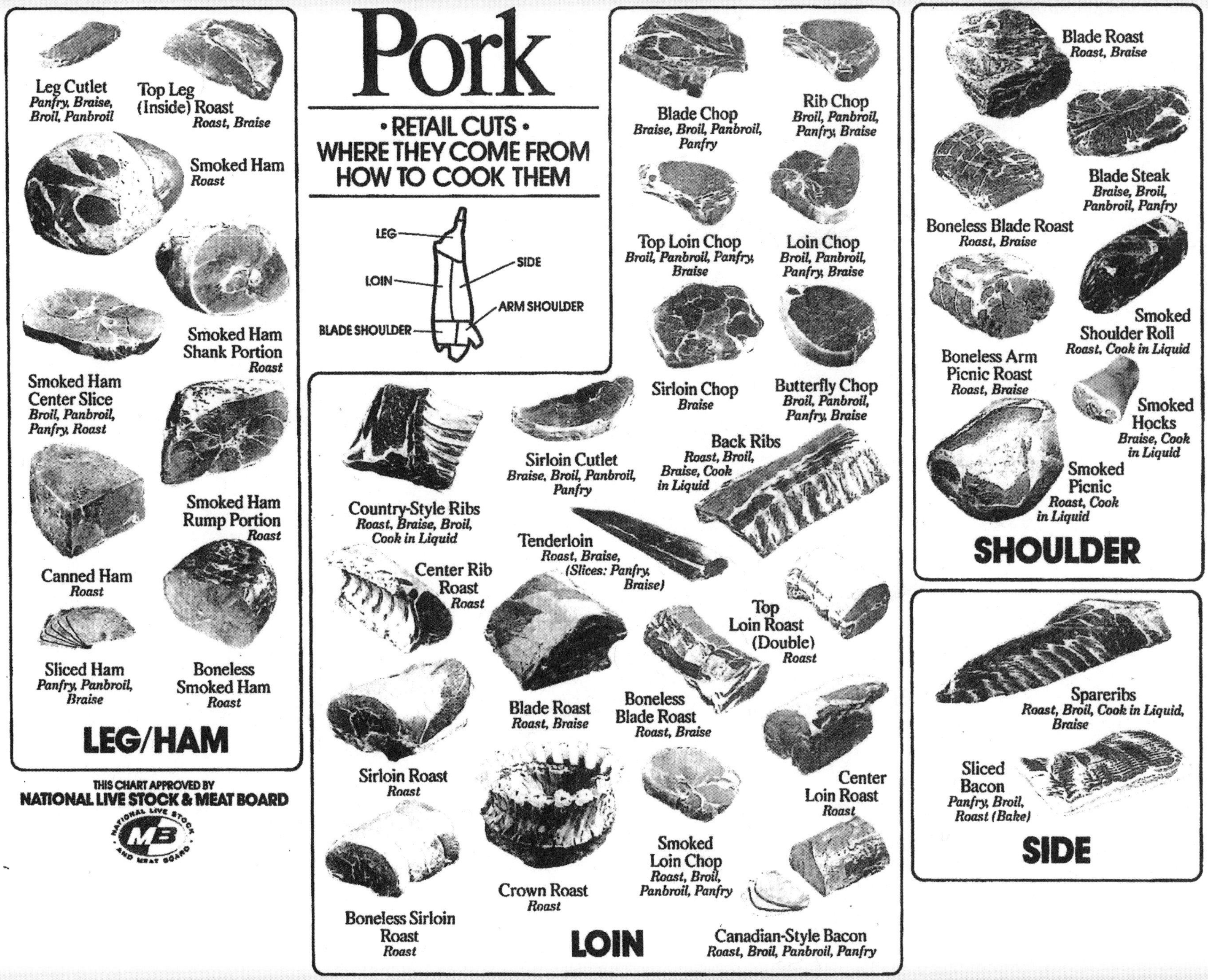
Pork
• RETAIL CUTS •
WHERE THEY COME FROM
HOW TO COOK THEM
LEG
LOIN
BLADE SHOULDER
SIDE
ARM SHOULDER
Leg Cutlet
Panfry, Braise, Broil, Panbroil
Top Leg (Inside) Roast
Roast, Braise
Smoked Ham
Roast
Smoked Ham Shank Portion
Roast
Smoked Ham Center Slice
Broil, Panbroil, Panfry, Roast
Smoked Ham Rump Portion
Roast
Canned Ham
Roast
Sliced Ham
Panfry, Panbroil, Braise
Boneless Smoked Ham
Roast
LEG/HAM
Blade Chop
Braise, Broil, Panbroil, Panfry
Rib Chop
Broil, Panbroil, Panfry, Braise
Top Loin Chop
Broil, Panbroil, Panfry, Braise
Loin Chop
Broil, Panbroil, Panfry, Braise
Sirloin Chop
Braise
Butterfly Chop
Broil, Panbroil, Panfry, Braise
Country-Style Ribs
Roast, Braise, Broil, Cook in Liquid
Sirloin Cutlet
Braise, Broil, Panbroil, Panfry
Back Ribs
Roast, Broil, Braise, Cook in Liquid
Tenderloin
Roast, Braise, (Slices: Panfry, Braise)
Center Rib Roast
Roast
Top Loin Roast (Double)
Roast
Blade Roast
Roast, Braise
Boneless Blade Roast
Roast, Braise
Sirloin Roast
Roast
Center Loin Roast
Roast
Smoked Loin Chop
Roast, Broil, Panbroil, Panfry
Crown Roast
Roast
Boneless Sirloin Roast
Roast
Canadian-Style Bacon
Roast, Broil, Panbroil, Panfry
LOIN
Blade Roast
Roast, Braise
Blade Steak
Braise, Broil, Panbroil, Panfry
Boneless Blade Roast
Roast, Braise
Smoked Shoulder Roll
Roast, Cook in Liquid
Boneless Arm Picnic Roast
Roast, Braise
Smoked Hocks
Braise, Cook in Liquid
Smoked Picnic
Roast, Cook in Liquid
SHOULDER
Spareribs
Roast, Broil, Cook in Liquid, Braise
Sliced Bacon
Panfry, Broil, Roast (Bake)
SIDE
THIS CHART APPROVED BY
NATIONAL LIVE STOCK & MEAT BOARD

There are odors, both positive and negative, that are unique to this type of commercial enterprise, and this room, which we children quickly dubbed the "Pig Tail Room," nearly always evoked the positive.

Frequently, following completion of our evening meal and chores, we children would hurry to the Pig Tail Room, sit on empty crates or lard cans, and beg our Grandfather Jim to stir the cooking fat pieces in search of pig tails which we immediately devoured when he located them. Not infrequently, we obtained our objective by stepping out into the cold and carrying in one or more pieces of wood. Grandpa appeared to sense that he had a captive audience and never hesitated to recite a litany of stories relative to his exploits in the Civil War and big- game hunting in the Yukon.

Our oldest brother attempted, in vain, to convince us that Grandpa's stories lacked foundation. However, we younger ones could not remotely entertain the thought of being absent from the Pig Ta(i)le Room when there was the possibility of those crispy morsels surfacing in that kettle..

OUR TIN Lizzie

My patriarchal grandparents, William R. and Emerica (Boolman) Cultice, Cedarville, Ohio, 1915.

In 1912, for less than $200, our father had purchased a second-hand, 1909 Model T. Ford. According to him, he drove a short distance to his parents' home to show off his "Tin Lizzie." While his mother stood on the porch in awe, his father, Grandpa Sandy, walked slowly out to the front of the machine and rubbed the brass radiator cap. While chewing his tobacco, he asked, "Boy, how much did you say you paid for this thing?" "About $200, Pop," our father answered. Grandpa Sandy then walked to the rear of the machine, kicked the tire as he stared at the exhaust pipe, and said, "Boy, this contraption ain't gonna' make no shit for the garden."

In 1927, after more than fifteen million Model T. Fords had been manufactured, our father purchased his fourth and last "Tin Lizzie," an open touring car. A year before he had purchased a Model T Ford truck. Both of these vehicles, when parked, represented over-sized toys for me and my little brother Hank. We would take imaginary trips to the filling stations, the junkyard, grocery store, our grandparents, or to visit our Aunt Grace in Chicago. No place was too far.

When our family actually took a trip, we would usually stop at Vorhee's filling station for gasoline, which was ten cents a gallon. While the gasoline was being hand pumped into the tank, our mother would always place her handkerchief over her nose since the fumes caused her to become very nauseous. She would also close her eyes when we passed over a viaduct or bridge.

During construction season, we brothers would help ourselves to the many tools, supplies, and scrap wood in the bed of the truck. We learned early how to saw, drive nails, and construct crude automobiles, airplanes, and barns. We also used the earth tamps to crush tin cans and the handles of earth picks for ball bats.

During one of our imaginary trips, I took a wrench from the rear of the truck and removed the tap nut that secured the steering wheel to the steering post. The following day my father was driving in town when the steering wheel came off the post. Our father never questioned Hank or me about the potential accident. Hank was present the day before when I removed the tap nut; however, he never told our father that I did it. Sometimes, but not too often, little brothers can keep a secret.

Grandpa Sandy was adamant that he would never allow one of these "contraptions" to replace his horses King and Prince. As such, he almost looked forward to the opportunity in extremely cold weather to pulling the machines with his horses in order to get them running. This practice, as Grandpa well knew, would only be initiated after a teakettle of hot water poured over the engine block was unsuccessful. While the water was heating and Grandpa Sandy was slurping his second cup of coffee from his moustache saucer, he was prone to mention that he'd better hitch up King and Prince just in case the "contraption" didn't start.

Grandpa Sandy reluctantly learned to drive after much cajoling on the part of our father. However, he never learned to put the engine into reverse gear in order to turn the "contraption" around. He just didn't like the idea of "that damn thing going someplace that he couldn't see," he always said. Therefore, when he did drive, we children would have to open a field gate in order for him to turn around in the field.

As a farm boy in the late twenties, I remember Grandpa Sandy saying that even though Model T's were a nuisance, "they still earned their keep." I guess he meant that with one wheel jacked up and a drive-belt attached, the "contraption" supplied power for grinding feed, pumping water, and running a circular saw for cutting firewood. Grandpa Jim also showed us how to build a narrow trough to put under the rear tire in order to hull walnuts.

When our father wasn't home, my brother Winston used the touring car for herding cows over some rough terrain. He said it was "like a horse with double-jointed legs," which sounded very funny. Brother Winston was fascinated with the "contraptions" and quickly learned the simplicity of their maintenance. He kept them, with a little help from our father on valve jobs, in perfect running order. His tools were a tobacco tin, snips, tire vulcanizing kit, baling wire, pliers, wrenches, and when our father wasn't present, a few "cuss words." It seemed like every farmer in our half of the county had a Model T, too.

When our family was about to set out for an extended ride in our touring car, especially in summer, and the isinglass curtains were removed, there was a scramble to avoid sitting on the left side of the back seat. Once, when we traveled to Winchester, Indiana, my brother Hank and I shared this seat. When we arrived at Grandma Peacock's place, our faces were replete with reddish-brown speckles, and she wanted to know if we had the measles. Our father assured her that we didn't and assured her that the blotches were merely a little second-hand, tobacco juice. Thereafter, in the words of our sister Evelyn, this seat would be known as the "measles seat."

HAPPY Warriors

After we had settled on our farm, we learned from Grandpa Jim that the creek flowing through our farm was very famous. Once we listened to his embellished tales of Tecumseh and his Shawnee warriors, we could not wait to look for arrowheads and reenact the lives of these tribesmen. He told us that Tecumseh had been born near our creek, and that he and his tribe had lived there for a number of years. In fact, Grandpa said, we could drink from the same spring where the Indians had drawn water.

My sisters were especially attentive when Grandpa Jim told us how Tecumseh fell in love with Rebecca Galloway, the daughter of a pioneer, and asked her to marry him. "Did she marry him?" my sister Rachel asked. "No," Grandpa Jim replied, "he died fighting in a war before they could be married." This facet of Grandpa Jim's Shawnee tale would become a magnet for coeducational play, as the girls would aspire to play the roles of Rebecca and Mrs. Galloway. For some unknown reason to me, they didn't seem to enjoy crushing corn kernels between two rocks and making corn cakes.

Our activities at Shawnee Creek usually began with the older boys cutting small birch trees to serve as teepee poles. The frame poles would then be covered with a well-worn Indian blanket from our tree house. After we small boys had gathered dry grass and twigs and placed them on a section of the exposed creek bed, the older boys would fashion a crossbow pot holder and light the fire. The girls were supposed to tend the fire while we boys divided into warring tribes and prepared for battle. This preparation, in addition to locating war clubs and reed ropes, mandated the application of body war paint made from squeezed walnut hulls, goldenrod weeds, and raspberries.

Tecumseh saving prisoners.

When the battle was over, the victorious tribe with its captured warriors and even an occasional horse or pony would return to the campsite, tie the captives to a nearby tree, and execute a war dance around the fire. When the captives accepted our conditions of surrender, we were ready for the "peace feast."

Since we generally did not have a utensil to cook our small pieces of meat in, we skewered it on a sharpened stick and held it over the fire. When the feast was finished, we passed the peace pipe around the fire for all to smoke, girls included. This pipe was usually fashioned from a cored-out corn cob and was filled with dried corn silk. When they were dry enough, we attempted, usually unsuccessfully, to smoke real Indian cigars, which were pods from the catalpa tree.

Sometimes one or more of us would walk with Grandpa through the area in search of arrowheads. Inevitably Grandpa would always be the only one to discover an arrowhead on any given walk.

Gee, we were all convinced our Grandpa would have been a great Shawnee warrior.

Holy Sunshine

It was a typical Saturday afternoon event during a string of hot, July days. The six of us had all agreed that a dip in our favorite swimming hole at Shawnee Creek would be the best and most inexpensive relief we could find from the oppressive heat.

Upon arriving at the creek we routinely checked to make sure that none of the livestock was presently upstream. When individuals other than family joined us at the swimming hole, the girls usually wore their bloomers, and the boys wore their cut-off pants or underwear. When we went skinny-dipping, however, it was protocol for the girls to disrobe and enter the water from behind a large, cottonwood tree that had fallen across the east end of the hole. The boys disrobed at the west end of the hole behind a clump of bushes and gingerly covered their "privates" as they quickly waded into the deeper sections of the hole. Once in the water only our lower anatomy was invisible.

Since this was a family swim, we all disrobed and enjoyed a nearly two-hour hiatus from the heat. However, when it was time for us to go home, we boys faced west for the girls to exit and get into their clothes. Almost immediately we heard them shout, "What happened to our clothes?" We boys would soon be asking ourselves the same question, "What happened to our clothes?" There we were shouting accusatory remarks from behind our respective nature shields.

My oldest brother, the surrogate parent, quickly surmised the severity of the circumstance and quickly quarterbacked

My mother two months before my brother Lowell's birth, March 1918, Cedarville, Ohio.

our plan of return to the safety of our house, which was more than five hundred yards from our location. We would travel some three hundred and fifty yards along the bed of the tributary, which went just beyond the tree-house elm. By heading in this direction, we would be shielded by the bushes and trees along its banks. When we reached the point beyond the tree house, we would turn westward up the livestock lane, move up behind the barn, and then, one at a time, race the remaining fifty yards to the back porch door.

Aside from several scratches from briars and berry bushes, all went well as we moved along the tributary while simultaneously trying to exhibit a measure of modesty by holding one hand over our pubic area and the other over the broadest portion of our anatomy. At last, we were behind the barn, a mere fifty yards from the haven of our house. Here, we were instructed to reverse chronological order, and my little brother was to initiate this Saturday afternoon "Charge of the Barebottom Brigade" by going first. As he turned the corner of the barn with the sun glistening on his backside, I quickly moved up to assess his speed and entry. In doing so, I also noted an automobile, not our Model T Ford, parked near the pump house.

As the porch screen door slammed behind my brother's bare bottom, I heard my mother scream, "Oh, my God," and very quickly I, too, raced past the foreign auto, up the steps, across the back porch, and into the kitchen past my mother who was being visited by our preacher, Rev. Simpson, and up the stairs to the safety of our bedroom. My two sisters and older brothers followed us in the order of assignment.

What was the reverend to think? Was this a band of undisciplined children who needed less exposure to nature and more exposure to the scriptures? We all stood near our respective hallway doors, as Rev. Simpson departed with these words, "Hilda, try very hard to have the children in Sunday school and church tomorrow."

Reciprocity

Whenever kids from the city or a neighboring farm defeated our team in a game, we would try to figure out how we could beat them by playing the game over again.

A couple of weeks after my brother Hank and I had lost our baled-hay fort in a water pistol fight against the Boysell boys who lived up the lane, we contrived for a re-match. After consulting my mentor-brother Winston, we were thoroughly convinced that our defensive strategy was good enough, and we had lost the battle because they had not fought fairly. In short, each team was to only have two guns, and it was fair if one soldier had both guns and the other team member served as a scout. However, when they charged our fort, they were each carrying two water pistols. Our brother Winston, in defense of his little brothers' honor, went to the barn with us a few days before the re-match and showed us how to arrange the baled-hay fort for additional protection and advantage. Without telling my little brother, he also secretly told me how we could gain a "ballistic" advantage when the shooting started even if the Boysell boys dared show up again with two guns apiece.

Even to my young mind it was a very simple plan. He would be working on the killing floor in the slaughterhouse during the week, and all I needed to do was to bring an empty can and lid to him, and he would take it from there. However, in an effort to keep it an "away game" status, I was not to tell our little brother Hank because he might be prone to leak the plans to our sisters, or even worse, to our father.

Sometime before the re-match, I picked up the can from the slaughterhouse and placed it in the fort. When the Boysell boys showed up at the cattle trough to fill their water pistols, they did not seem to be surprised that we were also going to be two-fisted gunslingers this time.

As before, the Boysell boys would be making their assault from the north end of the hayloft, down the ladder in front of the cow stall manger, and through the box stall to where we had our fort at the south end of the barn. Also, as before, the team that stayed the driest would be declared the winner.

Shortly after concealing ourselves in the fort, we emptied our pistols and refilled them from the can. Our plan of defense, this time, was to allow them to get through the box stall door before we opened fire. So, when they banged the hatch door at the top of the ladder, we were confident of victory. In a few seconds when they crawled through the box stall door, we rose up from behind our barricade of bales and gave them a four-gun withering assault of two-day-old pig piss. Not only were they both drenched, but Junior had taken a direct hit in the face and was writhing on the stable floor. While crying and spitting, his brother quickly surrendered for both of them, and my brother and I helped take his little brother back to the cattle trough to wash out his eyes. Once Junior was stabilized, we still needed to get the odor of battle off of our shirts and overalls.

We walked rapidly to our swimming hole, took a full-clothes-on dipping, and ate blackberries until our clothes were dry. It had been a good day! We not only avenged our earlier defeat but also had won an "away game" at home. Big brothers, we agreed, surely come in handy sometimes, don't they?

THE BIG School

By September of 1928, I would no longer have to stay at home and watch my brothers and sisters go off to school. My day had arrived. Early on that September morning, ably assisted by my mother, I made sure that my school bag contained all the essential items for a very eager first-grader: pencil, writing tablet, eraser, and most important of all, the paper bag containing my pickled, pig-ear and mustard sandwich.

During the summer and on our walk to the school that first day, my brothers and the Boysell brothers had exercised every opportunity to profile our teacher, Mrs.Stevens, as something just short of being a witch. Conversely, my sisters and Bonnie Boysell insisted that she was really very nice and only boys who were bad were ever spanked. Once at school, I found Mrs. Stevens to be very nice and very fair. She told us that it was all right for us boys to chase the girls on the playground just as long as we didn't shove or hit them. This rule was exactly like the one at our house, and I would quickly learn many other rules were the same—wipe your feet before you enter the door, put your hand over your mouth when you cough, don't wipe your nose on your sleeve, don't drink out of the water dipper, don't use cuss words, don't whistle or shout in class, don't pee on the toilet seat. Failure to comply could lead to what Mrs. Stevens referred to as "learning reinforcement." Before the first snowfall, a few of my classmates and I, all boys, would learn that the teaching instrument for this instruction was the paddle hanging at the end of her desk. At this juncture of my school career, I was puzzled by two things. One: How could Mrs. Stevens, who did not have any children, have the same rules as my parents had at home? Two: Don't girls ever receive a spanking?

Although I couldn't copy them very well, Mrs. Stevens wrote what she called "mottos" on the board for us to learn and memorize. Some examples were: "A penny saved is a penny earned," "Honesty is the best policy," and "Don't put all your eggs in one basket." My brother Winston said Mrs. Stevens thought if we learned these mottos we probably would someday have character. Since I didn't learn all of them, I guessed that I'd never have character, whatever that was.

I liked Mrs. Stevens and I was sure she liked me. She always gave me a part in our holiday plays. When we had our Easter parade and party, she was even very understanding when I explained to her that I couldn't be one of the Easter Bunnies because I had never found a rabbit's nest with eggs in it. She let me be a sheep in our Christmas play because, she said, "You have the best and loudest 'baaaah' of any of the sheep-sized boys in the school." I told her that I had spent a lot of time practicing for the part, and she just smiled. She smiled another time when she placed my hands in hers and told me that my hands were very "vocational." I had no idea of she meant by that big word; but, whatever it meant, it was better than telling me they were dirty.

We all understood the rule that we were not to whistle or shout in class in order to gain Mrs. Stevens' attention, but rather to hold our hand up until she recognized us. If you wanted to leave the room to go to the basement bathroom, in addition to raising your hand, you were to extend one or two fingers to indicate whether nature's call was of a liquid or solid nature.

Each year, the second-grade boys would attempt to exploit some unsuspecting underclassmen by adding a third signal. Instead of raising one hand, the intended victim was told he should raise both hands and cross his index fingers and wait for Mrs. Stevens to recognize him. When I did this, and Mrs. Stevens motioned for me to come up to her desk, the older boys could barely contain themselves. Once at her desk, she inquired if I had a stomach ache. If I did she said that I should go to the basement. I told her I didn't really have to go, and she sent me back to my seat. She was, like I always said, really smart. She had decoded this bathroom excuse early in her career and did not wish to discuss it before the entire room. The signal, as my brothers would later explain to me, was quite natural. If one finger meant liquid and two fingers meant solid, then crossed fingers meant that you were half-way between those two with nature's wind.

This school had a large playground with two sets of teeter-totters, two large slides, and two sets of monkey bars. The equipment was located behind the school, and the playground was bordered on the east by the homes of Tinsley Bell and Arthur Jefferson.

Tinsley Bell was a very grumpy man who didn't appear to like school children, especially boys who sometimes hit balls over his fence that rolled almost to the back door of his house. Frequently, he would keep these balls for several days or weeks, before they would mysteriously be found on the playground again. Mr. Jefferson was different from Mr. Bell. He seemed to enjoy watching us play ball, and he would always throw a ball hit over his fence back onto the playground. Once, or twice, when he noticed that our ball was badly tattered, he gave us a new ball. Mr. Jefferson said we shouldn't be angry with Mr. Bell because he had constipation much of the time, and he didn't feel very good.

Since his name was Bell and we didn't know what constipation was, we thought maybe our principal, Miss Bell, who taught third and fourth grades in the other classroom, might also have whatever it was since she didn't smile very much either.

When the bell sounded ending our recess period, we lined up quietly outside the building and marched into the building to the scratchy sound of John Philip Sousa's "Washington Post March." Once inside, we turned right into the coat hall; secured our coats, hats, scarves, overshoes, and lunches; turned left at the end of the hall; and sat in our assigned classroom seats.

On the south wall was a large clock with a painting of Martha Washington on one side and a painting of George Washington on the other side. Jack Burton, who was repeating the second grade, said that since our principal's first name was Martha, she must be related to President Washington.

Spring Hill School—I attended grades 5 and 6 here during 1933-35.

The front wall of our classroom had a very large painting of Christopher Columbus' three ships. Since I lived on Columbus Street before we moved to our farm, I wondered if maybe I might be related to him.

Between the school and Lighthiser's grocery there were several homes under construction during my first year at Orient Hill. My father had contracted for the cement work for these homes. Several times when I went to the grocery to purchase Mrs. Stevens' lunch during our noon recess, I waved to my father while he was working. Mrs. Stevens would usually give me one or two pennies for my services. Knowing that she trusted me meant even more than the pennies; it made me feel very special to be asked to run this errand.

The school did not have outdoor jakes. Instead, it had two large rooms in the basement. In the boys' room there was a long trough secured to the west wall called a "urinal" and several small "jakes" with large doors on the east wall. There were also four places to wash your hands after you had visited the urinal or "jake." However, the fourth grade boys, who were very sophisticated about such matters, let us know early that you only needed to wash your hands if you peed on them while you were using the urinal. It was not, according to the fourth graders, a good idea to try and hold a paper lunch bag in one hand while peeing in the urinals.

Mr. Edwards, our janitor, was somewhat elderly and had a small office near the boiler room and the boys' "lavatory," as Mrs. Stevens referred to it. He had known my father for several years and would occasionally ask about my parents. Sometimes he would invite me in after school. When he did this, I'd be excited. This was true because when we were caught with gum or candy in our classroom, Mrs. Stevens always made us empty the gum or candy from our pockets into the waste can. Just before school was over for the day, Mr. Edwards would enter the classrooms to retrieve the waste cans and take them to the boiler room. When I arrived, he would talk for a little while and then ask me if I would like to rummage through the paper in the cans in search of unwrapped gum or candy. Of course, I never declined. In fact, it grew so productive—gum, baseball cards, candy, etc.—that I was unable to keep the secret. I don't know how Miss Bell found out about it, but she did. Since my twin sisters were in her room, I always believed that one, or maybe even both, of them told her.

I guess I learned a lot of things that year: like how to salute the flag; recite the Pledge of Allegiance; how to stand up straight in a corner; how to enjoy lunch by myself; and how to keep quiet at home about some things that happened at school. Finally, I concluded that if you were going to be away from home all day anyway, school was a nice place to live in, learn in, and feel loved in. In fact, other than having more kids to play with, it was almost like home.

THE Sanctuary

Our father, a neophyte farmer, was a contractor and as such, was fairly astute with respect to the design of any newly constructed or restored buildings on the property. He felt such buildings ought to be visually pleasing objects, especially the privy, and project an impression of comfort and completeness upon all who saw or utilized them.

Aside from the materials selected for this new building, there was the serious issue of whether the door should be hinged on the right or left side of the frame and whether it should open outward or inward. There were, of course, many other important factors related to the construction of this outdoor facility. However, we children, along with our grandparents, knew the most important factor was the estimate of how many yards we could safely navigate through rain and snow in case of an emergency.

Our outdoor facility, according to our mother, had many different synonyms. Depending upon the age, occupation, social standing, or where they were visiting from, it was called backhouse, outhouse, can, jake, john, Johnny, chick sale, library, sanctuary, throne room, or office. Grandpa Sandy, irrespective of the social circumstances, always referred to an outdoor facility as a "thunder shed." Since one of our father's several nicknames was "Jake," we children quickly learned not to employ that term for the facility.

The interior of our two-holer consisted of a single board with beveled openings and raised seat handles for easy removal and safety. The walls were traditionally whitewashed every year or two and periodically decorated with calendars and newspapers. The accessories ranged from newspapers and magazines to corncobs. Grandpa Sandy always insisted on having a plentiful supply of corncobs—a ratio of two red ones and one white one on hand.

Our mother had borrowed an outdated Sears and Roebucks catalog and ordered a carton of toilet paper. When she informed Grandpa about what she'd done, he was dubious about having store-bought "*hiney* fodder" in the thunder shed. Shortly after she placed the order, she received a return letter explaining that the company could not ship the toilet paper until they received the order number from the latest edition of their catalog. When Grandpa heard this, he snapped, "Hell, that don't make no sense at all. 'Cause if we had the catalog, we wouldn't need the paper."

We boys, not infrequently, feigned a sudden urge to "nature's call" to avoid what we considered to be an unpleasant task. This ploy, within our childhood, secret vocabulary, was conventionally referred to as "shitting a rest." Some unknown author and informer appeared to expose our ploy when the following poem was tacked on the wall above the toilet seat:

The Sanctuary

Beneath the spreading long fir tree
The weathered outhouse stands
A sanctuary where you're free
From labor's harsh demands
Of all the cities' luxuries
Tile, porcelain and chrome
None satisfies and gives relief
Like this fragrant shack at home.

—Anonymous

We really disliked going to the outhouse in the icy-cold of winter and always made the trip as fast as possible. Besides this, our older brothers insisted there were spiders, snakes, and several other types of critters down there that just couldn't wait for you to expose your most tender parts to them, especially in the dark.

Finally, after we boys had failed to respond positively following a step-four disciplinary action, we were sometimes assigned a period of solitary confinement there. This action, a kind of forerunner to our contemporary "time out" practice, consisted of being locked in the outhouse in order to "think" about our transgression. Our only chance at early parole was for a female to sense "nature's call." Older brothers seemed to enjoy our plight because they would come to the door, knock, laugh, and then go to the barn to relieve themselves. When you need them most, older brothers can sometimes be very cruel.

SHAWNEE Indians

According to Grandpa Jim, the greatest Indian known in history, Tecumseh, was born not far from our farm in a small bark cabin. He was one of two boys born at the same time. Since twins were rare among Indians, this incident, Grandpa emphasized, was very remarkable and carried religious significance. Even in his youth, Tecumseh became famous. His brother, Els-Kwan-Ta-Was (The Prophet), was afterwards a famous medicine man or shaman and was second in influence to Tecumseh. We children were excited to learn that these two remarkable people hunted and fished on the very land where we were living.

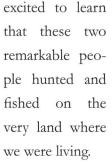

Curing venison in a Shawnee camp.

This Indian tribe, according to our grandpa, never contained more than 300 fighting warriors in all its villages. Yet it engaged the Americans in nearly two dozen fights. He went on to tell us that the Shawnee won over half of these battles. He said they could outfight and outmaneuver, man-for-man, the Iroquois, the Delaware, and the white backwoodsmen. We had some idea of who the backwoodsmen were but knew nothing of the Iroquois and the Delaware.

The Shawnee, he said, were hospitable, kind to their captives, and were extremely industrious. They were, he went on, not naturally hostile to white people, but they became embittered for many reasons. They were particularly bitter when a favorite Shawnee chief, Silver Heels, was murdered near the Ohio River by a backwoodsman from Kentucky. In addition, the death of Shawnee Chief Cornstalk, who was murdered while on a friendly visit with his son to the fort at Point Pleasant, was more than the Indians could stand. "And they did just what we would have done if it had happened to us. They went on the warpath to Kentucky and West Virginia with scalping knives and tomahawks, and they got an eye for an eye and a tooth for a tooth."

Grandpa Jim promised to someday take us to Old Town and show us the stone monuments that proved that the Shawnee really lived there. He told us that we should not believe that the Shawnee at Old Town were savages. He said they lived in comfortable log cabins, were well-clothed, and had gardens and orchards. If the white people had left them alone, they would have been living at the present time much after the fashion of the Iroquois in western New York.

Finally, Grandpa told us that a schoolhouse now stands where once the simple wigwams and the conical chamber of this remarkable and interesting tribe once stood.

FOR THE LOVE OF Rebecca

In 1798 James Galloway, Sr. settled on the Little Miami River two miles north of Old Town. The log house, which Grandpa Jim later showed us, bore the date 1801 on a stone over the door. A little west of the house, at Old Chillicothe (Old Town) lay the scene of possibly the most interesting events of this section, since this was one of the most popular places for the Indians from all directions to gather. It was here that Daniel Boone was held prisoner in 1778. He succeeded so well in ingratiating himself into the good favor of the Indians that they adopted him into their tribe. However, he soon escaped from them and fled to Kentucky to warn his people of the proposed onslaught by the Indians. Here too, Simon Kenton ran the gauntlet; and 1799 marked the famous Bowman Expedition in this locality. While all of these events are interesting stories in themselves, the story of Old Town centers on the Galloway family according to Grandpa.

The Galloways were near neighbors to some of the best known of the Indians who occupied that part of Greene County. This fact is worthy of special note as their family traditions are rich in interesting accounts of the friendships with the "Redmen" that were formed in those early days.

Galloway Cabin was relocated to Xenia, Ohio.

Grandpa Jim told us that the distinguished Tecumseh was a frequent and welcomed visitor at this house, and soon became very infatuated with the daughter, Rebecca. With true dignity, which was ever a character trait of Tecumseh, he approached her father and asked his permission to court her. Mr. Galloway, feeling that his daughter could perhaps more tactfully find a way out of the embarrassing position and still retain the goodwill of the Indians, which was important to sustain, referred Tecumseh to Rebecca. The chief fearlessly appealed to the girl herself. Was not he the great Tecumseh, the leader of his people? He offered her beautiful gifts of silver and ornaments dear to his people. She told him she could not work like the Indian women did, nor lead the wild life they did. He assured her that she need not work. Then she changed her tactics and told him she would consider his proposition if he would promise to lead the life of a white man and assume their dress and habits. This matter he took under consideration, but finally he told her, most sorrowfully, that he could not possibly do that. Taking up of the manners and customs of the white man would place him in everlasting disgrace with his people and as much as he desired the union, he could not bear the reproaches. And, thus we see the womanly daughter of the pioneer family fully able to turn aside the undesirable suitor but still retain a very necessary friend, for the friendship between Tecumseh and the family never waned, according to Grandpa Jim.

Early Delivery

When my father began wholesaling pork products in the winter of 1928, I begged for the thrill of going with him on a Saturday morning delivery when I would not be in school.

When my wish was finally granted, I was gently awakened by my mother at 4:30 a.m. I dressed behind the living room stove and felt extremely important to have the full attention of both parents at breakfast. After breakfast, my mother assisted with my winter clothing, tucked a folded blanket under my arm to keep my feet warm, and I went with my father to the slaughterhouse.

The delivery truck, a converted Model T touring machine, had a slatted rack about two feet above the floor and double-hinged doors on the back. While my father was loading the truck, he alternately whistled, talked to me, and repeated four words—north, south, west, and east—several times. When the rack and floor of the truck were fully covered with cuts of pork, tubs of sausage, and cans of lard, we headed for the north end of town. There were several neighborhood groceries in this section of town which, according to my father, conventionally purchased and paid cash for hams, tenderloins, backstraps, Boston butts, sausage, and lard.

"You see, Bo, these folks in this part of town are all 'high on the hog.'"

"Do you mean they ride on the hogs?" I asked.

"No, Bo," he replied, "they don't ride on the hogs, but they eat the parts of meat that are at the top of the hog." I understood his answer, and I was happy that he called me by my nickname, Bo.

In every section of town, I would look in the store's tobacco case for the brand that my father chewed, Red Horse. Also, in almost every store we visited I would press my face to the front glass of the candy case. The stores in the north section had mostly pipe tobacco and cigars. In addition, they seemed to have more boxed chocolates than penny candy.

The stores in the north section of the town almost always stood alone, while the stores in the south end usually housed the owner's family either in the upstairs or in the rear. The owners, about half of them women, were prone to purchase New York shoulders, fresh callies, pork loins, spare ribs, fresh side, ham shanks, sausage, and lard. These owners, according to my father, were a little more than "half-way up on the hog" because pork loins could be cut up into pork chops, which in turn, contained a large piece of backstrap and a small piece of tenderloin. Also, he informed me that callies and shanks, respectively, were the lower portion of the shoulder and ham. While my father would soon caution me about placing my face too close to the candy counters, I still noted that the tobacco counters in these stores had more types of products, including my father's Red Horse, than the stores in the north section. In addition, the candy cases in the south section appeared to have more penny candy and fewer boxes of chocolates.

When we reached the southwest section of town and stopped at the first store, my father took a small hog head and backbone out of the truck and carried them into the store which very much resembled the stores in the south end of town. In addition to these two cuts, the owner seemed to purchase cuts that were similar to those selected in the south section. My father referred to these purchases as being "a little more than half-way down on the hog." In this section, as my older brothers had already told me, I would not be permitted to go inside the stores, but rather would be expected to remain in the truck. Before my father carried the first items into the store, he instructed me to stay in the truck. If anyone opened any door of the truck, I was to say, "Hi, my daddy is coming right back." These restrictions, of course, meant that I wouldn't get to inspect the tobacco and candy cases, but they made me feel very, very important. My brothers referred to this part of the trip as "riding shotgun," whatever that meant.

The east section of town which embraced the descendants of runaway slaves moving north to Canada during the closing of the Civil War and an enclave of economically strapped whites known as Frog Hollow would be our next-to-last delivery area. Here, I would also remain in the truck. Nearly all of what my father referred to as "being low and inside on the hog"—heads, feet, backbones, neckbones, livers, hearts, kidneys, maws, ears, tails, and the staples of sausage and lard—would be sold in this part of town.

By this time it would be nearly noon, and I had mixed emotions when we headed for our final stop at the busy depot restaurant near the center of town to deliver a standard order of two hams, two shoulders, and one pork liver. I was sure I was going to enjoy my lunch—a glass of milk and pork barbecue sandwich—with my father in the warm restaurant, but I also knew we were going to walk across several sets of railroad tracks with hissing steam locomotives standing on them to reach the restaurant. My father, sensing my fear, would secure my hand in his until we were a few steps from the door of the restaurant. Once inside, I would again feel very important when Mrs. Bohl, the waitress, asked my name and said, "Are you your dad's helper?" I grinned through the sauce on my face and answered, "Yes." My father added, "Yes, he's a very good helper." I thought to myself, "Wait until I get to school on Monday and tell my classmates about this trip."

Uncle Remus

While many children our ages were reading and enjoying the book *Uncle Remus,* we children were being awed by a colorful local character named Remus Mace. Mr. Mace and his two assistants, "lieutenants," as my father referred to them, Bluenose Mulligan and Fourfinger Farley represented, according to our mother, everything that was illegal and immoral. She preferred that we not be in their company. However, when we were with our father in their company we felt safe and rather viewed Mr. Mace as a kind of a hero. This was especially true when this trio stopped by our slaughterhouse to warm at the stove and enjoy a handful of pork cracklings with their homemade tipple.

According to our father, the known illegal activities of this trio included hunting out of season and without a license, incarcerating small animals like weasels, raccoon, opossums, mink, etc., and employing ferrets to catch all of the aforementioned critters.

In addition, they hunted illegally at night. Bluenose and Fourfinger rode on the wide front fenders of Remus' "machine," armed with .22 rifles, and shot every rabbit that squatted before the bright headlights of the vehicle.

Their immoral activities, although somewhat in vogue during this era, embraced making moonshine—known locally as "rotgut," bootlegging, selling animal carcasses without a license, and it seemed, just about every vice that mothers didn't want their children to know about.

When we boys first visited Remus' house with our father, we were dumbstruck by the beautiful and loud-barking hunting dogs and cages filled with every type of small animal. We had one unofficial hunting dog, and there were more raccoons in one or two of those cages than we had caught in a full year of trapping. For us, it was like visiting a ball park to watch our first big-league game.

At the time of our visit, we overheard conversation relative to a pending coon-hunt training session for several young whelps. We were all invited to come along. Wow! Was it possible that we boys could convince our father to convince our mother that we might learn some hunting secrets if we were permitted to tag along on this great venture? Even though our mother gave her reluctant approval, she undoubtedly believed we would learn more new "cuss words" than hunting secrets during the night's adventure.

The adventure started just across the road from the forbidden area of the wooded swamp. Had our mother known, this starting point by itself, would have been enough for her to deny our request. When our father drove us to the starting point of the event, by flashlight we saw Uncle Remus, Bluenose, and Fourfingers standing beside two cages. One of the cages had five whelps in it, and the other cage held a large raccoon.

Shortly after we saw the cages, Uncle Remus took a burlap bag with a piece of rope tied around the middle out of his "machine" The bottom half of the bag, Uncle Remus explained, contained the straw bedding from several coon cages. He proceeded to pour about half a gallon of water onto the bag while it was flat on the ground. He then instructed Bluenose to drag the burlap bag through several fields and wooded areas for approximately one hour to a predetermined point where the whelps would eventually "tree the raccoon."

As soon as Bluenose departed, Uncle Remus moved the raccoon's cage within two feet of the dog cage. Immediately the whelps began barking and hissing. This, our father explained, was just the beginning of the big fight that would take place when the dogs and raccoon arrived at the finishing point.

"Bluenose" Mulligan shows off his dogs and their trophies, circa 1932.

About forty-five minutes after Bluenose left, Uncle Remus put the caged raccoon back in his "machine," and he and Fourfingers led the five whelps to the spot where Bluenose had started dragging the burlap bag and removed their leashes. The dogs instinctively picked up the scent of a raccoon and raced off for the kill.

Our father drove behind Uncle Remus' "machine" to the finishing point. We watched by flashlight, as Remus removed the raccoon cage from the machine, pulled on a large pair of engineer's gloves, took the frightened critter out of the cage, snapped a rather long chain onto its collar, and released it. Simultaneously he yelled, "Get up that tree, you SOB." I guess the raccoon knew that when she was called by all three of these names that she was destined for trouble so she scampered vertically up a large oak tree to a height of about twenty feet. Remus then drove a large nail through the bottom link of the chain at the foot of the tree. By then, we knew the dogs were approaching because their barking was becoming increasingly louder. When they finally arrived, they continued their howling and attempted to climb the tree in an effort to reach the raccoon. Slowly, as they howled, Uncle Remus pulled the raccoon out of the crotch of the tree and forced her to encounter the whelps.

Once at ground level, the raccoon placed her rear end toward the base of the tree and bloodied all of the whelps' noses with her clawed, front paws.

When Uncle Remus figured the whelps understood that coon hunting could be a very dangerous game, he allowed the raccoon to scamper back up the tree to a position of safety. Before he pulled the raccoon down again, he placed the caged dogs back in his "machine" and said, "Next time we'll let these mutts chase her into the water, and one or two of the SOB's might just get killed."

That sounded even more exciting. Of course, we boys wondered if we could convince our father to convince our mother to allow us to watch. I guess I also figured I would need some assistance in understanding why the raccoon and the dogs all had the same name, SOB.

WORK, WORK, AND Play

"The early bird gets the worm" was not the wake-up call at our home. Instead, we children would hear, "If you have any work to do today, you ought to have it finished by noon and start planning for the next day." This phrase, we children interpreted to mean, that aside from our daily routines, there were other specified chores to attend to, and if we were on task, we were "sprung for fun" for the remainder of the day.

In an attempt to alleviate the oppressive aspects of the many and varied tasks assigned, our curiosity would frequently seek a method of lessening the chore by discovering a new method that would shorten the work-time, which, in turn, would make it more fun.

These chores were of a seasonal nature, and every season we boys would each have a favorite. Even though our father leased out our small farm on an owner-tenant basis, we boys were understood to be the unsalaried, "hired hands."

In the spring we helped prepare the garden for planting and sometimes we drove the horses that were pulling the field plow and corn planter. Other times, in return for several gallons of maple syrup, we were assigned to Mr. Avery to help with the sap sled or to haul wood to his "maple sugar camp."

To employ the pun, we all saw this as the "sweetest" of all of our spring assignments because we would inevitably be playing on the woodpile inside the camp, savoring the aroma of the boiling sap, listening to the stories of the men tending the vats, and enjoying a piece of chicken that had been roasted in the ashes of the fire box beneath the sap vats.

Our extra chore responsibilities in the summertime consisted mainly of gardening, haying, herding, keeping crows out of the cornfield, helping with the threshing, and hoeing pea vines in the cornfield.

By 1930, both of my older brothers had attained the "rite of passage" age of twelve, which in our family, qualified them to fire a .22 caliber rifle. We brothers all eagerly looked forward to this age since it would not only qualify us to hunt but would also allow us to shoot crows in the cornfield. Fathers, like mothers are also very smart, and our father had the crow-shooting work-sport combined with the tedious task of hoeing pea vines between the rows of corn.

The remaining tasks of gardening, haying, herding, and threshing often occupied us brothers of all ages. My favorite work-game was serving as waterboy for the hoards of men and the tractor that visited our farm in late July to thresh our wheat or oats. Boys under twelve were not considered old enough to work near the threshing machine and steam tractor that was the power base for this seasonal event. As such, I was given the job of carrying water to the tractor near the barn and to the men in the fields. I used the conventional method of conveying the water, by tying several one gallon jugs of water together, draping them over Coli's back, and dropping most of them off at the steam tractor. After doing that, I would gallop off into the fields to quench the thirst of the sweaty field men and to tell them what time it was using my father's pocket watch. At the close of day, in my mind, I was absolutely essential to the success of this annual event. It sure was more fun than hoeing pea vines near our swimming hole.

The fall season, not unlike the other three seasons, issued in a new series of extra work duties, such as making sure that all the animals had extra straw bedding and that the ice covering the livestock watering trough was not frozen over. We made corn husking a competitive game; enjoyed the accolades we received from gathering, hulling, and drying walnuts; and sweated profusely under our added garments while cutting our winter's supply of wood for fuel. However, the most eagerly awaited activity of the fall, in fact, of any of the seasons, was the advent of custom butchering, when our slaughterhouse would resound with the squeals of hogs and the fractured English of one, or more, of the employed butchers. Upon returning from school, the aroma of freshly cooked lard and the sweet, smoky odor of hams, bacon, and sausages coming from the smoke house motivated us to quickly change our clothes, complete our daily chores, and head for an exciting visit to the slaughterhouse to read the name tags on the butchered carcasses and check the holding pens to determine how many we might expect to find hanging upside down the following evening.

My older brothers were well along in their apprenticeship here and were prone to flaunt their skills before their younger brothers, sisters, other relatives, or anyone else that they could coax inside to observe them. Our mother, in keeping with her Quaker heritage, was reticent to visit the slaughterhouse while it was in operation.

As one who was still too young, I'd dream about the day, hopefully before too long, when I would be in my brothers' boots and handling all of these dangerous tools. Meanwhile, I pondered, "How will I ever get all of this action to school for my turn at 'show and tell'?"

GETTING TO THE "Bigs"

When several neighbor or city kids, including girls, gathered at the farm for an "away game" on Saturday afternoon, the older boys would lay out the field, set up the rules, select the players, and finally determine the positions that each participant would play. The older boys, being more knowledgeable about the game, sometimes filled burlap bags about one-quarter full of dirt or sand, folded them three times, and used them for bases. These boys usually made sure there was some type of an outfield fence that only they could hit the ball over. The older boys contended they could do this because we were playing "barnlot baseball" and not sandlot baseball. Since I didn't know what sandlot baseball was, I guessed the older boys must be right.

Our sister, Rachel, and some of the other girls who were more athletic than some of the boys their ages threatened not to participate unless all of the girls and younger brothers were permitted to hold our pick-handle bat head in a vertical position. Then the older boys would be required to hold the handle head in a horizontal position. Since the baseball being used was frequently not round but rather somewhat egg-shaped, this rule, the girls insisted, would make a fair game.

When players were being selected, I would sometimes try not to notice that some of the girls would be chosen before the boys my age. My only consolation, I guessed, was that my little brother Hank would be the last one waiting in the player pool, and he would be playing right field for his team. I was experienced at both of these positions.

Most of the time in this position, you watched all of your teammates catching and throwing the ball during the game. If the ball was hit in the air to your position, you instinctively lost it in the sun, picked it up, and threw it to the centerfielder or the first baseman. Ground balls were even easier for the right fielder. If the ball was hit past you, it nearly always bounced or rolled through the wire fence for an automatic two-base hit. Of course, you were responsible for climbing over the barbed wire fence to retrieve the ball. Climbing over barbed wire fences, as almost every farm boy knew, could be extremely dangerous to your health, especially your masculinity. It seemed to me that right field might be a better position for a girl to play, but on second thought, I guess it would have been dangerous for her, too.

Rachel Cultice, Isabell Miller, & Evelyn Cultice, 1930.

I really liked baseball and sometimes I would crawl under our Atwater-Kent battery-powered radio in the corner of our living room, position the headphones, and listen to part of a baseball game being broadcast from Cincinnati. The Reds became my favorite team, and someday I hoped to see a "big league" game in Crosley Field where they played. A couple of years earlier, when our family drove all the way to Cincinnati, I had to go to the zoo with my mother, sisters, and little brother because, according to my father, I wasn't old enough to understand baseball like my brothers. I don't remember, but my sister Evelyn said that I cried during the tour of the zoo until our mother bought us ice cream. On that day especially, I wanted to find out why the ball in a big league game always bounced off the outfield fence. In our barn-lot games it always rolled or bounced through the fence. I needed an answer!

One Sunday, after church and our main meal, my father took me to a local sandlot ball game. He seemed to know the first names of the two umpires and all the local players, and he and the other persons sitting near us yelled at the players on both teams during the game.

I also noticed, like my father, that nearly every player on both teams was chewing tobacco and spitting on the field. My father told me that some of these players received a small amount of money for playing ball on Sunday afternoon but not as much as the "big league" players.

I guessed if I ever expected to be a "big leaguer," I would need to get out of right field, hit and throw the ball better, and learn to chew tobacco and spit on the field. I told my father I was going to grow up, become a "big league" ball player, and make lots of money so he wouldn't ever have to work again. He smiled, rubbed my head, and said, "I'm sure you'll be a very great, big leaguer."

A few days later, I sneaked a fist full of raisins from the kitchen pantry and stuffed them into my left cheek. I then picked up a half dozen small rocks from the yard, put them into my overall pocket, and retrieved the pick handle from the rear of the Model T truck. As I strutted around the lot, wearing my ragged baseball cap and toting the pick handle and rocks, I announced, "I'm the greatest batter in the world."

Then, I tossed a rock into the air, swung at it, and missed. "Strike one!" I yelled. Undaunted, I took a second rock out of my pocket and said again, "I'm the greatest batter in the world!" I tossed another rock into the air. When it came down, I swung again and missed. "Strike two!" I cried.

I then paused a moment to examine the pick handle and the next rock carefully. I spat on my hands and rubbed them together. I straightened my cap and said once more, "I'm the greatest hitter in the world." I missed, "Strike three!" "WOW!" I exclaimed, "I'm the greatest pitcher in the world."

On "Smitty"

It was necessary, as a result of the expansion of the slaughterhouse, for our father to employ an additional full-time butcher. For this position, our father employed a retired butcher who had operated a general store on Detroit Street for more than three decades. The new employee, Ed Schmidt, was small in stature, had bright blue eyes, a hearing impediment, and had bid farewell to most of his "chompers" several years before. He was seldom without a cigar, lighted or unlighted, clinched between his gums and his vocabulary tended to be weighted toward profanity.

Although "Mr. Smitty," as we children called him, was not a good storyteller, he seemed to hold our attention because he usually had a small bag of hard candy in his pocket. If we boys went outside to the woodpile and brought back enough wood to fuel the hog-scalding tank or the lard-rendering kettle, he would usually give us a few pieces of hard candy. Some days we boys would promise to have the wood inside when he arrived for work the next day. When we forgot our promise, he would give us the candy anyway and say, "Here's some candy for you lazy farts for bringing me in such damn good wood."

Smitty was very patient with us when we tried to help him clean the hog carcasses after they had been winched out of the scalding tank and placed on the floor of the slaughtering room. We learned where we should use a small scraping bell on the animal's carcass and how to remove the toenails with the "foot jerker."

After Smitty had been working for a few months, our father began to tell us stories about him when he owned his store on Detroit Street. Our father said that Mr. Schmidt always kept boxes and barrels of produce and meat on the sidewalk in front of his store and pedestrians frequently had difficulty working their way through the maze of goods when passing in front of the store. Besides this, he strung guy wires from the front of the store to the lampposts on the sidewalk and hanged dressed rabbits, poultry, etc. from them.

According to our father, Mrs. Green, a frequent and crotchety customer, was contemplating the purchase of a dressed rabbit. To insure its freshness, she pulled its legs apart and sniffed the interior of the carcass. Then she said, "Mr. Schmidt, this rabbit doesn't smell very good!" In anticipation of her negative comment, Smitty supposedly responded, "Well, if I did that to you Mrs. Green, you wouldn't smell a damn bit better."

GRANDPA Sandy

This entire work could easily have been written about my patriarchal grandfather, Sandy. Whether the scene or situation was economic, medical, political,

The Stock Market collapse in October 1929.

religious, or social, Sandy always seemed to be able to cut directly to the core of the issue with a concise, caustic, or comical comment.

Six years after Grandma Emerica died and the stock market took a massive drop on October 24, 1929, Grandpa Sandy came to live with us. Our father attempted to dissuade him from doing this because the only space we had for him was in the cellar. This space could only be reached by a door recessed in the floor of our back porch. Grandpa Sandy, however, was not to be deterred. Not only did he move into our home, but he convinced our father to allow him to bring along his cow Lulabelle and his two horses King and Prince. While we children did not really get excited about the idea of having another cow to "jerk" morning and evening, we just couldn't wait to have two more horses to lighten our workload and brighten our outdoor games on the farm. I guess we thought the idea of the horses was just the "cat's meow!"

It was obvious shortly after Grandpa Sandy moved in that the well-established house rules were not applicable to him. There were many and varied infractions which we children attempted, in vain, to call to the attention of our parents. In his room downstairs, Grandpa had a spittoon, which he was not supposed to have, and a "thunder mug," which he was supposed to use and didn't. As he said, "I prefer to spit in and shit out!"

In the kitchen, he consistently drank from the water dipper, rather than pouring the water into a glass. At the table he ate his food, including peas, with his knife, tucked his napkin into his waist instead of his collar, and ladled cold, red-eye gravy from the icebox onto his cold, apple pie for breakfast. Once, to the chagrin and consternation of our mother, when a discussion of the prevailing Depression was taking place at our supper table, Grandpa took out his false teeth, held them up, and said, "We'll all know that things have really gone to the dogs when I'm staring at these in a pawn shop window." Given all the things Grandpa got away with, we children couldn't understand why Grandpa became upset when we stirred raspberry jam into our mashed potatoes in order to give them a little color.

By 1930, many unemployed men resorted to selling apples on the street.

We always had time for one, or more of Grandpa Sandy's fabrications, especially if he was the butt of the joke. One evening when he was having supper with our family and we were having pork chops, which was very rare, he proceeded to entertain us with this tall tale. He said when he was small he was a very mean kid and his brothers, sisters, neighbor kids, and their family dog would not play with him. Eventually, however, his parents were able to get the family dog to play with him. Ever curious, we immediately asked Grandpa Sandy how they got the dog to cooperate. "Well," he said as he put down his coffee cup and smiled through his handlebar moustache, "they tied a pork chop with a piece of string and looped it around my neck." We children laughed in unison. At that point, our father looked at his father and said, "These kids already have more pranks than we can keep an eye on."

I liked very much to visit with my Grandpa in the basement and listen to his stories about when he was a boy and he used to drive a team of horses and a snow sled to the school to rescue his little brothers and sisters during a big snow storm. He said sometimes the snow was so deep that he could drive the team right over the tops of fences.

Sometimes, when I was in Grandpa's room, he would "accidentally" drop a nickel into his spittoon. Then he'd let me keep the nickel if I took the spittoon to the manure pile in the barnyard, emptied it, rinsed it out at the pump house, and brought it back to his room.

Grandpa also told me how his parents, when he was my age, used to take care of his sickness and injuries at home. He said before they knew Doctor Harris, if he had a sore throat or cold, they would have him gargle or sniff salt water. And when he had a cut or puncture, they would put a poultice of bacon rind or a cud of chewing tobacco on the injury. He also said that when he was my age, his family was so poor that they couldn't afford to go to the doctor's. So, he said, when he or one of his brothers or sisters needed a laxative, his mother took them into a room, sat them on a "thunder mug," closed the door, pulled the blinds, and recited ghost stories to them. After he told me this kind of story, his blue eyes would twinkle and he would preen the curled tips of his red, handlebar moustache with his fingers.

Home and office of Dr. James "Jim" Harris, Clifton, Ohio.

Grandpa Sandy was in his early seventies when he came to live with us, but he was still very strong physically and capable of putting in a full day's labor. Like our father, Grandpa exhibited a lofty work ethic. Once, I recall, when we brothers and Grandpa had returned to the house with horse and wagon after a day of fence building at the rear of the farm, our father queried his father Sandy relative to his sons' efforts. Grandpa pondered a while, spat on the wagon wheel, and replied, "Walter, them damn boys ain't worth the salt in their bread." Of course, if you knew Grandpa like we did, that came fairly close to being a compliment.

After we had worked the horses, Grandpa frequently would make sure that we took them to the watering trough before we removed their harnesses. His reminder was somewhat conventional: "Remember, boys! You can lead a horse to drink, but you can't make him water!" We boys would always be laughing before he finished.

My brother Winston said that one time when he and our brother Lowell were painting a room in the slaughterhouse, Grandpa Sandy entered and said, "There can't be any work going on in here because it's too quiet." When he had gone, Winston said to Lowell, "What the hell did Grandpa think we were painting with? hammers?"

Grandpa had been a butcher all of his life, and he was very knowledgeable and helpful when he was working in the slaughterhouse. Sometimes, he and our father would disagree about whether a hog should be split in the modern way for pork chops or backboned for tenderloins. Either way, Grandpa was prone to say, when we boys were present, "Now boys, if you want to grow up and be successful in life, all you need to do is put your backbone up someday where your wishbone is now."

Our father's brothers, Uncle Frank and Uncle Charlie, and his sister, Aunt Laura, enjoyed sharing stories with us about their father, Sandy. Aunt Laura told us that when her father went to Doctor Harris' office and received a prescription, he would bring it home and place it behind the clock on the mantle. When Grandma Emerica told him it was time to take his medicine, he would always ask her to read the instructions on the bottle. When she told him that he was supposed to take two pills every four hours, he would object and say, "I'll be damned. I'm not going to do that. I'm going to take four pills every eight hours. They're mine. I paid for 'em, and I'll take 'em any damned way I like."

One time, when Grandpa was experiencing a loss of hearing, he hitched Prince to the buggy and drove over to Clifton to visit Doctor Jim Harris. According to Uncle Frank, he entered the doctor's office, sat down, and explained to Dr. Jim that he was having difficulty hearing. When Dr. Jim queried him relative to the acuteness of the impairment, Sandy allegedly answered, "Well, Doc, it's so bad that I can't hear myself fart!" Doc replied, "Is that right, Sandy?" They then entered into a rather lengthy dialogue relative to the price of hogs per pound at the Cedarville stockyards and the price of corn per bushel at the Springfield granary.

During the discussion, Doc wrote out a prescription and Sandy paid him two dollars. When Sandy was about half-way out the door, he turned back to Doc and said, "Now look here, Doc, is this here medicine really going to help my hearing?" Doc quipped, "No, Sandy, it won't! But it sure will make you fart louder."

Our Uncle Charlie told us that when his father, Sandy, lived with his family for about two years, he and a neighbor, Marty Martin, used to sit, whittle sticks, chew tobacco, and joke about their respective spouses. Sandy contended that Emerica was not a very good housekeeper because sometimes when he went to the kitchen sink to piss, it would be full of dirty dishes. He also said that when he put his arm around his cow Lulabelle and told her he loved her, that she always gave more milk. And, he thought Grandma ought to know that. When Marty asked Grandpa if there was anything Grandma could do that Lulabelle couldn't do, he allegedly pondered a while and answered, "Yes, Lulabelle can't walk into water up to her rear end without getting her spigots wet."

Grandpa also told Marty about the time he made this big scarecrow, and the crows still stole his planted corn seed. Grandpa said he was told that his scarecrow was not ugly enough to frighten the crows away. "So," Marty asked, "what did you do about it?" Sandy smiled, and replied that he put a photograph of Grandma's face over the face of the scarecrow. "Did it work?" Marty asked. "Sure did," Sandy replied. "It not only kept the crows out this spring, but her face was so dour, that some of those SOB's brought back the corn they stole last spring!"

Seriously, though, grandpas are really smart! When our father asked Grandpa one time where Hank and I and our two playmates were, he replied, "I'm not sure, but they are probably up in the hayloft having a circle jerk!" I guess Grandpa was a kid once, too!

SHOTGUN Revelry

A "revelry" usually greeted a newly-married couple a few days after they returned from their honeymoon. I had never participated in a "revelry," but I understood that after the couple had gone to bed that everybody marched around their house making as much noise as possible. Then, after the newlyweds opened the door and invited the neighbors in, they usually served cake, candy, and cigars. If they didn't serve some type of goodies, the participants would play various types of pranks on them.

The whole event—staying up late at night, making as much noise as you possibly could, eating cake or candy, and playing tricks on adults—was a seven-year-old boy's dream. Eva Bocklett and her husband Fred were recently wed and the folks were gearing up for an old-fashioned "revelry" on their second night back.

The night of the event our family joined the celebration. Hank and I beat out a din with lard can lids. Our sisters tooted whistles. Our older brothers lighted fire crackers. Our father fired-off several shotgun blasts, and our Quaker mother marched with her hands clasped over her ears. Like our father, most of the men, my brother Winston said, were shooting shotguns because "they make the loudest noise."

While our family was eating supper a few days later, my sister Rachel referred to the event as "a shotgun, wedding revelry." While laughing, our father responded that it was a "wedding revelry" not a "shotgun wedding." My brother Winston also laughed as our mother frowned at both of them. I hoped that my brother would tell me sometime why he was laughing. He was only thirteen at the time, but he knew a lot of the same things that grown-ups did, and he almost always told me because he knew I wouldn't tell our parents.

Sometime later, my brother, with all of his adult knowledge, tried to explain to me that our grandparents had had a "shotgun wedding" because our grandfather didn't want "to be a daddy." Our grandmother's mother wrote him several letters inviting him to the wedding. When he didn't answer, she had the county sheriff take him an important piece of paper. After he read it, he changed his mind.

"So, after they were married, did the neighbors give them a big revelry with lots of shotguns?" I asked. No, my brother replied. "Well," I asked, "why was it called a shotgun wedding?" "I'm not sure," big brother replied, "but I think it was because Grandmother's mother mentioned something about a shotgun in each of her letters to Grandpa."

GLAD Rags

During the Great Depression, any type of dressy clothing was referred to as "glad rags." However, at our house and at Grandma Delie's house, "glad rags" included any type of household article or clothing that had been fashioned from a feed sack. These sacks, available at local mills and feed stores, for the most part were made from soft material such as muslin or huckaback and carried attractive exterior patterns. Wholesalers and retailers alike seemed to compete for business as much with the pattern of the sacks as with the quality of the contents.

A public park in St. Louis, Missouri, accommodated multiple shanties in 1933.

In our respective homes, feed sack curtains graced the kitchen windows; feed sack dish towels hung at the kitchen sink, and folks toweled-off with a large "glad rag" following Saturday evening's stand-up tub bath in front of the open oven. In addition, there were glad rag mattress covers, bed sheets, and pillow slips in some of the bedrooms.

Finally, burlap doormats invited those entering at both the front and back doors "to please wipe your shoes before entering." Burlap was a very coarse fabric, made from hemp. It was generally not used for clothing, but employed outside the home. We used it at the outbuildings and in the slaughterhouse.

In 1929, during our second grade class' Christmas play, I wore a shepherd's cloak that Grandma Delie had made from burlap. During the Christmas vacation, Doctor Harris visited our house and treated me for a severe rash on my neck and shoulders. He told my mother that it could have been a lot worse if I hadn't been wearing my winter "long johns."

L to R: Winston Cultice, Ralph Truesdale, John Ernst, Walter Cultice, & Lowell Cultice, 1933.

Earlier that year Grandma had made a pair of knickers for me and my little brother Hank. I could hardly wait to show them off at school because my grandma made them. However, Hank, who was only five, according to our father, said he wasn't going to wear his knickers unless our mother allowed him to go to school, too.

My twin sisters were prone to boast about the numerous "glad rags" that Grandma had made for them a few years earlier. Almost without exception, they would relate how she made each of them new dresses with matching bloomers and how eager they were to wear them to school on Monday. Much to their surprise, the Watson twins arrived at school that same Monday wearing matching "glad rags" dresses. Later, on the playground, while they were on the teeter totter, one of my sisters noticed that the Watson twins also had matching bloomers. My sisters traditionally concluded their rendition of the incident by contending that their outfits were superior to the Watson twins because Grandma Delie was real smart and used a prettier feed-sack pattern.

Holiday Events

Both at school and at home our family would recognize several of the holidays during the year. My brother Hank and I would sometimes patiently listen to our grandparents and parents extol the merits of "the good ole days"; attempt to dispute, despite the candy and gifts, the existence of the Easter Bunny and Santa Claus; and try to anticipate the accompanying "sibling abuse" that our older brothers would attempt to perpetrate upon us.

While we children would all be out of school on New Year's Day, my recollection is primarily of listening to the noise and watching the rockets "bursting in air" from our sisters' west bedroom window upstairs.

By Valentine's Day of 1930, I was in the big, two-room, two-class elementary school named Orient Hill. My second grade teacher's name was Mrs. Stevens, and I had liked her ever since I entered the day after Labor Day. My twin sisters were across the main hall in Mrs. Bell's fourth-grade class.

Our mother permitted each of us to purchase a valentine for each of our classmates and our teachers. My sisters helped me select my valentines and write the correct spelling of the names on the envelopes. Mrs. Stevens' valentine was very special and it read: "Dear Valentine, why beef when there is so much at stake? Promise me you'll be my valentine." She laughed when she opened it and said, "This valentine is so appropriate." I wasn't sure what she meant by "appropriate," but I was really glad she thought it was funny.

I remember that Easter was namely about church, flowers, and the Easter Bunny. In fact, just before Easter the previous year, Grandpa Sandy had told Hank and me that if we wanted to catch the Easter Bunny, all we had to do was "to hide in the grass and make a noise like a carrot." Almost eight, in an effort to continue the fruits of the Bunny's gift basket, along with my brother Hank, I was fighting off the attempts of my older brothers and sisters to convince me that this "egg-laying rabbit" was not for real. The day after Easter, my older brothers offered me a small chocolate egg which the Easter Bunny had forgotten to give me. I, of course, was unaware that they had hollowed out the center of the egg and inserted a hen turd. I quickly popped the entire egg into my mouth and started chewing on it. They had already started to laugh, but when I gagged, spit it out, and yelled "This tastes like shit," they rolled in the grass convulsing with laughter. Finally, after they had given me another "shitless egg" to take the bad taste out of my mouth, and I had promised not to tell anybody about what they had done, they said, "Now you're smart enough not to believe in the Easter Bunny." Somehow, in retrospect, I guess I still wasn't too smart. Instead of sharing the incident with my little brother, I should have kept my promise so I could laugh and roll in the grass while he gagged next Easter.

We all perpetrated and were the recipients of assorted April Fool's Day pranks and jokes. For some reason, most of the intended "fools" were on guard for our attempts to fool them.

Memorial Day would find our family visiting cemeteries and placing freshly-cut flowers on relatives' graves and listening to our parents relate numerous stories about their lives. Our mother conventionally placed one, or more, flowers on the graves of military veterans. She would encourage us to accompany her and place additional flowers on the graves. Some years this practice would be held just before we enjoyed a family picnic at the edge of the cemetery or in a nearby park.

We all looked forward to Independence Day when we could play with matches. My older brothers' friends would annually get firecrackers for them at a very cheap price. My sisters appeared to be satisfied to light and twirl sparklers. Hank and I felt really grown-up when we held a small, "punk" firecracker in one hand and it exploded. Larger salutes, M-80's and cherry bombs were restricted to our older brothers, however. They would use these devices to blow up boxes, tin cans, and glass jars. The latter two, of course, mandated a quick withdrawal and concealment before the obstacle was shattered by the explosion. Hank and I frequently begged our older brothers to allow us to ignite these powerful firecrackers especially after they had been secured under a tin can since the can usually was blown several feet in the air.

We younger brothers were nearly in orbit ourselves, when our older brothers and their friends offered us an opportunity to simultaneously light a cherry bomb under what appeared to be two upright coffee cans about ten feet apart on a gravel surface near the woodshed. What we didn't know was that the cherry bombs and wicks had been covered with paraffin and placed under a Quaker Oats box that was nearly filled with semi-liquid, cow manure. After threatening to tell our father, we small brothers refused to help wash the entire side of the woodshed and headed for the swimming hole for a brief swim and a laundering of our shirts and overalls.

Of all the Halloween pranks that we brothers were privy to, none could ever supersede my brother Lowell's, which backfired on his seat. It seemed that he and some of his classmates had gone into the west end of town on the eve of Halloween, divided into two teams, and attempted to establish bragging rights by turning over backyard outhouses for a given period of time. I don't remember which team won, but I do remember the next day that a county sheriff's car pulled into our property, and a deputy got out and talked to our father. When the deputy was gone, our father took my brother to the woodshed, closed the door, and we could hear the smacks, and my brother yelling that he understood why he was being punished. Later, when my brother recovered, he said that our father didn't whip him because he helped turn over an outhouse last night, but rather because he didn't knock on the privy door before he helped push it over. According to the sheriff's deputy, there was a tiny grandmother inside who needed the assistance of some neighbors to get out of the privy, which was on its back and had an outward swinging hinged door.

Other than at school, I don't recall that our family celebrated Armistice Day. I suppose we younger boys were silently grateful that our older brothers and their friends hadn't concocted some dangerous "away game" that would have caused our sisters to weep as they placed flowers on our graves.

Thanksgiving memories are replete with our family gathered around the dining room table and enjoying several traditional dishes. 1930s Thanksgiving, however, is the most memorable. Ably assisted by my father, I convinced my mother to cook eight of my pigeons instead of two chickens for our main dish. At the table, with our parents' approval and participation, we traded with one another in order to have an abundance of our favorite piece or pieces. It was fun, inexpensive, and very rewarding for this junior poultry dealer.

Even before I went into the first grade, we brothers would hitch Rex or Coli to the snow sled, go to a small clump of trees near the creek, saw down a six to eight-foot pine tree, and haul it back to the house for Christmas. We had a few commercial decorations on the tree; however, most of them were fashioned from papers, dried cranberries, and popcorn.

Every Christmas, without exception, our family would receive a large box of candy from our Aunt Annie in Indiana. In a way, this gift amounted to a mathematical motivator. At first opportunity, when unsupervised, we children would open the box, count the pieces, and divide by eight, and stake a claim to our 10-piece grid on the top or bottom layer of the box.

Our mother's parents, Grandpa Jim and Grandma Delie, would usually arrive at our house shortly after supper on Christmas Eve and park near the entrance, off the road. They would still be in the living room when we children went upstairs to bed. At first, we tried to audit conversation downstairs by gathering near the heat registers in the living room ceiling. When we were not successful in doing this, my brother Winston outlined another plan for the following year. The plan called for Hank and me to keep Grandpa in his chair for one of his "less-than-true stories," Evelyn and Rachel to sit on Grandma's lap and talk about their favorite Christmas recipes, while Lowell and Winston went quietly out the back door and around the house. Then, using a flashlight, they'd look under the blanket on the back seat of Grandpa's Model T Ford. When most of the presents they saw were under the tree the next morning, our brother said, "I think I know where Santa parked his sled last night."

There were few holidays, as indicated earlier, when our older brothers did not target Hank and me for one of their pranks. Two years earlier, our brothers knew that Hank and I had asked Santa to bring us a pony for Christmas. They also told us that we should leave a note in Hank's "wish stocking," and Santa would probably grant our wish. The pony, they said, would be in the stable with Rex and Coli. My older brothers were up, out to the stable, and back in the house, before anyone was out of bed on Christmas morning. They, of course had placed several "horse apples" in Hank's "wish stocking." I followed Hank downstairs, and he took the shortest route to his "wish stocking." He peered in, backed up while holding his nose, and started to cry. Through his laughter, my brother Lowell said, "I guess Santa brought your pony, but he got away."

HOMEMADE Guns

I envied my older brothers and their friends who seemed to be able to make almost any type of toy or sports equipment that they needed. Almost every boy near where we lived had a slingshot that he had made. My brothers would cut a forked branch from a tree and shape it to size with a pocketknife. Then they would find a discarded inner tube and cut a couple of rubber strips about a foot long from it. They tied one end of each strip to one of the forks and attached the other end to a leather pocket, usually made from the tongue of an old shoe.

Before my brothers could go hunting, they needed bullets for their slingshots. We smaller boys were given the task of collecting rocks in coffee cans for this purpose.

Most of the older boys were pretty good shots with these homemade guns, and they would sometimes "bag" a rat, gopher, or rabbit on the first shot. After the novelty of slingshots had worn off and the older boys were into rifles, they passed the slingshots down to their little brothers (at our house it was my sisters) or taught them how to cut the forks and rubber strips to make them.

As novices, we spent quite a bit of our time shooting tin cans and glass jars that we had placed on top of fence posts. One of our favorite "away games" was to attempt to hit the large glass insulators at the top of the power poles along the gravel roads. When we did this, we didn't have to worry about running out of ammunition. However, we did have to worry that our parents would find out about our mischief and remind us of the consequences.

When Hank and I asked our brother Lowell to make us each a homemade rifle so that we could play cops and robbers, he told us that he couldn't do this unless we had two clothes pins to use for the triggers. The next Monday, while we were helping our sisters hang the day's wash on the clothes line, we each managed to pocket a couple of clothes pins. My brother sliced an old inner tube into ammunition for our guns. He cut the tubes into one-inch wide strips forming large rubber bands and knotted them in the middle. Then the bands were stretched from the notched end of the gun barrel to the clothespin trigger. The gun's one-piece handle was made of scrap wood from our father's contracting truck.

There, of course, were no written rules about using these weapons when we played. However, it was a rule to always aim shots at the feet and never at the face. We brothers seemed to enjoy it most when we could target and hit some member of the family or a playmate right in the broadest part of their trousers or dress.

Once, when our Aunt Grace was visiting from Chicago, Hank accidentally shot her under the chin, and the rubber band slid down into her bosom. She just laughed as she pulled it out and said Hank was just "a chip off the old block." I didn't understand what she meant because we didn't use chips and blocks to make our rubber guns.

Setting the Table

It did not hold, as my older brothers had promised our parents, that when we moved to the country they would fish, hunt, and trap and my parents would never need to go the grocery store again. However, all three of these industries, at the rural level, were a major source of excitement and did, at various times, decrease our food expenses.

We fished year round, chopping holes in the ice on Mr. Sutton's pond in the winter in order to catch small pan fish. During the warm months we would frequently catch enough frogs or turtles to constitute an entire meal for our eight-member family.

Rabbits, squirrels, ground hogs, pheasants, and pigeons were very prevalent on our farm and in the woods on the surrounding farms. At first we would attempt to shoot them with our first gun, an air rifle, which usually only frightened or stunned them. However, after reaching the "gun passage age" of twelve and receiving our first .22 caliber rifle, we enjoyed much more success.

Occasionally our hunting safaris did not include a rifle but only a flashlight. When we accompanied our father on stock buying trips to area farms and noticed the presence of many pigeons, knowing they were a real nuisance to the farmer, we sought permission, minus a firearm, to remove them free of charge. We had a unique method of capturing them for our family table and/or selling them to a local poultry dealer to earn our own spending money.

We brothers were probably more serious about our trapping exploits than most of our rural peers. In addition to rabbits and squirrels, we were successful in trapping raccoons, opossums, muskrats, and skunks. We corresponded with snare and steel trap companies in St. Louis and Chicago and two major pelt buyers in other cities.

Our winter evening meal at home would occasionally consist of groundhog or raccoon fare, but my father would not permit "any critter with a rat-like tail" to gain a pot position in, or on, our kitchen stove. At the time of our first store-bought haircuts, we brothers, however, learned that one of the barbers at Del Johnstone's shop, Brownie Herr, was very fond of baked possum or muskrat stuffed with sweet potatoes. He agreed to trade us haircuts for these carcasses. As a result, our parents may have entertained the thought that we might be gaining a measure of business aptitude.

Our excitement was always heightened when we sensed the distinctive musk odor of a skunk in the cold morning air. If we were successful in trapping this critter, especially a star skunk, we knew that we would be a few dollars wealthier following the tedious task of removing the pelt. We also knew, that if we were sprayed by the musk it would mean washing our clothes in vinegar, a canned, tomato-juice bath, and spending a night or two sleeping in the tree house. We always felt really lucky when we caught these rascals on a school-day morning. Sometimes it must have seemed to our parents that we were more jubilant about the day out of school than the catch.

My Heroes

In retrospect, my heroes at age seven were six in number. One of my first heroes was a playmate of both my older brothers. His name was Ernest Hillyard, and he visited our farm almost every week. He would help my brothers with their various chores, and he was very polite. My par-

Section 1

"All the News That's Fit to Print."

The New York Times.

THE WEATHER
Generally fair today and tomorrow; moderate to fresh southerly winds.
Temperature yesterday—Max., 60; Min., 53.
For weather report see Page 31.

Section 1

VOL. LXXVI....No. 25,320. NEW YORK, SUNDAY, MAY 22, 1927. FIVE CENTS In Manhattan Bronx and Brooklyn | Elsewhere TEN CENTS

LINDBERGH DOES IT! TO PARIS IN 33½ HOURS; FLIES 1,000 MILES THROUGH SNOW AND SLEET; CHEERING FRENCH CARRY HIM OFF FIELD

COULD HAVE GONE 500 MILES FARTHER

Gasoline for at Least That Much More Flew at Times From 10 Feet to 10,000 Feet Above Water.

ATE ONLY ONE AND A HALF OF HIS FIVE SANDWICHES

Fell Asleep at Times but Quickly Awoke—Glimpses of His Adventure in Brief Interview at the Embassy.

LINDBERGH'S OWN STORY TOMORROW.

Captain Charles A. Lindbergh was too exhausted after his arrival in Paris late last night to do more than indicate, as told below, his experiences during his flight. After he awakes today, he will narrate the full story of his remarkable exploit for readers of Monday's New York Times.

By CARLYLE MACDONALD.

Copyright, 1927, by The New York Times Company.
Special Cable to THE NEW YORK TIMES.

PARIS, Sunday, May 22.—Captain Lindbergh was discovered at the American Embassy at 2:30 o'clock this morning. Attired in a pair of Ambassador Herrick's pajamas, he sat on the edge of a bed and talked of his flight. At the last moment Ambassador Herrick had canceled the plans of the reception committee and, by unanimous consent, took the flier to the embassy in the Place d'Iena.

A staff of American doctors who had arrived at Le Bourget Field early to minister to an "exhausted" aviator found instead a bright-eyed, smiling youth who refused to be examined.

"Oh, don't bother; I am all right," he said.

"I'd like to have a bath and a glass of milk. I would feel better," Lindbergh replied when the Ambassador asked him what he would like to have.

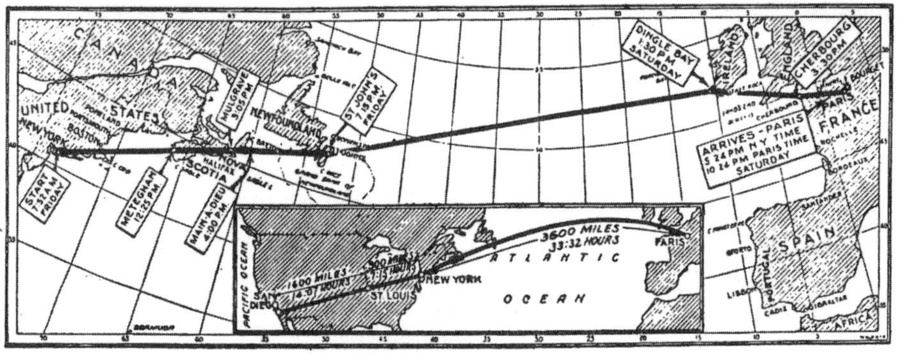

MAP OF LINDBERGH'S TRANSATLANTIC ROUTE, SHOWING THE SPEED OF HIS TRIP.

LEVINE ABANDONS BELLANCA FLIGHT

Venture Given Up as Designer Splits With Him—Plane Narrowly Escapes Burning.

BYRD'S CRAFT IS NAMED

Lindbergh Cheered at Ceremony—Commander, Now Last in Field, Waits on Weather.

Through no fault of his own, Clarence D. Chamberlin, who with Bert Acosta established a world's non-stop flying record a few weeks ago, will not fly the record-breaking monoplane in an attempt to establish a second New York-Paris non-stop flight.

G. M. Bellanca, designer of the plane, and Charles S. Levine of the Columbia Aircraft Company, owner

LINDBERGH TRIUMPH THRILLS COOLIDGE

President Cables Praise to "Heroic Flier" and Concern for Nungesser and Coli.

CAPITAL THROBS WITH JOY

Kellogg, New, MacNider, Patrick and Many More Join in Paying Tribute to Daring Youth.

Special to The New York Times.

WASHINGTON, May 21.—The triumph of Captain Charles A. Lindbergh in flying from New York to Paris without a stop created a tremendous sensation in the national capital and found immediate response in a host of official messages and statements congratulating the daring aviator upon his achievement.

President Coolidge expressed his

CROWD ROARS THUNDEROUS WELCOME

Breaks Through Lines of Soldiers and Police and Surging to Plane Lifts Weary Flier from His Cockpit

AVIATORS RESCUE HIM FROM FRENZIED MOB OF 25,000

Paris Boulevards Ring With Celebration After Day and Night Watch—American Flag Is Called For and Wildly Acclaimed.

By EDWIN L. JAMES.

Copyright, 1927, by The New York Times Company.
Special Cable to THE NEW YORK TIMES.

PARIS, May 21.—Lindbergh did it. Twenty minutes after 10 o'clock tonight suddenly and softly there slipped out of the darkness a gray-white airplane as 25,000 pairs of eyes strained toward it. At 10:24 the Spirit of St. Louis landed and lines of soldiers, ranks of policemen and stout steel fences went down before a mad rush as irresistible as the tides of the ocean.

"Well, I made it," smiled Lindbergh, as the little white monoplane came to a half in the middle of the field and the first vanguard reached the plane. Lindbergh made a move to jump out. Twenty hands reached for him and lifted him out as if he were a baby. Several thousands in a minute were around the plane. Thousands more broke the barriers of iron rails round the field, cheering wildly.

Lifted From His Cockpit.

As he was lifted to the ground Lindbergh was pale, and, with his hair unkempt, he looked completely worn out. He had strength enough, however, to smile, and waved his hand to the crowd. Soldiers with fixed bayonets were unable to keep back the crowd.

United States Ambassador Herrick was among the first to welcome and congratulate the hero.

A NEW YORK TIMES man was one of the first to reach the machine after its graceful descent to the field. Those first

ents sometimes invited him to stay for supper. When my brothers, always as an "away game," staged a rodeo contest, he won nearly every time. He also was the best shot when they were targeting tin cans or crows with their .22 rifles. In fact, I once saw him knock a tin can off a fence post behind him while using a rear-view mirror. He could ride horse back under the lowest limb of our tree house, grasp the limb, and scamper up and into the tree house in less time than anyone else, including my brothers. I aspired to doing all of those things someday while the other kids watched and said, "Wow."

Another hero was my brother Winston who almost always won first or second place in the games that we played. He was also very smart. He always seemed to know when, and just how hard, we would be punished when we transgressed the established intramural or extramural rules. In fact, sometimes he could predict exactly how many swats we would receive with a conventional instrument of correction—a fly swatter, waist belt, razor strap, etc. I guess he figured his pre-warning would afford his little brothers an opportunity to locate some cardboard to place inside the seat of our overalls. We would, of course, eventually learn how he could be so accurate with his predictions.

I, like all my boyhood playmates at any location, was totally enamored with Babe Ruth and probably knew his full name, George Herman Ruth, before I knew my father's. Whether we were batting, throwing, running, catching, or sliding, we were always Babe Ruth. His record of 60 runs in 1927 was instrumental in my learning to count to that figure before I attempted to master the alphabet. Besides this, a guy needed three Jimmy Foxx bubblegum baseball cards or six "aggie" marbles to get his hands on a Babe Ruth card.

In that same year, 1927, another hero entered my life. This hero had flown an airplane named "Saint Louis" all by himself all the way across an ocean. It was more than I could comprehend. When I learned that you could receive a large "Lucky Lindy" coin by mailing in several Tootsie Roll wrappers, I was quick to respond thanks to my mother's help. Almost immediately, my little brother and I stopped flying our homemade airplanes over the cattle watering trough. Instead, we took them to our swimming hole and pretended we were our new hero, Charles "Lucky Lindy" Lindberg.

The afore-mentioned were all heroic figures in my young life. However, my greatest hero was my father. He was, at this impressionable age, the biggest, stron-

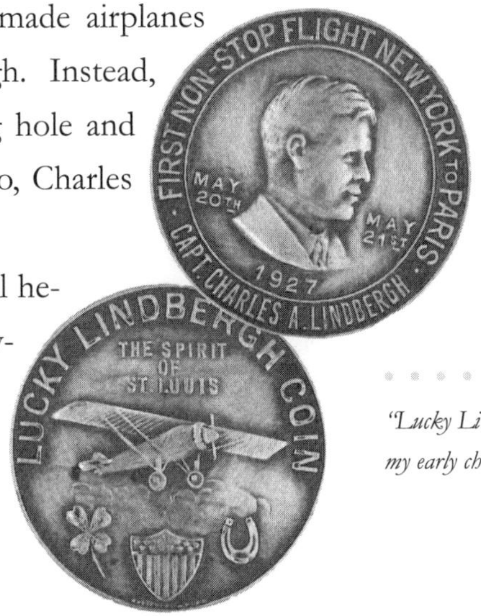

"Lucky Lindy" was one of my early childhood heroes.

gest, bravest, and smartest person I would ever know in the world. He was so big that his shoes would leave footprints in the soil or snow, and I could not fill one print with both of my feet. He was so strong that he could carry me and Hank as far as we had declined to walk. He was not afraid of the biggest, meanest bull either. When he put his fingers through the ring in the bull's nose, the bull would gently follow him wherever he wanted to go. Lastly, he was so smart that he seemed to always know where we had been, what marginal activity we had engaged in, and that our eyes were still open when we were supposed to be asleep upstairs. Boy, oh boy! I surely hoped I'd be that smart someday.

HOME ON THE Range

Our kitchen, similar to many homes during this era, was the center of our household, especially at meal time. The large cooking range was in constant use from early in the morning until the dishes were washed after supper. Most of the food that was cooked on the range or in the oven was prepared by our mother at her Hoosier cabinet or dough cabinet or by my father in the slaughterhouse. The vegetables and fruits were grown or picked wild on the farm, and the meat was raised or hunted on the farm.

Shortly after my mother had graphically illustrated for me just where our family was on the hog—mostly east and west—I began to tune-in more attentively by the coded vocabulary of my older brothers and sisters relative to our daily meals. Firstly, they told me that in the north end of our town the folks referred to what they ate as their "menu." I thought that "menu" was an interesting word, but when they also told me that folks in the north end of town ate dinner at night, lunch at noon, and didn't eat supper at all, I became very confused. Mostly, I wondered what they ate out of their dinner buckets at night.

Pork was the main meat dish at our table. However, with our custom butchering, we occasionally enjoyed beef, veal, lamb, and wild game. On rare occasions, when we did not have a meat entree, our father, once he sat down, would scan the table and ask, "Where's the hog?" This question, of course, was always good for a laugh.

At our meal, our father would always insist on having cream in the cream pitcher. "Milk," he insisted, "is for kids, calves, and kittens." The most unacceptable word at our table was "tough!" In short, it was alright to classify the meat as a "little tight," but the term "tough" was an unacceptable term to those in his chosen vocation. He clearly did not want to hear it.

The words in our coded meat vocabulary were a combination of "slaughterhouse" and sibling ingenuity. Our parents, of course, did not know the meaning of many of these coded words in our "meal" vocabulary.

Moo juice and bread, in one form or another, were on our table nearly twenty-one times a week. In addition to these two staples, in a given week, one might expect to find any of the following:

Breakfast	Dinner	Supper
Oatmeal	*Rabbit Food*	*Strong Food*
Shingle "J"	*Rattlers*	*Stringers*
Fried Mush	*Lickers*	*Oysters/Fish*
Sticky Stuff	*Canned Gas*	*Rocky Mountain Oysters*
Smart Food	*Fried Spuds*	*Blackberry Soup*
Cackleberries	*Sow Belly*	*Pisser Stew*
Chin Bacon	*Force Meat*	*Baked Maws*
Fried Spuds	*Loud Food*	*Jar Fruit*
Scrapple	*Jar Vegetables*	*Fried Spuds*
Hot Mush	*Fly Swatter Soup*	*Smashed Spuds*
Indian-Dog Bread	*S.L.O.P.*	*Paunhaus*
Rabbit Food	*Roast Butt*	*Sweet Food*
Soppin's	*Cake/Pie*	

While we were dining on these, mostly offal delicacies, our father would school us in the art of separating the meat from the bones. According to him, "the bones should be so clean that when you throw them out to the dog, the dog will look at them, pick them up in his mouth, and throw them back into the house."

The supper menu was sometimes seasonably varied to accommodate one or more visitors, especially our Aunt Grace from Chicago and our Aunt Annie from Indianapolis. They would usually visit every other year. We children, having been previously sworn to secrecy, could barely contain ourselves at supper as Aunt Grace extolled the wonderful flavor of Rocky Mountain Oysters. The next year we children would need the same measure of containment as our Aunt Annie raved about the tenderness and flavor of the beef or lamb "tender groin."

I guess our meal motto was "we can eat anything that won't eat us." In concert with this philosophy, we children were led to believe that every type of meat we ate—sweet food, smart food, strong food, etc.—would improve our mental or physical condition.

Once, when my brother Lowell asked Grandpa Sandy if everything our father said about the meat improving our condition was true, Grandpa supposedly responded, "You kids are eatin' real good and you little farts don't need to squeal about what's on the table." So, I guess that took care of about the only parts of the hog that didn't show up on our table.

We children still had one more question that we needed answered. If eating sweetbreads made us sweet, eating pig's feet made us fast, eating brains made us smart, and eating heart made us strong, that was ok! However, if we ate too many Rocky Mountain Oysters, would we be apt to go nuts?

I regret that these special recipes were lost to posterity.

HOME Games

Winter, summer, spring, and fall every field, creek, building, and plot of ground on our farm was the potential site of one of our conventional or innovative games. We were afforded limited time for such activities and lost little time in an effort to enjoy such time to the fullest.

Our playmates, in addition to family members, were drawn from the neighboring farms, the city, and a few black children who resided on the north side of the multiple railroad tracks.

In retrospect, our games could have been classified as home and away games. That is, the games we played when our parents were home, and the games we played when our parents were away from home.

For several years, the respective Quaker-Methodist backgrounds of our family prohibited us from playing the conventional games of baseball, basketball, and football on Sunday. This restriction, as interpreted by my older brothers, only applied if our parents were at home at that time.

There was always a shortage of equipment for these games, and the eagerness to play was consistently the mother of invention. Handles of earth picks taken from our father's contracting truck were regularly substituted for broken ball bats. Baseballs were routinely taped with friction tape from the same source.

Our basketball goal was a discarded barrel hoop that was nailed onto the south side of our barn. It was located here because there was a high "goose-neck" type electric light at the southwest corner of the barn.

My father had never played football, didn't understand the rules, and didn't want his sons to engage in the sport.

Therefore, when we had an inflated football and it was not in use, it was concealed underneath the granary. When we did not have an inflated football, we rolled up a burlap bag, tied it securely with binder twine, and continued the game.

Sometimes, the inflated bladders in our footballs and basketballs would sustain a leak or puncture. When this happened we would unlace the cover, remove the bladder, patch the leak using an automobile tire vulcanizing kit, place it back in the cover, inflate it, and sew up the laces. When the original bladder deteriorated to the status of non-repair, we would sometimes substitute a hog bladder from the slaughterhouse. Fortunately, the butchering, football, and basketball seasons ran concurrently every year.

Nearly overlooked in this narrative of conventional games were our early spring baseball games in the various pastures. When the milk cows were first released to graze in the fields, there were two givens. One, for several days the milk from the cows would taste of the wild onions they ingested. Two, there would be many un-solidified, cow-dung patties scattered over the field. Each year, at least one, or more, unknowledgeable playmates would be invited to join us in a baseball game in one of these pastures. However, before the intended victim arrived, our gang, using lard-can lids for home plate and the three bases, would have the field carefully laid out. Without exception, there would be a fresh cow patty concealed under second or third base. When the victim, through a hit, walk, or intentional error reached the preceding base, a pre-arranged signal would be given that encouraged the runner to advance and always with a fast slide. As the runner was sliding into the base, the defenseman, with or without the ball, would edge his toe under the lid and flip it aside. Once in a while, the defenseman's foot would be too near the patty and both individuals would be calling for timeout. Meanwhile, the players on both teams convulsed with laughter.

Away Games

In the previously listed home games, we held fairly fast to the conventional rules and regulations. However, when our parents were away, we generously enacted or modified the rules, usually to the advantage of the Cultice kids, as the contest progressed. These creative contests were ordinarily held on Sunday afternoons when our parents and sisters were ten or more miles away from home and had placed our oldest brother Winston in charge during their absence.

Since our farm was a haven for stray cats and dogs, many of whom became quickly domesticated on meat scraps and cracklings, there was always a choice of cats to choose from when we were going to play our "Cat in the Carpet" game. The game itself was quite simple. We took a small carpet or rag rug from the house, placed it flat on the grass, put our chosen cat and a small container of milk in the center of the carpet, and patiently held on to the four corners of the carpet. When the cat became preoccupied with the milk, with a swift upward motion and downward snap, we simultaneously sent the cat and the container nearly fifteen or more feet into the air. The scoring was likewise very simple. Each two-man team received one point for every revolution the cat made on its way up or down, one point if the cat landed feet first on the rug, and unlimited single bonus points for the number of times you could snap the helpless critter back into orbit before it could scamper off the rug.

Chicken racing, on the ground and in the air, was another form of entertainment. We would scratch starting and finishing lines about twenty-five feet apart in the dirt between the poultry house and the woodshed. After running down what we each considered to be the fastest leghorn in the coop and bringing the excited critter to the starting line, we would wait for the signal to release our potential winner.

This contest eventually went airborne when we placed a small, rectangular-shaped starting box on a fence post. The box had a hinged door at either end. The signal to start authorized the "pilot" as we referred to ourselves to open the front door to release the chicken for flight, and, as was usually necessary, to also open the rear door in order to administer a much needed prod. The rules were inordinately simple. You could not touch the bird after it flew the coop, and the bird that flew the greatest distance in any direction before it landed was declared the winner.

My oldest brother Winston always seemed to win any type of chicken race. I thought he just had a good eye for fast chickens. Many years later his secret was revealed. He was, in racing parlance, "doctoring" the critters. In short, before each race, he would stuff a pinch of hot Zanzibar pepper in the bird's cloacae. He was the only brother who had access to the seasoning cabinet in the sausage room.

While the conventional types of horse racing and jumping contests frequently took place on the farm, the "at home games" were frequently broadened into rodeo-type contests when our parents and sisters were away. Utilizing calves and small steers born on the farm and purchased for slaughter, imitating our western heroes of Gene Autry, Ken Maynard, and Tom Mix, we would ride along side these running animals, lasso, or dive onto their necks, wrestle them to the ground, and quickly bind their four feet. This practice, in true barnyard parlance, was known as "hog-tying." Again, the rules were simple. It was a time-based contest and would be judged by anyone present who owned a watch. More often than not, none of us had a watch and we would have to go into the house and borrow the alarm clock.

Since Monday was a major slaughtering day, the barn and adjacent feed lot would usually be replete with various steers, heifers, cows, and bulls on Sunday afternoons. The bulls, however, were kept and fed in a separate pen. The main feeding lot had a long, feeding trough in the center which accommodated ten animals on each side.

Having gained some insight into the relationship between male and female bovine, my brothers quickly calculated that by withholding the feed from the females until Sunday afternoons, we might witness some "real live barnyard action."

The plan, when executed, called for the feed to be placed in the trough. Then, when each cow or heifer had its head between the stanchions, we would open the gate and allow the bull access to the harem of cute, young heifers.

The contest became a favorite of the area boys, especially our peers from the city. The event was eventually given the title of "Barnyard Circus." This title, of course, was little more than a cover for what was actually taking place.

We brothers enjoyed collecting nickel and dime wagers from unsophisticated urban attendees who did not understand the scene from the bull's perspective. In short, several cute heifers dining at the feed trough are no substitute for a worn out milk cow in heat.

Early History Lesson

It was conventionally hot in the upstairs bedrooms in our home during the summer months, and we children, with an Indian blanket in tow, frequently retreated to the front porch or lawn to spend the night.

Our parents agreed to our bedroom relocation only after we agreed not to utilize the front porch light. My sister Evelyn appeared to be the future scientist in the family when she suggested that we could carry out our plan by increasing our evening's catch of fireflies. Sisters can sometimes be real smart. Thereafter we went to sleep by the light of our Ball-Mason jar firefly lanterns, the fragrance of honeysuckle and fruit tree blossoms, and the ever-present serenade of cicadas. We boasted to all that we didn't even have to get up to turn out the lanterns. "Yeah!" our little brother Hank said to Grandma Delie. "We don't have to get up and turn out the lanterns, 'cause the fireflies all die just before it gets light in the morning."

Oblivious to the lack of a mattress and the ubiquitous critters—mosquitoes, spiders and assorted unnamed bugs—we talked about our friends, planned our pranks for the next day, and relieved ourselves in the adjacent orchard instead of walking to the privy at the back of the house.

Sometimes, on really clear nights after we had gone through the aforementioned routine, we would relocate on the front lawn at the edge of the orchard. Resting on our blankets, Hank and I would listen attentively as our older siblings attempted to convince us that Grandpa Jim was really joking when he told us that the moon was yellow because it was made out of cheese.

We quickly learned within the constellation of stars to identify the Big Dipper and the Little Dipper and fell asleep scanning the heavens for a fireball meteor that we could brag about to our friends the next day.

One evening, after staying for supper, Grandpa Jim and Grandma Delie were about to leave in their Model T and Hank and I were pointing out the Big Dipper to them, when Grandma Delie told us that Negro people sometimes refer to the Big Dipper as the "Great Gourd in the Sky." She said she would tell us more about the name on their next visit.

Sometime later she told us that she was born during the Civil War when black slaves were trying to become free by moving north on the Underground Railroad. She told us that they hid in basements and barns during the day and traveled at night. Grandma Delie said that the leader of the slaves, Harriet Tubman, told them that if they followed "The Great Gourd in the Sky" they would soon gain their freedom.

Upon reflection, while I could understand why the slaves wanted to be free, I was probably somewhat confused with Grandma Delie's story. Firstly, I was certain she was born during the "Silver" War not the Civil War. Furthermore, the gourds in our garden only grew on vines, not in the sky. Finally, all of the railroads north of our farm were above ground.

It did make some sense to me, however, if the slaves were riding the railroad north to get their freedom, that's probably why they were still living on the north side of the tracks in our town.

A NEW Arrival

It was a rather warm day in May when I went to the rear of the farm to drive the cows to the barn for their evening milking. In the edge of the wooded area near the creek, I spotted Sarah, who had been pregnant and was expecting her first calf during the month. Since she would not allow herself to be driven out of the area, I drove the remaining cows to the barn lot and told my father that Sarah appeared to be sick.

My father allowed me to accompany him back to the wooded area where Sarah was attempting to give birth. Although I had observed our pet cat and dog giving birth, I was unusually excited because I had never watched a calf arrive in the world before.

When we approached Sarah, her flanks were moving in and out and she was moaning. She appeared to be in a lot of pain. I watched in awe as my father simultaneously talked to and petted Sarah in an effort to calm her. While he was doing this, I saw a calf's nose appear. Then came the mouth, complete with a tip of tongue protruding. My father grasped the two front feet that appeared next and gently pulled each time Sarah moaned and contracted.

Finally, the calf, with its legs folded underneath its body, lay in the grass behind Sarah. As she turned around to attend to her new baby, I noticed a shiny, almost translucent membrane protruding from her backside. I remember asking my father about the membrane, and he attempted to explain to me, in a kid's language, about the whole process.

Although time has erased the details of his description of the process, I distinctly remember my eagerness to inform my classmates and Miss Stevens, my teacher, about the event on my first day back at school after the birth.

ANIMAL Shelter

The isolation of the road east of our home made it a depository for unwanted animals, especially cats and dogs. Folks from the city would usually tie these animals in a burlap bag and drop them alongside the road at night. Frequently, these critters would migrate to our farm for food or drink.

We children would occasionally wheedle our parents into adopting a cull or runt, hand feed it in a cardboard box behind the kitchen stove, and hope to keep it as a pet when it reached maturity. We had many opportunities for adoption because there were at least two litters of kittens and two stray dogs, sometimes with puppies, on the property nearly all of the time. In addition to table scraps from our kitchen, these animals feasted well on meat scraps from the slaughterhouse and their natural diet of mice, rats, birds, and young rabbits. Our parents, almost without exception, prohibited us from receiving these critters as gifts. However, our father, on a few occasions, permitted the adoption of large tomcats in order to purge the rear of the slaughterhouse of huge rats. These rats, when pursued by smaller cats, would consistently mutilate or kill them.

Some of the female cats would rest on the foundation sill with their mouths opened wide, and we boys would squirt milk from the cows' teats directly into their mouths. When they had their fill, they would lick the residue off their faces and paws, jump through the open window behind them, and return the next morning or evening. Several weeks after they had romanced with a prowling tomcat in the hayloft, they would sometimes bring their brood back to the barn sill for a family dinner. The kittens instinctively opened their mouths and following their dinner, always tidied up as mother watched. I guess mother cats are super smart. Where else could you take your entire brood out for a free dinner and have them receive a milk bath at the same time?

An insurance salesman, Milt McFay, once gave my mother a dog and promised her that the dog would not suck eggs. However, after the dog had chased several hens out of the chicken house and then devoured several eggs, my father made him take the dog back.

When I was about eight years of age, a collie pup visited our backdoor. After it had been at our home for a few days, I asked my father if we could keep it. He allowed me to keep it and said I should give it a name. When I asked my brother Lowell to help me with the puppy's name, he replied that it was just a "homeless slut" and that is what I should name it. So, I did.

When folks visiting our farm asked me what my dog's name was, I would answer "Slut." Sometimes a few of them would laugh, but most of them just rolled their eyes and asked, "Where did you get the name 'Slut'?" I would always reply that I got it from my brother Lowell. I told Grandpa Sandy that my dog was real smart and her mommy and daddy were probably very smart, too. He replied that she was probably out of desire by degradation. Those names sounded real good, but I thought she only needed one name.

HOLD On

Harold "Bud" Stark was also among my heroes at this stage of my life. Bud owned and flew a small, single-engine, open-cockpit monoplane that he occasionally landed and took-off from a large field north of the barn.

When he circled low over our farm, we children would line up atop the barnyard fence and wait for the landing. As soon as he had landed, taxied his plane to the area near the barn, and turned off the engine, we would be allowed to lift the fuselage skid off the ground, face the plane north, and drive the stakes that secured the tie-down lines.

In my young mind, Bud dressed in full flying gear—helmet, goggles, scarf, jodhpurs, leather leggings, and gloves—must have been a pilot hero in World War I who shot down a lot of enemy planes.

Take-offs were even more exciting. Bud would ask us to invite our playmates to watch the event. In fact, we and our playmates were almost essential to a successful take-off. After Bud primed and started the engine, all present would locate a handhold on the tail fins and hold the plane stationary while he accelerated the motor speed. When Bud gave the awaited hand signal, we would all let go while simultaneously tumbling to the ground. Then we would quickly get to our feet and cheer—sometimes pray—as the plane skimmed over the power lines and railroad tracks at the north end of the farm.

Blériot Monoplane in a field. Circa 1909.

Bud had lost several toes on his left foot as a result of an earlier plane accident. His second accident, however, was fatal. He was flying to northern Ohio to attend the funeral of a friend and fellow pilot who had been killed in a plane crash, when he, too, became lost in a severe storm, crashed, and died.

SPECIAL Treats

We had few treats growing up during the Depression, but we always looked forward to the rare occasion when our mother made root beer, fudge, or ice cream.

After she bought the ingredients for root beer, she told us that she could not finish the job until we children had gone out and collected pop bottles that people had thrown out. I was usually able to get a dozen, or more, along the road east of our house. This was a place where people parked, petted, and threw out condoms, ice cream cartons, and pop bottles.

After the bottles had been washed and bleached, our mother, ably assisted by our twin sisters, started the root beer. She poured sugar, root beer extract, yeast, and water into a large kettle and brought it to a boil. When she did this, the entire house smelled of root beer. We were always very eager to taste it but knew that it would be several days before we could do anything but smell that great aroma. We children knew better than to drink warm root beer. Once, my brother Lowell drank warm root beer, and our father told us that it worked on him so fast that he ran out the back door of the house, barfed at the pump house, and shit his pants before he got to the outhouse.

Sometimes, when our father and older brothers had gone back to the slaughterhouse after supper, our mother allowed us to help make chocolate fudge. She would get out all the ingredients and follow the recipe on the side of the Hershey's Cocoa can. She allowed our sisters to mix the milk, vanilla extract, cocoa, and sugar and put them in a saucepan.

Hank and I eagerly watched while we took turns stirring as the mix was boiling. From time to time, our sisters would test the consistency by dropping a small amount into a glass of water to see if it formed a soft ball. If it did, the mixture was poured into a cake pan and placed in the icebox or outdoors to harden.

We usually played dominos while we enjoyed the fudge, and mother always held some back for our father and older brothers when they returned to the house about nine-thirty. I liked the fudge best when our mother allowed us to stir peanut butter into it while it was boiling.

Our father always enjoyed the fudge the most when it had walnuts in it. Since I always wanted to please our father, I would sometimes crack walnuts and bring the half-jar of kernels to our mother in the kitchen and ask if she thought our father would like some homemade fudge. It didn't always work, but once in a while it did.

In the Depression years, even homemade ice cream was a special treat, not an every day, every week, or every month fare. Our ice cream freezer consisted of an outer wooden tub, an inner one-gallon can, a gear unit, and handle. Our mother's recipe included sugar, cream, eggs, and vanilla extract. Sometimes seasonal fruits were added. She would bring the mixture to a boil on the wood stove and set it aside to cool sufficiently so that it wouldn't melt the ice when the rock salt and ice were packed between the container can and the outer wooden tub.

Hank and I did the turning at first, and then our older brother when the turning became harder. By then, the ice cream was changing in texture. Sometimes a thick, folded burlap bag was placed on top of the freezer and one of us sat on it while the last of the turning took place. The extra weight held the freezer down when the turning was difficult. Finally, when the gear unit was removed and the top taken off the canister, all of us children wanted to lick the dasher. Once, while Hank was licking the dasher, Grandpa Jim told a story about a little boy who cut his tongue on a dasher and wasn't able to eat his ice cream when it was served. My brother said he wasn't afraid because he liked to drink it after it had melted anyway.

BILL Quirk

Bill Quirk was one of those fortunate individuals that the Depression did not put out of work. According to our father, who had known him for years, Bill had seldom, if ever, worked more than a few days at any type of employment. He would perform small jobs in the area, invest in some homemade "rotgut" and he and his squaw, "Snag" Halstead, who lived in Frog Hollow in the east section of town, would spend a few days and nights camping out in the thicket at the east end of our farm.

While camping out, he and Snag slept under and worked out of his 1924 Star sedan, frequently serving as lookouts for the bevy of bootleggers who plied their trade in the woods around the swamp almost nightly. Since we knew him, he would frequently come to our house during the night seeking a "horse tow" rather than risking exposing the identity of the bootleggers whose vehicles were in difficulty. We boys would seldom, if ever, see the driver of the "hooch car" and would receive a full dollar for our "see, hear and speak no evil" service. According to our brother Winston, Bill usually bartered his emergency service for someplace between one-half and a full gallon of "sauce." Since few of the wholesalers dealt in any amount under a full gallon, Bill was able to sustain his campout for several days. Our Grandpa Jim, following the theft and cannibalizing—tires, tubes, windshield, battery—of his Model T machine in the swamp area, threatened to render bodily harm to Bill, after the county sheriff failed to arrest him for serving as a lookout while Grandpa's machine was being dismantled. Bill had worked for Grandpa Jim for a short time, and Grandpa was not unfamiliar with his character. Bill, according to Grandpa, was so slick that he could "out fox" a whole band of gypsies who would occasionally stop at the swamp until the county judge rendered them a "sundown sentence."

We children would sit on our front lawn fence and wave to Bill and Snag as they drove by our house going or coming from the swamp area, and they would acknowledge our greeting. However, Snag, who had a central incisor missing, would sometimes be holding her bloomers out the window in a windsock position on their return trip. My brother Winston said they had been "poontanging" and she was drying her drawers in the wind. I wondered why she just didn't put them on the clothes line when she got home.

Sometimes, not always by accident, our livestock would stray off the property on Saturday night. When this happened, we brothers, in lieu of attending Sunday school, would be assigned the task of locating the livestock and driving them home. With our oldest brother in the role of scout, we brothers were filing into the swamp one Sunday morning in search of three Duroc sows who were about to farrow. When our brother threw up his arms and turned around, we froze in our tracks. We peered around him to see Bill and Snag on a discarded oil cloth table cover. Brother Winston turned his head, put his hands to the sides of his mouth and whispered, "It's Bill and Snag and he's packin' her pudding." Our brother then asked Bill if he had seen our Duroc sows in the area, and Bill replied, "No, I ain't, boy, but I'll be done here in a tad, and I'll he'p you look for 'em."

Loving Pigs

During the winter of 1930, our father and Ernest Truesdale had constructed two 8'x20' hog houses. Each house, he said, would accommodate three sows. The houses were mounted on 2'x6' sled runners and could be conveniently located on the farm. In March, he purchased six Duroc sows that were due to farrow toward the end of April. The boxes, pulled by a team of horses, were located on a small lot behind the slaughterhouse with the front facing south. Our father told us that the doors always faced south to keep out the north wind and allow for the most sunshine during the day. Two removable partitions were placed inside each house, creating three separate pens for the sows to farrow and nurse their piglets. Again, using small fence sections, three outside enclosures were erected in front of each house.

Our father estimated that if the Duroc sows were on their best behavior, we might have as many as forty or fifty hogs to slaughter by the time butchering season started in the fall. After we had helped our father place a covering of straw on the inside floors and secure the feeding troughs in the outside enclosures, we eagerly looked forward to the arrival of the six sows.

In late April the first sow gave birth to nine piglets. Our father said we should get a small container of stale cracklings from the slaughterhouse and include them in her feed. He said the cracklings would grease her mouth and she would not be tempted to cannibalize her piglets right after they were born. Grandpa said this was true because he and his father had always followed this practice successfully. Years later, in my vocational agriculture class, I would learn that the cracklings were really a protein supplement for the sow.

During a six-day period, the remaining five gave birth to an additional forty-five piglets. Within the six litters, there were four "culls" or "runts" that were struggling to gain access to a teat and, therefore, to survive. After two of them died, our father gave the remaining two to Hank and me and told us if we took care of them we might each have one. With the unsolicited maternal advice of our sisters Evelyn and Rachel, we obtained a box, blanket, bottle, and nipple and placed the piglets behind the kitchen stove. We fed them milk before we went to school and when we returned in the late afternoon. While nurturing them, we began to ask our brothers and sisters what we should name them. Brother Winston suggested that we name them "Runt One" and "Runt Two." Our sister Rachel objected to this name because her nickname was "Runt," and she didn't like the idea of having another "Runt" in the family, especially a pig. Our father suggested that since they were both male Duroc piglets that we might want to name them "Duey" and "Rocky." So, we did and two weeks later they were back with their brothers and sisters, fighting for milk at their mother's table.

FINDLAW Family

This disjunctive family was known to nearly all of the folks living several miles east of town. They had formerly lived in a small village where my father operated his first meat market. My father said the mother would bring all eight children into his market on Saturday evening, seat them on the floor, and have my father cut each of them a piece of ring-liver pudding. After she had served them, she would call out, "Now, chil'ins, 'es you'll had 'pud'?"

My Grandpa Jim, also knew this unusual family and their speech pattern of shortening a word, syllable, or word groups in what amounted to a homegrown language.

Grandpa Jim told us that one time when he was driving by the small farm home of this odd family, one of the children, while running and waving his arms, approached his buggy and said, "Eey mis'er! Eey mis'er! Your bug' 'eels turnin' roun'; your big' 'eels turnin' roun'."

Another time, Grandpa Jim told us, the Watkins' salesman knocked on the front door of the home several times without getting a response. Suddenly, he said, a child leaned out of an upstairs window and shouted, "Eel, damn, mis'er. Tain't nobod' ta 'ome."

Brother Winston said that Grandpa Jim told him that the children, both girls and boys, sometimes played in the rain without their clothes and, on one occasion, he had observed one of the younger boys "shuckin' his nubbin" under a small shade tree adjacent to the road. According to Grandpa, when the family sold any type of livestock, they would always get cash in order to divide the money evenly. By this he meant that each member would take one piece of paper currency, regardless of denomination, until it was all distributed. After this, they would distribute the silver and copper coins in the same manner. Even Grandma Delie told us of the time that she saw two of the little children sucking milk from the teats of a mother goat that was standing on the front porch of the home. Grandma also said that the family shared their kitchen with the chickens and rabbits that they raised for food.

Having listened to our grandparents relate many and varied tales about this unconventional family, our father felt the need to relate a few more from his earlier experiences with them. It seems that the family, following the butchering of two hogs and the curing of the hams and side meat, attempted to smoke the meat in their "jake" by building a fire underneath the seat of the "jake." In doing so, they burned the "jake" to the septic area. Our father said he was invited by a county health official to view the disaster and render an opinion relative to the consumable status of the meat. According to our father, he did not find the destruction of the "jake" to be as interesting as the family's efforts to create a substitute facility for it. They had sawed a hole in the corner of the dining room floor, built a box-type seat over the top of it, and placed a large galvanized tub beneath it in the basement.

Our father's favorite story about this unorthodox family was also associated with his first meat market. It was customary during this era for many farm families to barter their produce—butter, chickens, eggs—when they came to town on Saturday evening. The butter, which was churned at home, would infrequently contain a few short cow hairs. But the butter from this family almost always contained several hairs. As such, my father advised Mrs. Findlaw to be more careful with respect to the presence of these hairs.

According to our father, the following Saturday evening when several of his regular customers were in the market, one of the Findlaw children, carrying a five-pound crock of butter, burst through the front screen door and shouted, "Eey, mis'er! Eey, mis'er! You want ta buy some good ole country butt'? Ther' ain't no 'airs in mom's butt!"

GRANDMA'S Lament

Grandpa Jim and Grandma Delie had a combined garden and orchard of nearly two acres. While their garden, like ours, grew the conventional vegetables, their orchard, had cherries, gooseberries, and elderberries in addition to apples, peaches, pears, and grapes. We children enjoyed visiting with Grandpa and Grandma in the late summer and eating our fill of these fruits under the guise of helping with the harvest.

Some years Grandpa would need to hire additional help to cultivate, maintain, and harvest their vegetables and fruits. He was prone, much to the objection of Grandma, to employ a local vagrant, Dirg Beech.

According to my brother Winston, one day when Grandpa Jim was not going to be home, he hired Dirg to cut weeds and asked Grandma Delie to feed him dinner, which she did. When Grandpa came home, Grandma complained to him that while Dirg was sitting on the pump-house platform eating his dinner, she could see his "tallywhacker" through a hole in his ragged overalls. Grandpa roared with laughter and said, "Delie, I asked you to feed him dinner. I didn't ask you to look at his tallywhacker."

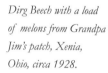

Dirg Beech with a load of melons from Grandpa Jim's patch, Xenia, Ohio, circa 1928.

In the grandparent's basement there were nearly a dozen ceramic crocks aligned against the east wall. Several of these crocks contained Grandma's homemade sauerkraut, sweet and sour pickles, and deviled beets and eggs. However, the majority of them, much to the chagrin of Grandma, contained Grandpa's homemade wines—made from any fruit or flower that would ferment. Dandelion was his specialty. Grandpa's winery was contrary to Grandma's Quaker heritage. Year after year she complained that she almost had to beg for enough fruit to can and make jam and jelly.

Whenever Grandpa boasted that there were never dandelions in their lawn, Grandma would frown and quip, "No! They're all in the basement doing the work of the devil."

Supper Slips

Our mother, in the tradition of her mother and grandmother, was rather determined that we children would gain a measure of culture in addition to good manners. As a result, while we were gathered around the table for our evening meal, we were sometimes offered an opportunity to recite a few lines of verse, tell a joke, or define a new word that we had recently learned. We children learned that a recitation, especially when one of our aunts was visiting, might bring a reward of ten cents or more. It appeared that if your recitation was amusingly forward or flippant and you were not immediately excused from the table, that you stood a good chance of getting the top prize of twenty-five cents.

Not infrequently, we children would rehearse our respective presentations before supper to determine if they would pass censorship and speculate on the size of our prize. Older siblings, especially brothers, occasionally enjoyed using this pre-supper rehearsal to set up their younger siblings.

It is impossible, after three-quarters of a century, to recall many of our recitations. However, a few of them might be worthy of note. When our aunt from Chicago was visiting, Winston, in a bold effort to appear grown-up, asked, "What is the stinkiest day in the week?" When my brother Lowell who already knew the answer and appeared to be seeking some type of reciprocity, challenged him with the correct answer, "Saturday," and demanded to know why. Winston responded, "Because it has 'turd' in the middle of it." The only rewards he received were a few muffled snickers from his siblings, objectionable stares from both parents, and the honor of finishing his supper after the table had been cleared and the dishes washed and put away.

Although she didn't qualify for a prize, my sister Evelyn entertained the family one evening with the following: "Did you hear about the girl who always wore a dress the same color as the man's hair when she had a date?" She continued, "Whenever she had a date with a blond-headed man, she always wore a white dress. When she went out with a black-headed man, she always wore a black dress, and when she went out with a red-headed man, she always wore a red dress. One night she went out with a bald-headed man and didn't wear anything."

Every member of our family belonged to the "clean plate club." That is, if you ladled food from a serving dish onto your plate, you were obligated to ingest every morsel. On an evening when my brother Hank was not hungry, and my brother Lowell was attempting, somewhat unsuccessfully, to ladle fried potatoes onto his plate, Hank blurted out, "I told you already that I don't want any f….'n fried potatoes!" He would later return to the kitchen, but it would not be to finish his supper. Instead, he, like his three older brothers, would have that dreadful experience of having his mouth washed out with that awful yellow soap.

In what appeared to be an attempt to upstage his older brother Winston, brother Lowell asked, "Did you hear about the hunting dog that had a flat tire? He was pumped up by an Airedale." This one, surprisingly enough, received only a step two response from our father.

Having watched my tadpoles mature in the livestock watering trough over several weeks, and unknowingly set up by my older brothers and their friends, I announced at the supper table one evening that "even though my tadpoles now had four legs, they were still able to flagellate real fast." My older brothers nearly choked with laughter while pretending to enjoy their macaroni and cheese; my sisters wanted to know what that new word meant, and my parents, without a word, maintained mutual, blank expressions.

My sister Rachel, without being set up by an older individual, probably epitomized the innocence of these supper literary forums when she asked, "Billy Ballard called me a pussy on the way home after school, and I told him I was not a cat. Is there something else that's called a pussy besides a cat?" "Yes," our mother immediately replied, "a pussy is a young English girl who is not married. Billy probably said that because his mother is English." "I didn't know that," responded our father. "Do you mean that you didn't know that Billy's mother is English?" our mother queried.

We children had always known that our mother had been a teacher and she was very, very smart. However, this time, she had not only answered our sister Rachel's question, she had, judging by the expression on his face, taught our father a new synonym.

FAULTY Equipment

My brother Hank and I, not unlike many other boys our age, had always been fascinated by bright, red fire engines, especially when we saw them going to a fire with sirens at full decibel. As such, seasonally, when Santa was within earshot, we would let him know that a toy fire truck was very high on our respective list of wishes. For some reason, Santa didn't respond to our request, and we began to think of how we might simulate this exciting action. We were already adept at simulating the motor noises of trucks, tractors, and the occasional monoplane that flew low over our farm. Thus, knowing we were already equipped with a built-in water tank and hose, why couldn't we set a small paper box on fire, retrace a short distance away, activate our sirens, race to the scene of the fire, take out our hoses, and put out the fire? This practice went very well when we were using a small box. However, when a larger box was ignited, we did not have sufficient water volume in our initial squirt to knock the blaze down to where we gained control of it and eventually extinguished it.

At this point, it occurred to our young minds that what we really needed was a pumper truck. Then, as though by divine providence, one day an idea came to my little brother Hank. I'm almost embarrassed to write that I didn't think of it first. In his active mind, as with the hose, we already had a built-in "pumper. Instead of whipping out our hoses at the site of the fire, we would extract them before we raced our trucks to the "fire," pull our foreskin forward, while simultaneously pinching the opening together between our thumb and index finger to insure against loss of much needed water and tank capacity as we raced to the fire. As we screeched to a halt at the box fire, employing the thumb and index finger of the other hand, we quickly squeezed the bloated prepuce. This action not only gave us control of the fire but also an internal sense of relief. It was, as we soon discovered, essential for all the "junior firemen" to stand on the same side of the fire. Aim was of the utmost importance.

Shortly after we had mastered this fire truck game, my brother Hank invited his first grade classmate Rodney Roach for a Saturday afternoon of play. We played several games. When interest began to wane, my brother suggested we liven things up with this innovative activity.

After a demonstrated practice drill, including an explanation of the rules to Rodney, he began to cry and said it wasn't a fair game because he didn't have a "pumper truck." As he cried we were unable to get him to tell us why some cruel person would not allow him to be a "pumper truck." We attempted to take away his tears by promoting him to fire chief. This pacified him for a little while; however, when he arrived home, he began to cry again.

The rest of the story, as almost every youngster knows, is conventional history. Rodney told his mother why he was so upset. His mother told his father, who, in turn, called our father; who, in turn told our mother; who explained to us in her guarded, Quaker manner that we shouldn't be playing with matches.

When the day was over, we were certain of two things: Rodney would never grow up to be a fireman, and this activity, if engaged in again, would always be scheduled as an "away game."

THE GREAT Flood

Our father told us that a few years before he was born, Shawnee Creek, which ran through our farm and later through the southwest area of the town, overflowed and several people died as a result of the flood. He said Grandpa Jim was about twenty years old at the time and had helped clean up after the disaster.

According to Grandpa Jim, as a result of the terrific flood that came on May 12, 1886, twenty-eight people lost their lives. The storm occurred between eight and nine o'clock at night. Shawnee Creek, usually just a small stream which passed through a populous part of the city, was converted by a cloudburst into a torrent of water which descended like an avalanche upon the homes of many living in Barr's Bottoms. At ten o'clock the fire bells sounded the alarm, and soon another alarm sounded. Dense darkness reigned everywhere, but the calls of those in distress could be heard above the roar of the storm and surging waters. "It was," Grandpa said, "a night of wild terror and horror." Huge bonfires were built, the shadows of which gave added eeriness to the scene. There were many heroic deeds that were performed that night in an effort to save the drowning. According to our father, our Grandpa Jim was among those on record who pitched in and helped.

Twenty houses were swept away in Barr's Bottoms, near the Little Miami depot; only three remained. Orrin Morris, his wife, and three of their five children, former neighbors of Grandpa Jim, perished. The house bearing the family floated down the stream until it struck the solid masonry of a bridge, and then all was still. Two children of the family were rescued. The next morning the sun came out bright and warm, disclosing a scene of utter desolation.

For a time Xenia was cut off from all communication with the outside world. The office of the mayor was converted into a temporary morgue in which the bodies of the dead lay in somber array. While Grandpa didn't boast about his rescue efforts, our father said he was very much a part of this historic event.

TRAINS CAN BE Dangerous!

When our mother was growing up in Xenia, she and her parents, Grandpa Jim and Grandma Delie, would frequently ride the train to and from Richmond, Indiana, to visit relatives.

Grandpa Jim considered himself to be a quasi engineer, conductor, brakeman, etc. and always seemed to enjoy telling stories about the multiple lines that criss-crossed our small town. One of these lines, he said, entered town on the east side of the exceptionally wide Detroit Street, which was a bit unusual not only for our town but also for our state.

When the train consisted of several dozen freight cars, it would effectively block east-west traffic on five streets. With the advent of the automobile in the first quarter of the 20th century, drivers would occasionally park on, or near, the tracks and the engineer would have to stop the train while the police located the drivers and instructed them to move their autos. In addition, older boys would sometimes open the doors of autos parked between the curb and tracks forcing the train to stop.

Grandpa said it was not an uncommon sight for a mixed freight-train and passenger train to come through town, and for the engine to stop at a point opposite the court house while passengers got off and on at the Detroit Street Station. Then old Mr. Coggswell, the conduc-

Engineer waiting for the policeman to move automobiles off the track on South Detroit Street.

tor, would give the signal for the brakeman on the top of the train to transmit the same to the engineer to start on the journey to Springfield.

When we told Grandpa how we placed pennies on the track for on-coming locomotives and cars to flatten, he cautioned us against this type of activity. In fact, he said, "Railroad trains are dangerous." When he was about twenty-five years old, Grandpa told us there was a terrible railroad accident near the train depot during a heavy rain storm. While the wind was blowing severely, a woman who lived near the depot was walking uptown to buy groceries. She had a jug in her hand and was carrying an open umbrella. Since she was walking into the storm, she had the umbrella well down over her head. She was coming along the tracks when five cars backing toward her ran into and over her. All of the cars and even the locomotive passed over her. He said it was very sad because she was the mother of six children.

About ten years before the lady was killed, Grandpa told us that a railroad employee, Mr. McCreary, was killed when he accidentally fell off the bridge on South Detroit Street and struck his head on a pile of stones at the bottom of the street.

When we told Grandpa that our oldest brother Winston had hopped a ride on a slow freight train near our swimming hole, Grandpa frowned and told about his neighbor, Mr. Murray, who was a brakeman who was crushed to death between two freight cars near the stock yards a few years earlier.

JUNIOR Chef

About a month after school was out in 1930, Hank and I came downstairs for breakfast and discovered that the rest of our family had eaten and left the house. However, via the west kitchen windows, we saw our mother in the orchard picking mulberries, much to the disdain of several early birds.

Since Hank was aware that I already knew how to fry eggs and make shingle-J, he asked me if I would prepare his breakfast. When he did this, I asked him if he still had the nickel that he had shown me the day before. When he responded that he did, I told him I would make his breakfast but it would cost him five cents. He gave me the nickel and I proceeded to add wood to the stove, spoon some bacon drippings into the skillet, and fry two eggs for each of us. Hank wanted his fried on both sides, but mine, in the words of our father, were fried with "their eyes open." When the eggs were finished, I scattered a little salt on the hot stove lids and tossed on several slices of bread to make the shingle-J.

When we had finished breakfast, we went to the orchard to help our mother pick mulberries, and mother thanked me for cooking my little brother's breakfast. At that moment, Hank started to cry, and told Mother that I had charged him a nickel to cook his breakfast. Mother, of course, then directed me to return his nickel, which I reluctantly pulled from my overall pocket.

At this stage of my life, I just guessed that little brothers didn't always appreciate the culinary talent of an older sibling.

What's in a Name?

Ably assisted by our older sisters and brothers, my little brother and I soon learned the code of potential discipline at our home. Our father, in the footsteps of his father, consciously or unconsciously, exercised a four-step approach to the issue. This approach was somewhat akin to an educational or corporate evaluation process. That is, you were notified, advised, warned, and sustained the consequences.

Firstly, when he wanted the attention of one or more of his sons, he called out "Boy!" At that moment, we boys all knew to direct our undivided attention to our father. If he then designated one or more of us by our first name(s), the others were free to move on.

At this juncture, Step Two, of the procedure, those of us who had been detained, would be advised that our conduct, physically or verbally, was out of concert with our parents', grandparents', uncles', and aunts' expectations. It always seemed that those folks had been rather saintly when they were small.

When our father, at Step Three, addressed us by our first and second names, we began to scan the immediate area for any, and all, possible objects that were available for punishing us. If we did not see any, we might still avoid the final step.

Finally, when he addressed us by our first, middle, and last names, we knew we were at Step Four and there was no "court of last resort." At this stage, we didn't bother to scan the area because he was already grasping the source of punishment in his right hand. He never shouted or appeared to be angry when he was administering our discipline. In fact, when he finished, he would put his arms around us, tell us he loved us, and ask if we understood why it was necessary for him to punish us. Very quickly, we learned to cry at first contact and shout that we understood. This acknowledgement would tend to cut down the length of the punishment. Before he released us, he would ask if we had any questions. I don't remember ever having any at the time.

While the call "Girl!" would stop my sisters in their tracks, I don't recall ever seeing my father spank them. I do recall, however, that they were at Step Three several times. I guess I concluded that girls are smarter than boys about such matters.

In retrospect, we children were most fortunate that our father without the aid of psychologists and psychiatrists understood the art of administering discipline affectionately. Later, when we learned that our father and five of his brothers and sisters were all called by their middle names, we asked him why. He replied that he didn't know. We children, however, quickly concluded that Grandpa Sandy's kids must have been pretty bad if they were that close to getting a spanking all of the time.

Our grandfather, of course, looked very favorably upon this type of discipline. "Sometimes the shortest route to a kid's mind is right straight through the seat of his pants." Once Grandpa suggested to our father that he ought to fetch a broom, take us to the woodshed, and give us a good lickin'. When our father responded that we hadn't done anything wrong, his father supposedly stated his philosophy more emphatically with these words, "Well, by God, they will sooner or later, and look how far ahead of them you'll be." Grandpa's theory, in retrospect, was not too far off the mark.

Speedway

Necessity being the mother of invention, we were always on the lookout for new games to play or modifications of those that were already familiar. One of these games, called "Speedway," consisted of several well-worn, automobile tires from the unauthorized dump across the road from the forbidden swamp east of our farm. Running barefoot, we guided these tires with our hand, or a short stick, in our barn lot and on the gravel road in front of our house. All of this activity, of course, was accompanied by our verbally simulating the cranking, rattling, and backfiring of our family's open touring "machine" and our father's truck. Then, when it was time to attend to our chores, or when we were called into the house, we would open the barn doors and park our respective "automobiles" on the right side of the granary.

This activity was very popular with our playmates from the city, and they all aspired to having "automobiles" of their own. When Hank and I talked with our brother Lowell about getting tires for our friends, he said that we should charge five cents for each tire. Later, since their parents didn't want them to bring tires home with them, our brother Lowell suggested that we charge them a stick of chewing gum for each tire stored in our barn between visits. Big brothers, it seemed, could be really helpful once-in-a-while. Thus, at any given time, there would be six to ten extra "automobiles" parked parallel to the granary with the inscribed names like Hod, Bill, Froggy, etc. crudely chalked over the trademark—Goodyear or Montgomery-Ward.

While the speedway activity was an approved "home game," it too, in the absence of our parents, quickly converted to an "away game." In short, our older brothers and their friends encouraged us to curl up inside our tires while they rolled them. Now, we were the real drivers of our "autos." This was a great deal of fun and led to several races in the barn lot. Later, however, they took us up to the crest of the hill on the gravel road and gave us a starting shove. Rolling unattended, we younger boys would be dusty, bruised, and ditched along the incline. But, occasionally one of us would remain curled up inside the tire for the full fifty yards, and we would have bragging driver rights until the next winner survived the "fun."

Hod Hook, who had never won the event and seemed to be near tears after his most recent unsuccessful attempt, asked Ralph Teasdale, one of the older boys, what he had to do to win. Ralph told him to switch from a truck tire to a touring machine tire because touring machines were faster than trucks. When he still failed to win, Ralph told him he needed to get a new driver.

THE BIG Parade

Our summer of barefoot activities in 1930 consisted of farm work, tree-house antics, skinny dippin', and berry picking. In June several local civic clubs announced that

Showing off one of my prized pigeons.

they were going to sponsor a pet show on the last day of July at the local park and that they were going to give awards in several categories.

My brother Lowell had just completed a harness and a four-wheel wagon for our pet goat and decided he was going to enter the contest. I, too, wanted very much to be in the pet parade and contest by entering one or two of my pet pigeons. When we told our father that we both wanted to enter the contest, he suggested that we put several pigeons in a poultry crate and haul them on the wagon during the parade. My brother did not like the idea because he needed to be seated on the wagon in order to properly drive the goat. When we told our mother of our plan, she suggested that we train one or more of my pigeons to perch on the goat's back during the parade. By doing so, I could ride behind my brother on the wagon. We tried several times, unsuccessfully, to train two pointer pigeons to perch on the goat's back while it was walking. We even offered the birds ground corn if they would co-operate, but they refused. Finally we won their cooperation by putting a small amount of cracked corn in a small, open box that we secured to the top of the goat's collar.

We finalized the bird's training for the pending parade by placing lesser amounts of corn in the box and measuring how far the goat could walk before the pigeons knew that they had been duped. After several trial-and-error runs, one bird, even when the box was empty, would remain perched on the goat's back, patiently waiting for a refill. Now, we were ready for the big day of the parade.

The poet and popular radio emcee from Cincinnati, Edgar Guest, was going to serve as judge for the parade, and we were confident that he would reward our creativity.

When the judging for the day concluded, our entry was awarded third prize in the open field entries and first prize in the unusual pet category. Our sisters suggested that we might want to rename the goat "Edgar" and name the pigeon "Corny."

THE DOCTOR IS Out!

Our farm was approximately a dozen miles from Dr. Jim Harris' office, so whenever conventional family illnesses or minor accidents happened, home remedies were utilized. Our mother and father knew a lot of these remedies, but our grandparents knew a lot more.

In the summer of 1930, when I was helping Joe Harner load hay on his wagon, I stuck a tine of the pitchfork through the webbing between my second and third toes. Mr. Harner took his cud of chewing tobacco out of his mouth and had me press it against the puncture. He then removed his red bandana from around his neck and wrapped my foot.

Later in the summer, while we were all attending our annual family reunion in our Uncle Charlie's large orchard, several girls, including my sisters, punched a hornet's nest with a stick and were all stung one or more times. Fortunately, this happened after the picnic so there were plenty of tobacco-cud-poultices to medicate the stings.

Except in winter, insect bites were almost an everyday occurrence on the farm, and we children shared the same treatment for them as our pets and livestock. We thought that this was true in other families too because we used the "bag-balm" on our cows' udders and teats when they were sore or cut, and our sister Evelyn had overheard Grandma telling our mother that Mrs. Murray had used the same stuff on her breasts several times.

Serious lacerations in the slaughterhouse and on the farm that needed stitches were attended to by Dr. Harris. However, if Dr. Harris' services weren't needed, the remedy for chapped hands, abrasions, and lesser cuts was liquid from the bile duct of a hog or steer. Consequently,

Dr. James H. Harris, Clifton, Ohio, 1929.

a bile duct could consistently be found hanging on a small hook on the wall of the killing floor in the slaughterhouse.

When we encountered chiggers, our mother would have us rub a salty bacon rind over the area for half an hour. At other times, a lighted cigarette or cigar would be held over the entry hole and the chigger would back out.

In the late spring, after the brood sows had furrowed, we boys were given the chore of cleaning the furrowing sheds. In the process of performing this chore, we would become infested with hog fleas. Even though we wore protective clothing, these critters would find their way through to our skin and make a home for themselves on our head or any other area that had hair on it. Hank and I felt sorry for our big brothers who had already reached puberty. When we finally finished, we remedied the situation by going to the swimming hole and jumping in with all of our clothes on. In a few minutes, we would be laughing and counting the fleas floating on top of the water.

When our father was doing contracting work in the summer and was exposed to cement, he would sometimes develop an abscess, "boil" as our grandma called it or "carbuncle" as our grandfather called it. Our mother would treat the abscesses by applying hot, towel compresses. Later, she applied a black ointment from a flat tin box that smelled like tar.

When we children had really bad chest colds or pleurisy as our grandma called it, our mother would mix lard and mustard on two pieces of cloth and plaster them onto our chest and back before we went to bed at night.

One day after school when I stopped at my grandparents' to pick up their milk pail, I noticed that my grandfather was wearing what looked like a diaper under his chin tied in a large knot on top of his head. Grandma told me he had "quinsy." I already knew that eating too many green apples would give you a bad bellyache so I asked Grandma if Grandpa had eaten too many green, quincy apples from the orchard, and she said, "No! He's been smoking too much Prince Albert in his pipe."

Grandpa Jim enjoyed telling us about home remedies when he was small! He told us that when he was a boy he was able to get rid of the chicken pox because his folks had him lie down and made live chickens fly over him. He said his mother tied a dirty sock around his neck overnight to rid him of a sore throat. When he complained to his folks that he was having nightmares, they placed a Bible under his pillow before he went to bed. After that, they stopped his leg cramps by having him turn his shoes upside down before he crawled into bed.

Finally, the worst one, he said, was the remedy for measles. His folks brewed tea from sheep droppings. After straining it, they made him drink it just before he went to bed. I guessed that some folks were afraid they were going to get measles, and that's why they counted a lot of sheep before they fell asleep.

FIRST Funeral

Our family reunions were held annually in August and we attended every year. There would always be several tables laden with homemade food and gallons of iced tea and lemonade.

Some of our best times at these reunions were spent with Grandpa Sandy's sister, Aunt Matt. She was always laughing, exchanging jokes with the men, and spending a great deal of time participating in the games we children were playing. We particularly enjoyed a game called "Find Abe." A hat would be passed among the adults, and they would place all of their pennies into it. Then, while we children hid our faces, the pennies would be scattered over a designated area of the lawn. When given a signal, we would crawl on our hands and knees and try to find as many pennies as possible. We always knew that Aunt Matt would be standing or sitting in the grass where the pennies were most densely seeded.

When we told Grandpa how much fun we always had with Aunt Matt, he began to tell us about his sisters and brothers. He told us that Aunt Matt and her twin sister, who was already dead, were born three years before him. He said he also had three other sisters and brothers who died before we were born. We children, especially my twin sisters, Evelyn and Rachel, found Grandpa's story about his brothers and sisters to be very interesting.

Shortly before Valentine's Day in 1930, our father told Grandpa that Aunt Matt had died and our family would be driving to Springfield for the funeral. When our family entered Aunt Matt's house, Grandpa, our father, Uncle Frank, and Uncle Charlie sat near Aunt Matt's open coffin, which was resting in the far corner of the living room. We children, with our mother, stood before the coffin for a few moments. Then our mother herded us to the far side of the living room where we were seated with a number of relatives that we recognized from the family reunions.

Occasionally, while the organ played and a lady sang a hymn or the preacher raised his voice, some people, mostly ladies, would wipe the tears from their eyes and utter inaudible words. Before the coffin was closed, several persons who had arrived late expressed their sorrow to Grandpa as they said good-bye to Aunt Matt. At the cemetery our father parked near the gravesite, and we children remained in the "machine" while our parents attended the burial service.

Since this was the first death and funeral of a close relative that we had experienced, as our parents had anticipated, we had a number of questions that would need answering on our way home. Question: "Was Aunt Matt going to heaven?" Answer, "Yes!" Question: "Will Jesus allow Aunt Matt to come down from heaven to be with us at our next family reunion?" Answer: "Jesus will allow her spirit to be with you at the reunion!" Question: "What's going to happen to Grandpa Sandy?" Answer: "We're all going to keep on loving him and take real good care of him!"

TRY Again

In September 1930, I returned to the big school for a second try at the second grade. I was afraid that the other kids would tell me that I was dumb, even though my mother had told me that it wouldn't happen.

For the most part, the year would be about the same as the previous year. However, some things were different. My twin sisters would no longer be in Miss Bell's room across the hall, and they would not be carrying school tales to my mother and father. That was going to be a real relief, but I guess I had not given much thought to the fact that my little brother Hank was going to be in the first grade in the same room. He and I quickly agreed on a program of mutual silence about school events when we were eating supper. And, to the best of my recollection, Mrs. Stevens did not find it necessary during the entire year to gain our attention with anything other than her engaging smile and pleasant voice.

I attended Orient Hill School in grades 1-4.

Oddly enough, Hank and I discovered that at school, unlike at home, we could work on projects for a long time without arguing or fighting. We even served our respective stints of "Pee Patrol" in the basement lavatory without having to report one incident to Mrs. Stevens.

At Halloween time, we each brought a small pumpkin to school to help decorate our room. At Thanksgiving, we brought empty Quaker Oats boxes so that we could make Pilgrim's hats to wear in our school's parade.

The first week of school, I had introduced my little brother to our janitor, Mr. Edwards. Mr. Edwards liked him right away and invited him to stop in his office after school.

At Christmas, even though I was still in the Blue Jay's reading group, Mrs. Stevens asked me if I would like to be one of the three wise men in our play. She also said my brother's "baaah" was improving, and he would be one of the sheep in our play. At the supper table that evening, when I told everyone that I was going to be a wise man, my brother Lowell laughed and said that it would probably be the first time in the history of the school that a Blue Jay ever became one of the three wise men. Everybody, including my parents, thought it was funny too.

MY FRIEND Froggy

Besides my classmates at school, the person I spent the most time working and playing with was Johnny "Froggy" Halstead. Froggy was the younger brother of "Snag" Halstead and, of course, lived in the Frog Hollow enclave in the east end of town. Frequently, on Saturday mornings, he would walk across the railroad tracks and the north field to our farm. Before we would get seriously into the morning's play, he would help me with my chores in the woodshed, poultry house, or barn. When he did this, I would usually ask my father for permission to give him a double fistful of cracklings and a pinch of salt and pepper. He was almost always hungry when he arrived.

Sometimes when he came to spend a few hours at the farm, he would bring several of his Negro friends—Kirk Bird, George Dorge, or Henry Simons—to also help and play. When this happened, Froggy and I would sometimes tie a rope around the waist of our Negro playmates and pretend they were slaves. When the chores for the day were finished, they, too, were rewarded with cracklings and/or hot pigtails plucked from a kettle of lard that was nearly ready to be drained off into the crackling press.

During the spring of 1930, Mrs. Shaw, the school district's visiting nurse, sent a note home to my mother and informed her that I had contracted head lice. She suggested that my mother purchase a bottle of larkspur and check the heads of all members of our family. My mother, of course, found this to be embarrassing and attempted to learn from whom I might have contracted the infestation. When the school nurse concluded that mine was the only case, my mother quickly concluded that my friend Froggy must be the carrier. The next time Froggy came to our house, my mother thoroughly checked his head and clothing before I was permitted to spend time with him. Mothers, as I always say, are really smart. So, when Froggy would come over during the summer, I would meet him at the swimming hole for a quick skinny-dip before we started our chores.

During my second year in the second grade, Froggy developed a very serious cough and sometimes he would spit up blood when we worked hard or played really hard. As soon as my mother learned of this, she said he would no longer be coming to our farm. I was very saddened by this and missed his company very much. Two years later, when I was in Miss Bell's fourth grade, my Aunt Aline read Froggy's obituary in the evening paper and told me that he had died from T.B. I had no understanding of what she meant by "with T.B.," but I guess by this time, I was becoming accustomed to having special people in my life leave me to go to heaven.

Singing for Cookies

My mother and her parents, Grandpa Jim and Grandma Delie, were all very fond of Stephen Collins Foster's music. In fact, Foster had departed this life in 1864, the year Grandma Delie was born. Grandma had several of Foster's songs stored in her piano bench. Whenever we children would visit, we would beg to work the pedals on her player piano while we sang her two favorite songs:

My Old Kentucky Home
Stephen C. Foster
The sun shines bright in the old Kentucky home;
'Tis summer, the darkies are gay:
The corn-top's ripe, and the meadow's in the bloom,
While the birds make music all the day.
The young folks roll on the little cabin floor,
All merry, all happy and bright;
By 'n'-by hard times comes a-knocking at the door,
Then my old Kentucky home, good night!
Chorus:
Weep no more, my lady
Oh, weep no more today!
We will sing one song for the old Kentucky home,
For the old Kentucky home, far, far away.
They hunt no more for the possum and the coon,
On the meadows, the hill, and the shore,
They sing no more by the glimmer of the moon,
On the bench by the old cabin door.
The day goes by like a shadow in the heart,
With sorrow, where all was delight,
The time has come when the darkies have to part-
Then my old Kentucky home, good night!
The head must bow, and the back will have to bend,
Wherever the darky may go;
A few more days, and the troubles all will end,
In the fields where the sugar-canes grow.
A few more days for to tote the weary load-

No matter, 'twill never be light;
A few more days till we totter on the road,
Then my old Kentucky home, good night!

Grandpa Jim was born in Kentucky, and he would usually put his pipe down long enough to join the song-fest on this Foster favorite:

'Way down upon de Swanee Ribber,
Far, far away,
Dere's wha' my heart is turning ebber,
Dere's wha' de old folks stay.
All up and down de whole creation,
Sadly I roam.
Still longing for de old plantation,
And for de old folks at home.
Chorus:
All de' world am sad and dreary,
Everywhere I roam;
Oh, darkies, how my heart grows weary,
Far from de old folks at home!
All round the little farm I wandered
When I was young.
Dem many happy days I squandered,
Many de songs I sung,
When I was playing wid my brudder,
Happy was I;
Oh, take me to my kind old mudder!
Dere let me live and die.
One little hut among de bushes,
One dat I love,
Still sadly to my memory rushes,
No matter where I rove.
When will I see the bees-a-humming
All round de comb?
When will I hear de banjo turning,
Down in my good old home?

When we had finished singing, Grandma Delie would always give us one or two large oatmeal cookies and a glass of milk.

My mother and her parents, James W. and Fidelia (Peacock) Mullen, in Xenia, Ohio, 1902.

Sassafras

Grandpa Jim said he could always tell when winter was nearly over because his neighbor, Mr. Gorham, would bring him a brown, paper bag nearly full of sassafras roots. When we children went to our grandparents we didn't have to be told that Mr. Gorham had brought over his spring delight. We could tell by the invigorating aroma coming from Grandma's kitchen.

While we were visiting, we children would sometimes beg for an extra cup of sassafras tea before we left for home. Our grandparents and Mr. Gorham, much to our delight, would seem to entertain us with conversation about sassafras. "Too much sassafras will make your blood thin," Grandpa Jim would say. And Grandma Delie would laugh and say, "Too much sassafras tea before bedtime will probably make you pee the bed." They seemed to know everything about sassafras.

Sassafras seedling.

Mr. Gorham said that the Shawnee Indians gathered and boiled sassafras roots in order to make medicine and told us he would show us how to identify sassafras trees and dig out the roots. He also explained, and Grandma agreed, that the tea is a little bitter when the roots are boiled for the first time. However, according to both of them, you can boil the same roots several times after that, and the tea will just keep getting better and better.

When Mr. Gorham came to our farm to help us locate and gather sassafras roots, he explained that it was the soil that determines the quality of the sassafras. He took us deep into Eavey's woods and up against the side of a hill. "On hills," he went on, "chop one off. Then jerk it. Or crack it like a whip and it opens the soil and cracks right out. That's sassafras. The bigger the sassafras tree, the bigger the root, and the redder," he confided in us. He sure knew everything there was to know about sassafras. "You know, it's a change in the spring, like a change of oil to your pa's machine." And then he thinks again how it is, "Kinda like taking off your winter underwear," he says.

MOTHER GOES TO Heaven

Shortly after my brother Winston's birthday on the fifth of March in 1931, our mother, on the pretense of being overly-tired, would go to bed before we children were required to go. By the end of March, she was confined to her bed, and Doctor Harris was visiting her twice a week. We children were constantly being cautioned with respect to walking softly, closing doors gently, and speaking quietly in the house. In addition, we were not to play in the southwest corner of the yard that was proximal to our parents' bedroom.

During early April, when our mother was awake, we visited her bedside before we headed off to school. At night, if she was still awake, we would again visit her bedside for our evening prayers.

One Friday afternoon as Hank and I walked over the crest of the hill in our road, we noticed a black sedan parked in front of our house. As we drew closer to the front gate, we saw a man dressed in black, carrying two large satchels onto our front porch. Our father opened the door for him to enter; closed the door behind him, and while walking toward us, informed us that Dr. Harris had just left, and that our mother was dead. Through my tears, I noticed that our black and white cat "Spot" was crouching on the sill of the bedroom window that was near the front porch door.

Our father walked with us around the house and we entered the back door. Once inside, we were surprised to see our uncle from Cedarville and learn that we would be staying with him and Aunt Laura for a few days. While Hank and I were there, our cousin Ruth gave us several good scrubbings in this big, long, white tub in their bathroom. Aunt Laura took us to Hartman's Clothing Store for new clothes, and Uncle Will took us fishing in a small gorge right behind his poultry house. They really kept us busy and made sure that we had a good time.

On April 14th, our mother's birthday, we returned to our home about noon and ate dinner in the kitchen with several relatives. Then our sisters gave us each a single pink rose, and we walked with our father into the living room to say good-bye to our mother. When we stopped in front of her coffin, we noticed there were already four pink roses spread softly over her folded hands. Our father hugged us as we placed our roses beside the others. We then returned to the kitchen and waited while scores of people seated themselves on chairs placed throughout the downstairs and on the front yard. Our parents' bedroom served as the family room during the funeral, and Hank and I sat on opposite sides of our father. Before the funeral, my brother Hank and I had agreed that we would not cry unless our father did. Shortly, after Mrs. Stout, from our church, sang two hymns our mother had requested, "The Old Rugged Cross" and "In the Garden," he pulled his handkerchief from his inside coat pocket and we followed his example.

Hank and I sat on the fold-down seats in the rear of the family limousine and observed the procession of automobiles behind as we drove the fifteen miles to the cemetery at Clifton. Following the graveside services, we returned to our house where many friends and relatives had dropped off assorted covered dishes and desserts. We had not been home very long, when our father excused several ladies working in the kitchen and directed all of us children to take our usual places at the table. Our mother's chair, of course, stood empty. Our father nodded and pointed to her chair, as he extolled her many attributes and acknowledged how much we would all miss her. He concluded by saying that even though our mother was gone and we still had a mortgage on the farm, we would remain here as a happy family if we all continued to do our share of the work. But, he added, "If one or more of you get in trouble with the law, you will all have to go to the county orphanage." Hank must have thought our father was referring to the military orphanage where a few years earlier our friend's wandering dog "Tippy" was caught and castrated before he returned home. As soon as our father mentioned the orphanage, Hank clasped his hands to his crotch and said, "Oh, no! I'm too young for that."

Mother

STRAIGHT TO Heaven

Since the first day of school, I had delivered a quart canister of milk to my grandparents' house every other morning on my way to school and picked up the empty canister on my way home. Grandma and Grandpa had several neighbors who lived southwest of them, and the women frequently socialized during the day. Grandma and the women in the neighboring homes were always very cooperative when our school was selling candy, magazines, or seeds to raise money for a school project.

About the time in April when our mother was confined to her bed, I became aware that Grandma Delie was no longer meeting me at the front door when I picked up the empty canister after school. When I mentioned this to our father, he told me that Grandma Delie had been very ill for over a month and that she had not been told that her daughter, our mother, was dead. He also said that her caregiver, Mrs. Jenkins, was told not to tell her.

On the first day of school following our spring vacation, I stopped at Grandma Delie's to pick up the empty canister, and Mrs. Jenkins opened the door and asked me if I would like to see my grandma. She walked ahead of me into the downstairs bedroom and asked me to stop in the door frame. Grandma Delie was sitting up in bed. Mrs. Jenkins had been brushing Grandma's long, gray hair which fell to her waist. I had never seen Grandma Delie when her hair was not in a large chignon. Mrs. Jenkins explained to me that Grandma could not touch or hug me because she had a bad case of the flu. While we were talking, I noticed that Grandma's face was very drawn and she had very dark skin under her eyes. She thanked me for delivering the milk and asked about my sisters and brothers. I was glad that she did not ask about our mother. If she had, I guess I would have told her that I thought our mother was sleeping.

On April 24th, exactly two weeks after our mother's death, and without ever knowing that our mother was dead, Grandma Delie died in her sleep. At the funeral parlor, according to our father, Mrs. Jenkins said, "Grandma did not suffer. She just closed her eyes and went straight to heaven."

I was puzzled about who would deliver her milk up there every day, but I was sure that God would really enjoy her large oatmeal cookies.

Spots Also Goes to Heaven

We younger boys always had several fish, turtles, and frogs in the livestock water container located in the barnyard.

A short time after Grandma Delie's funeral, my brother Winston told me that one of my frogs was floating on the surface of the water trough and appeared to be dead. When I asked him which frog, he said he didn't know because they all looked alike. I hoped that is wasn't Spots because he was my favorite. I had caught him when he was very small. He had been injured. While I did not know for sure, it appeared that he had been bitten by a snapping turtle because one of his hind legs had a scar on it just above the knee. Unfortunately, Spots was the one that was dead.

Remembering the details of my mother's and Grandmother's recent funerals, I decided that Spots, too, would receive a funeral and I immediately assumed the role of junior undertaker. I put Spots in a quart jar, filled it with water, and secured the lid so that the birds, cats, and chickens could not harm him. Then I hid the jar in the woodshed. The next morning I scavenged for an appropriate box to use as a coffin. Eventually I pulled an abandoned, cigar box from the trash container behind the poultry house and placed it near the jar in the woodshed. During the day, I determined that I would bury Spots near my swing which was located between the livestock scale and the road. After I did, I'd be sure to place a cross over his grave so that everyone who passed by would see it. That afternoon, after I got home from school, I dug a shallow grave before I fashioned a small device from sticks and strings that would enable me to lower his "casket" into the grave just as the undertakers had done after my mother died. Then, I needed flowers. Eventually I remembered that there were roses inside in the hallway. After removing about a dozen petals from the roses and putting them in my pocket, I solemnly went to the woodshed, picked up the cigar box and jar, and walked to the burial site. Once I got there, I opened the jar, removed Spots, and placed him in his "coffin." Before I lowered him into his grave, I covered him with the rose petals. As I lowered him into the grave, I tried to remember the words to the songs that we sang at my mother's funeral, but I couldn't. Instead, I said my bedtime prayer:

Now I lay me down to sleep,
I pray the Lord my soul to keep,
If I should die before I wake,
I pray the Lord my soul to take.

I was glad that there wasn't anyone there to see me cry as I covered the "coffin" with dirt and placed a small cross over the grave.

I'm not sure why I did not ask anyone to help me with Spot's funeral or even tell them that there was one. Later, I told my father and he said that Spots was probably glad that I had seen to it that he had such a nice funeral.

Royal Flush

Our Grandpa Sandy was anti-indoor privy from the very first time that our father mentioned that he planned to construct a bathroom in the house, complete with a large bathtub and toilet bowl. Once installed, however, Grandpa seemed to enjoy the hot and cold running water that allowed him to adjust the temperature of his bath water. Somewhat reluctantly, he acknowledged that it was a little more convenient than dipping water from the reservoir at the end of the kitchen stove and standing in a galvanized washtub before the open oven door. He also admitted, after my brother witnessed him spitting tobacco juice in the wash bowl and flushing it down, that the bowl and the faucet were both "mighty handy gadgets."

However, his major hang-up with the facilities, determined even before they were installed, was the toilet bowl. At one time he had suggested to our father that the "damn thing would be pretty useful if it were to replace the wooden seat in the thunder shed. "Then," he said, "I could get back to using corncobs instead of toilet paper."

Due to an unfortunate accident, he decided never again to use the indoor toilet for his "necessary relief." According to my sister Evelyn, who heard him yelling in the bathroom and using cuss words that she had never heard before, it was pretty scary. As Lowell told us, Grandpa had finished his "business," and before he got off the seat, he pulled the handle and got a "royal flush." The extremely cold water from our deep well filled up the toilet bowl and engulfed his testicles.

When I heard about Grandpa's "royal flush," I was unable to figure out how he was seated on the bowl. When I asked my father, he laughed and said, "Someday, son, you'll find out."

King and Prince

About a week after our mother died, Grandpa Sandy's children, including our father, concluded that it would not be in his best interest to remain living at our house. As such, he was going to be relocated to our Uncle Charlie's farm which was only four miles from where he had lived before he came to live at our home. In addition, since he too, had not been feeling well, he would only be about two miles from Dr. Harris' office.

Grandpa Sandy indicated that he would only cooperate in the proposed move if his horses King and Prince were relocated to his son's farm. He said that he was the only one who could feed them. So, a few days before Grandma Delie's death, we waved goodbye as the truck carrying Grandpa, King, and Prince pulled out of our barnyard gate and onto the road.

Grandpa Sandy's health grew progressively worse. By the middle of May, Dr. Harris had restricted him to the house and eventually confined him to his bed.

Grandpa Sandy disregarded Dr. Harris' orders and daily got out of bed to go to the barn and feed King and Prince. "Those horses," Doc told him, "are going to outlive you and very likely eat the grass off of your grave if you don't stay in bed!" Doc told Grandpa that if he didn't stop being such a contrary "old fart" and stay in bed that he was going to die and he was not going to feel a damn bit sorry for him, but he would, however, send some flowers for his funeral.

According to our father, Doc told him during Sandy's illness that Sandy was probably the most cantankerous patient that he had treated in more than fifty years of practicing medicine. By the first day of June, Sandy had fed King and Prince for the last time, and at noon on June 15th, he belonged to the ages.

Just prior to Grandpa's funeral service, Doc Harris extended his condolences to our family. Then he walked our father to the head of Grandpa's casket to point out the spread of flowers that he had promised Grandpa if he didn't follow his instructions and stay in bed.

King and Prince, as Doc Harris had predicted, lived more than five years beyond Sandy's passing before they were sold to a local knacker.

Special Supper

Our Aunt Grace, who had traveled by train to her father Sandy's funeral, would be visiting our farm for a few days before her return to Chicago. When we brothers heard that she was coming for a visit, we also knew that we would be sleeping in our large tree house. Likewise, the male Duroc shoats, including Duey and Rocky, were very likely going to have to surrender their masculinity in the form of "high pockets" for one evening's supper since Aunt Grace always looked forward to this special treat when she visited our house.

Hank and I began to discuss how we could convince our father that Duey and Rocky should be spared from this impending fate of the twenty-two male shoats. Hank and I, ably assisted by our sisters, calculated that if each of Duey and Rocky's brothers gave up two oysters, that Aunt Aline would have a total of forty oysters to cook for Aunt Grace's special supper. This number, we pleaded, would be enough for a full family supper. If our father didn't think that forty oysters would be enough, then we said that we wouldn't eat any at supper, and Rocky. We then appealed to his sense of compassion with this question, "Don't you think Duey and Rocky

The Pennsylvania Railroad Depot was a hub for several of the nation's leading railroads. Xenia, Ohio, circa 1927.

that would make a total of forty oysters for only seven persons. While our father appeared to be favorably impressed with our mathematical progress, he didn't appear to be persuaded with the idea of sparing Duey and ought to grow up to be a daddy some day?" "We don't keep hogs on this farm very long," our father replied. He then suggested that we reread the short verse that was posted near the meat grinder in the slaughterhouse:

I had a pet pig when I was small
But he grew up and spoiled it all
My mother saw bacon, my father saw ham
I last saw Jake in the frying pan!

We children learned this short verse when it was first posted in our father's newly constructed slaughterhouse. So, it was not necessary for us to continue our plea for Duey and Rocky's exemption from their pending entrance to barrowhood and eventually to hog heaven.

Hank and I knew that we going to be holding Duey, Rocky, and their twenty brothers when they were castrated, and they were all going to do a lot of squealing during the process. We agreed that we would hold one another's shoats and that way it would probably be a little less difficult for us to have it happen.

When it was all over, Hank and I carried the bucket containing the "high pockets" into the house where Aunt Aline washed, filleted, and placed them in a crock of salt water. That evening, Hank and I went into the kitchen, removed the lid from the crock, and tried, unsuccessfully, to identify Duey and Rocky's contribution to tomorrow evening's special supper.

The next evening at supper, when our father told Aunt Grace that Hank and I had helped grow the oysters, we sat proudly and smiled. We really wanted to tell Aunt Grace that if things had gone our way, she probably wouldn't have had a third helping of oysters, but we didn't tell her.

IS EVERYBODY GOING TO Die?

In July of 1931, brother Hank's cat had given birth to a litter of seven multi-colored kittens. When the kittens were about two weeks old, they were devoured, except for their tails, by an unknown predator. He sobbed uncontrollably when he discovered this had happened. For a long time he even carried their tails in his overalls pocket to show people when he told them about the kittens' misfortune. The same month, I, too, witnessed the demise of several turtles and minnows that had been in our livestock trough since early spring.

In August, every hog on the farm, including Duey and Rocky, became ill and our father called Dr. Ayers, the veterinarian, to come and look at them. When Dr. Ayers arrived, he quickly determined that they all had a severe type of intestinal problem, called cholera, and they would all probably die in a day or two. We boys were given the task of digging a long trench into which we threw each hog as it expired, Duey and Rocky included, and covered each with a thick layer of dirt, just as Dr. Ayers had instructed us to do.

At this juncture of my young life, I was in need of some assurance with respect to the future. As such, I queried my father, "Is everybody and everything we know going to die? Are you, too, going to die?" He put his arms around me, hugged me for a longer time than usual, released me, and said, "No! We are not all going to die. We have had our share of bad luck, but things will get better before too long."

By the fall of 1931, I was in Miss Bell's third grade class; thousands of unemployed transients were caught, some of them near our farm, illegally hopping "rides" on the nation's railroads. Several hundred thousand children, (I was not one of them.), were roaming the country as drifters, and thousands of men (Our father was not one of them.) were queued up in bread lines across the country. We children, not fully cognizant of the national economic conditions, were eating beans and cornbread, inserting cardboard insoles in our shoes more frequently, and sporting a lot more patches on our clothing. However, as our father had promised when our mother died, we were still together under one roof.

Crowd of depositors gather in the rain outside Bank of United States after its failure.

Summer

In the summer of 1931, we children didn't know that there were eight million Americans unemployed. However, we did know that more men were daily stopping at our farm and offering to work for fifty cents a day. We believed there were thousands of men in the large cities selling apples on street corners because we had seen a few of these vendors in our small town.

Our father knew several families that had been evicted from their homes and farms because they were unable to make their monthly mortgage payments. He seemed to be particularly sympathetic toward the plight of the farmers. Mr. Reese's farm, he told us was auctioned off, and several neighboring farmers collectively purchased the farm and then gave it back to Mr. Reese. Our father said that these farmers were all fine people.

Mr. Dutton, from whom our father had previously purchased hogs, was about to lose his farm and offered to sell his hogs to our father for a few pennies a pound. However, our father could not help him because his slaughterhouse did not have refrigeration.

Our family was very familiar with the practice of bartering, and we watched it grow in popularity during the Depression. As the previous owner of a retail meat market, our father had always accepted eggs, chickens, and butter in exchange for meat. He enjoyed a good laugh, however, when he heard that one of the small hotels in town had accepted vegetables, ham, and eggs in exchange for a room.

Gardening during the spring and summer was a very serious undertaking and was closely supervised by our father. We boys had worked long hours to prepare, plant, hoe, and water more than a half-acre plot next to the orchard. While our older brothers used their .22 rifles to discourage the birds, especially crows, from disrupting our highly cultivated patch, brother Hank and I fashioned a pair of slingshots in an effort to get a piece of the action and a measure of fatherly approbation.

At this stage of the Depression, even though we had lost many loved ones, we felt very fortunate. Our father had a job. Our local bank had not closed. We had a big garden, and the grain was ripening in the fields.

We children, however, thought the idea of having a "Hoover buggy" to drive into town would be a lot of fun.

Heavenly Soles

Our father was too proud to accept any type of welfare clothing during the Depression, so our family, relatives, and friends participated in a hand-me-down swap system. Things were passed along until they practically disappeared. In fact, sometimes items were little more than patches on patches.

Generally the shoes I wore were passed down from my brother Lowell and were consistently well-worn and too large because he was four years my senior. Sometimes when I got holes in my shoes, one of my older brothers or sisters would help me cut a piece of cardboard to fit inside. This repair was good for two or three days in dry weather, but snow or rain destroyed the repair in an hour or so.

Occasionally my father would give me a quarter and I would walk to the 5 & 10 cent store and buy glue-on soles and heels for my shoes. My classmates always knew when I was wearing them because they made a "clippity clop" noise when the front came loose.

Mr. Grooms had a shoe repair shop near the railroad depot, and I was glad when my father told me to stop at his shop. It was a small shop that smelled like leather and had a low bench with an upside-down iron leg and foot sticking up out of it. He was a tall man with bushy, red hair and a matching handlebar mustache. He laughed a lot, liked children, and knew a lot about Presidents. He told me that George Washington's men at Valley Forge would have been glad to have had my well-worn shoes. He also told me that before Abraham Lincoln was President, people didn't have left and right shoes so it didn't matter which foot they put them on. I asked him if that made them easier to put on in the dark. He laughed and said, "It probably did!"

I had a habit of wearing the heels of my shoes unevenly, and Mr. Grooms was not laughing when he explained to me that this was a waste of material. I told him I would try to wear the new heels straighter. He also said that if I wore high-top shoes it could strengthen my ankles and it might not happen.

Sometime in early December 1932, my brother Hank and I were walking home from school and I found seven dollars. It had dabs of cow manure on it, but it was real money. I told Hank if our father allowed me to keep the money, I was going to buy a pair of high top shoes with a knife pocket on the side, and then buy a new knife to put in the pocket.

My father said that he would hold the money for a week or ten days, and if it was not claimed, we would discuss what I could do with it. I'm sure that I told him more than two dozen times during the waiting period what I wanted to buy. When the interminable waiting period ended, my father told me that I could spend the money for the high tops, but that they would only cost $3.49. So, I suggested that maybe I should buy two pairs. He sounded like Mr. Grooms when he laughed and said, "Are you going to wear two shoes on each foot?" Then he grew serious and said, "Your little brother was with you when you found the money, and he deserves to have a new pair of high tops with a knife pocket, too."

That Saturday evening our father went with us to Joe Kennedy's shoe store on Main Street, and we grinned at each other as we rolled up our overall legs and were fitted with "dream shoes." When our shoes were finally laced up, Mr. Kennedy said that we could roll down our overall legs, but we didn't. We went back out on Main Street, and it seemed that everyone was admiring our new pocket-knife high tops.

CHARLIE Simms

According to Grandpa Jim, Charlie Simms' father was moving via the Underground Railroad from Ironton to Columbus, Ohio, when President Lincoln issued the Emancipation Proclamation in September 1862. On his northern journey he had been hidden during the day in attics, cellars, and haylofts. At night he and his fellow slaves were taken to the next "station" or home of a member of the Underground Railroad. According to Grandpa Jim, they often made the hazardous journey concealed in farm wagons.

Charlie's father was hidden in an underground station in Xenia, Ohio, at the time of the Proclamation signing and decided, along with several other slaves in his group, to make the town his home. His son, Charlie, Jr., born about 1875, received no formal education, but established himself as a reliable worker and worthy citizen. In addition, he had a very amiable personality and exhibited a talent for music and story-telling. Well-known in the town, he was the first Negro appointed to the town's police force when he was approximately twenty-five years of age.

Charlie liked to joke about the time before he was on the police force when he registered at the Xenia Hotel with a woman with whom he shouldn't 've. When he registered, instead of puttin' down his X which he does because he can't write, he put down his X and put a circle around it. When he was asked why he "done" that, he said, "Why you didn't expect me to sign my real name, did you?"

Charlie liked to tell how he avoided what some called mental illness. He was quoted as saying, "When I works,

I works hard. When I sits, I sits loose. When I worries, I go to bed."

opinion with respect to this latest wireless gadget, Charlie is alleged to have answered, "One good thing about radio

Xenia Hotel where Charlie Simms signed his name with an "X."

Our father would always laugh as he related to us how he once slowed down at Monroe and Third Streets only to be stopped at the next intersection by Charlie in the town's only police car. Our father said that Charlie approached his "machine" with the full, accusatory comment, "S.L.O.W. Stop, Mr. Cultice. Can't you read?"

In the middle twenties, Charlie like the rest in the nation was caught up with radio. When a citizen asked his

is that it never lets you go off the deep end. It always takes you so far, and then snaps you right back. For instance," Charlie continued, "I was almost moved to tears by the report of the arrival of President Harding's body back in the Capitol, when a lady came on and said, 'Constipation? I don't let it bother me.'"

Charlie and his boss, Sergeant Rollie Robinson, were sent to frog Hollow after a crazed man from Columbus had allegedly killed a man who fingered his backyard still to revenue officers. They got the crazed man holed up in a storm cellar, and there was no question at all about what to do. "Go in after him," said Sergeant Robinson to Charlie. Charlie thought for a long time and finally said, "Sarge, the more I think of it, I swear, the less I think of it."

An avid storyteller, one of Charlie's best yarns concerned a local Justice of the Peace, who conducting a trial in Charlie's presence, listened to the two town lawyers plead their respective sides of a case until it came time to eat. According to Charlie, the JP got up and tacked a piece of paper to the wall and interrupted, "Gentlemen, it is time to eat. I am going. You continue as long as you want to, and when you have finished, here is my decision."

Charlie responded to a call relative to a collision between a Model T Lizzie and a horse-drawn milk wagon in the north end of town. Upon arrival, he routinely took out his pencil and accident sheet to profile his report. The accident was at the corner of North Galloway and Pleasant Streets. When Charlie questioned a bystander and was told that the horse, with two broken front legs, was on North Galloway Street, he suggested, "Maybe we ought to just drag the poor S.O.B. around the corner to King Street before I write up this report."

On duty, or off, Charlie always had time to tell, and the locals always had time to listen to, his mother-in-law story. Charlie said he had never seen such a funeral as that of his mother-in-law who'd gotten kicked to death by a mule. "Why," he said, "the people came from all over Greene County, and the wake was so crowded people could hardly find a place to sit and sing." When the person he was tellin' it to would say, "Charlie, your mother-in-law must have been mighty popular in this county that people would pay such lofty tribute." Charlie would display his gold-filled, front incisor during his laughter and say, "Well, actually, most of the fellows didn't come for the funeral. They came to find out if they could buy the mule."

USE YOUR Napkin

Our Aunt Edna wasn't much of a story-teller, but she enjoyed reciting this story that her sister-in-law, Sylvia, told her. We children never tired of hearing the following story:

Sylvia's husband Joe was prominent in a large, fraternal order in Ohio. Almost every weekend Sylvia and Joe traveled to another town to visit their lodge and usually they were invited to have dinner with a lodge member following the afternoon meeting. They almost always accepted the first invitation. On one occasion, when they accepted, several other members of the lodge seemed a tad surprised to find out where they were going for dinner.

Sylvia and Joe sat in the living room of this attractive house with a bootleg drink and admired the furnishings. A large collie dog seemed especially to occupy much of their attention. After the usual pleasantries, they were invited into the dining room. The furniture was very attractive and the table was well-set. However, they were puzzled. The table was set with five places! The four of them sat down. Then the large collie hopped onto the empty chair and sat attentively through their host's dinner blessing. Meat and potatoes were passed around. Rover received his share with the meat daintily cut by his master. It was a fine meal and much appreciated to some extent by all present, including Rover. He behaved very nicely except he did not use his silver or napkin. As Sylvia recalled, neither did he take part in the conversation. He did, however, lick his plate clean. Sylvia and Joe stayed the polite time after dinner, said good-bye, and patted Rover. It had been, according to her, one of their more memorable evenings.

When my sister Rachel shared this story with our father, he suggested that maybe our family ought to have Rover come and live at our house for a few weeks. I guess he must have thought that Rover would help us children improve our table manners.

MORE PIG Ta(i)les

Near the lard-rendering kettle in my father's slaughterhouse was a poem written by James Whitcomb Riley. While we were seated on boxes beneath this poem, Grandpa Jim would tell us about old slaughterhouses that were built before our father built his. He said about seventy years ago there was a pork packing and shipping company that was owned by two men, which was located twelve miles south of our town. In addition, he said, pork packing on a large scale took place in Bellbrook, Ohio, which was only about eight miles from where we were. He said it began about a hundred years ago, when a brick pork house, known as Porkopolis, was built near the center of the village. Each twelve-hour work day, almost 250 hogs were received there from the slaughterhouse west of town.

These hogs were hauled in farmers' wagons that formed long processions. The wagons were piled high with clean, white, stark bodies. Noses were ornamented with blood-red icicles and a round, red wound in the white foreheads showed where the unerring blow with the hammer had struck them down. These wagons, with noisy drivers, filled the street all day long and often into the night. Once the cargo was delivered, it was weighed on the sprangled arms of the beam scales just within the doors of the pork house. The weight was announced in stentorian tones, like the town crier at an auction. Next huge, flying cleavers cut the hogs into hams, shoulders, sides, etc. This busy, noisy commercial endeavor created quite a lot of commotion in the old town of Bellbrook.

An old tavern stood on the corner, a short distance from the pork house. Up on the roof, alongside the big chimney, a bell hung in a pagoda-like house. It had hung there, Grandpa Jim told us, for almost one hundred years. The old bell had a peculiar roundelay when it was rung. A long time ago it was decided that the old bell was trying to say: "Pig-tail done!" which was repeated three times to each measure. So that old bell is tenderly associated with many pleasant reminiscences in the memories of those who lived in the old town in earlier days. Its fame is preserved in prose and poetry by local historians and bards, to which James Whitcomb Riley in his "*Ponchus Pilut*" has added:

"Yes, an' out in our backyard
He he'ps Lindy render lard;
An', wite in the fire there, he
Roast a pig-tailed wurst for me-
An ist hen th' old tavern bell
Rung, down-town, an' he says 'well
Hear dat! Lan' o Canaan, son,
Ain't dat bell say "Pig-tail done!""
Pig-tail done!
Go tell Son!-
Tell dat
Chile dat
Pig-tail done!

Frequently Grandpa Jim would insist that we children, and our playmates if they were there, attempt to read or recite a few lines of this poem before he'd give us a hot, crusty pig-tail.

MRS. Knocka

We boys did not receive any allowance for working in our father's slaughterhouse. Our father, however, would sometimes allow us to cut wood for some of our neighbors to earn money to go to town on Saturday and see our friends.

Sometimes, when we were cutting wood, my two older brothers would delight in shaking me off the end handle of the crosscut saw or assigning me the task of splitting red oak, which was very difficult to split. When this happened, I would begin to cry, and they would tell me I wasn't going to get my share of the money for the work; therefore, I wouldn't be allowed to go with them into town on Saturday evening for a big bag of popcorn and a western movie featuring Tim McCoy or Tom Mix.

One of the areas where we cut and split wood was near one of our off-limits fishing and swimming holes. I particularly liked it when we hitched the horses to the wagon, put in our broad axes, wedges, and sledgehammer, and our Aunt Aline, who was our caregiver at the time, did not fix us a bag lunch to take along.

My brothers would not tell me where we were going, but I was sure I knew at least four things. One: We were going to the small farm of a retired Methodist minister, Reverend Leo Knocka and his wife Lena. Two: If I used any cuss words while we were there, I wouldn't get paid. Three: If my brothers made me cry, Mrs. Knocka would scold them. Four: At noon, we would all sit down at Mrs. Knocka's kitchen table and enjoy her chicken dumplings and strawberry rhubarb pie. My brother Lowell said that Mrs. Knocka's chicken dumplings were so good that they would "make a hound dog run up and hug a rabbit."

Tom Mix, 1925.

Reverend Knocka had a small grove of locust trees on his farm, and he sometimes had us cut eight-foot fence posts. I liked it when we did this because the trees were not very large around, and we got three posts by sawing only twice. Besides, the pile of posts built up really fast. There were two other reasons why I liked to saw and split wood at Preacher Knocka's farm. We didn't have to split the rungs too many times because he had a large fireplace, and we didn't have to load it on our wagon.

When we finished the job, hitched the horses to the wagon, and prepared to leave, Reverend Knocka would give us a generous amount of money for our "good work." Mrs. Knocka would give us a small bag of hard candy, tell us to enjoy the movie that evening, and not to eat too much popcorn.

I really liked Mrs. Knocka, and she always made me think about my mother. I guessed her grown-up kids were glad that she was their mother when they were my age.

THE SLAUGHTERHOUSE Kid

When the visiting nurse, Mrs. Shaw, weighed Miss Bell's third grade class in October of 1931, the holes in my socks showed as I took off my shoes and stepped onto the scales. As she weighed me, Mrs. Shaw referred to me as the "slaughterhouse kid" and mentioned that she knew my father very well. While I was a little embarrassed by the holes in my socks, I was glad that she knew my father and recognized me as the "slaughterhouse kid."

Miss Martha Bell, or "Granny," as we referred to her when she was not in auditory range, ran a very tight ship and seemed, at times, to be devoid of a sense of humor. However, several of my classmates and I were afraid of the yardstick that she occasionally carried in class and used, in her words, "to measure her philosophy." We students guessed that "philosophy" must be the same thing as discipline, since she seldom used the yardstick during our arithmetic lessons.

Miss Bell didn't seem to be very happy when Mr. Miller, the circuit music teacher, came to our class every

Teacher

Thursday afternoon. I guess she thought he was wasting her teaching time because, according to her, our combined classes didn't seem to read music and sing very well. However, Miss Bell didn't seem to mind Mrs. Mason coming to our classes on Tuesday morning for our combined art lessons. One of my classmates, Marjorie Johnson, said that Miss Bell didn't like Mr. Miller because he was a very good-looking, young man.

We boys seemed to frequently answer questions that Miss Bell hadn't asked and when we did respond to her questions, we frequently gave the wrong answers. We never understood why she got angry when she didn't know the answers to our questions. I guess we didn't understand her anger because we didn't get angry at her when we couldn't answer her questions.

During an arithmetic lesson she asked if anyone knew how to tell how many feet were in a yard. Dick Douglas put up his hand and she called on him. Dick replied, "You count the number of people in the yard and multiply by two." We students had to stifle our laughter. Even Miss Bell caught herself grinning at his answer.

Another time when we were working on addition, Miss Bell asked me if I put my left hand in my left pocket and found two dimes and my right hand in my right pocket and found three nickels, what would I have? I quickly answered that I would probably have somebody else's pants on because I never had thirty-five cents at one time in my life.

Brother Winston had told me before I entered her class that she might ask such a question, and he had coached me carefully with respect to my answer.

A Bushel of Love

In the fall of 1931, our father and one of our neighbors, Frank Boysell, were looking at a new-born calf in our barn when Mr. Boysell noticed a bushel basket of cull potatoes that we had not taken to the root cellar. Mr. Boysell told our father that if our family was not going to eat "them taters," that there was a "sod wider" with several "younguns" who attended his Jimtown church who would be glad to have them, and he would be glad to take them to her.

Our father told Mr. Boysell that we were probably not going to need the potatoes and she was welcome to them. However, he told Mr. Boysell that it would not be necessary for him to take the potatoes to the widow because he would personally see that she received them.

Front row, L to R: Gerald Morris, Louise Morris, & Henry Cultice. Back Row, L to R: Wendell Cultice, Alpha Ford, & Edith Ford.

His gift basket was warmly received by the widow, and he was invited to spend an evening at her house the following week. Our father told us about this invitation which became a source of much curiosity within our home.

Before his departure on the evening of the invitation, we children, especially our sisters, made sure that our father's shoes were shined, his necktie was snug against his collar, and his cheek was free of his usual cud of Red Horse.

When our father told our oldest brother Winston that there was a very attractive sixteen-year-old girl living next door to the widow, our brother said he would like to meet her. Within two weeks, our father and brother were driving to Jimtown together one evening a week to visit their mutual friends. Each evening before they left the house for Jimtown, they flipped a coin to determine who would get to wear the overcoat and who would wear the hat because there was only one dress hat and one overcoat. Our brother told us that sometimes he would wait a long time for our father to come to the automobile for their ride home, and it was very cold when it was not his night to wear the overcoat.

After a few weeks, our brother's local, high school sweetheart saw to it that Winston's half of the dual, courtship ride was cut short. However, by that time, our father was making the trip not once a week but twice, on Wednesday and Sunday evenings.

When we children asked our father to tell us about the lady he was visiting, he told us she was very pretty and had three small children. Our sisters wanted to know if the lady and her children were going to become our stepmother and our stepsisters and brother.

Hank asked, "How many of her kids are boys?" "One," our father responded. "Is the boy old enough to play ball?" Hank inquired. "Not yet," our father said. "What about the girls? Are they old enough to play ball?" Hank continued.

NEVER ON Sunday

One Sunday just before Halloween, our father and sisters had gone to Winchester, Indiana, for the day to visit our Aunt Annie, who had been ill for nearly two weeks. Conventionally, our father appointed our oldest brother Winston to serve as surrogate parent during his absence. That day was no exception.

While Winston and his friend Dick Hodge were busy repairing Dick's Model T Ford, Hank and I caught half a dozen white leghorn hens. Ever curious, we wondered what they'd look like if they were another color. Since we knew there would be some paint in our father's contracting truck, we headed for it. Sure enough! We found what we needed. Before our brother knew what was happening, we took a bucket of paint and two brushes from the rear of the truck and proceeded to paint each of the squawking birds a bright green. Although we anticipated some form of punishment once our father returned, we decided our experiment had been worth it. By itself, this activity would have been enough to warrant punishment. However, the day had just begun and we could not foresee the events of the rest of the day.

Sometime after we had finished our sandwiches at noon, Hank's friends Elmer and Jim Thome stopped at the farm for a few hours of work and play. Temporarily we forgot about our morning adventures and the inevitable consequences of our actions, since we knew there always were consequences. By mid-afternoon, we were playing in the area near the tree house, and someone suggested that we ought to get some kitchen matches from the storage box in the tree house and build a small fire on the bank of the dry ditch that was located near the base of the tree containing the tree house.

As a result of our threshing event in early September, the ditch and the fence rows in the area leading to the barnyard had a small amount of chaff where the straw had been blown into a stack only a few yards from the main barn.

While our attention was directed to the fire, Elmer noticed that the chaff along the fence row leading to the barnyard was burning very rapidly. After our immediate efforts to trample the fire with our bare feet were futile, with burns on our feet, we raced to the tree house to get help from our older brothers. They and several other men who arrived to help were successful in pushing our father's truck a safe distance from the barn, but the entire fall harvest—corn, wheat, and oats—went up in smoke. All that was left were the smoke and ashes that a slight wind sent swirling skyward.

By the time the city fire department responded, the barn was burning toward the southwest corner. Fortunately the firemen saved our house from also catching on fire by directing a light stream of water onto the roof as well as onto the southeast corner of the house.

Alternately, Hank and I sat and stood on our front lawn and cried as we observed the heap of burning, smoking rubble that had been our barn. Before most of the men had gone, our Grandpa Jim and our minister, Reverend Knocka, showed up and stayed with us until our father returned from Indiana at about six o'clock that evening.

Hank and I were unable to convince our Grandpa Jim and Reverend Knocka that we ought to go into the house and put some cardboard in the seat of our overalls before our father returned home. Instead, when our father arrived and even before he was able to get out of the automobile, Reverend Knocka walked us toward him and explained that we small boys had been playing with matches and had accidentally burned the barn. He also pointed out that God had seen to it that his children were not harmed.

As I reflected on the event years later, I'm not sure if Reverend Knocka saved any souls that Sunday morning, but I know for certain that he saved two small boys from getting a well-deserved spanking that evening.

THE HOLIDAY Crisis

When the custom butchering season began in the fall of 1931, our father was aware that many of his regular customers were not going to be able to pay for their animal(s) to be slaughtered at his plant. Therefore, he encouraged the farmer(s) to barter his services by giving a portion of the animal(s) to him in exchange for his services. This practice allowed him to sell his portion of the animal(s) to the retail markets in the city for cash. This time-honored practice, however, did not produce the needed revenue for his business to grow as it had in previous butchering seasons.

Our father encouraged our sisters to hurry home after school to help Aunt Aline with the housekeeping chores. We boys, especially my two older brothers, were also encouraged to hurry home after school and attend to their husbandry chores before supper. After supper they would go with my father to assist in the processing of the animals that had been slaughtered the day before. Several times during the week, Hank and I would also go to the slaughterhouse to assist by cutting pork fat and rind into small cubes to be rendered the next day.

An unemployed man and his improvised shanty.

My older brothers suspected that our family was beginning to feel the pinch of the Depression when our father was, for the first time, slaughtering animals on Saturday afternoon. Frequently, we were also returning from church on Sunday, eating our dinner, and reporting to the slaughterhouse to work several hours in the afternoon.

Our Thanksgiving dinner, the first one without our mother, was enhanced by our sisters, who made two mince-meat pies. Aunt Aline had roasted a large, fresh ham and cooked sweet potatoes in maple syrup. During the meal-time prayer, although we did not discuss it afterwards, brother Hank and I were very grateful that the ham we were enjoying was not one of Duey's or Rocky's.

By the end of the first week in December, we children were unable to attend school because our clothes, shoes, jackets, and hats were worn threadbare. This was the most poignant facet of the Depression for our family.

About the 15th of December, our father arrived home about noon, came into the house, and asked Winston and Lowell to accompany him back out to the auto. When they returned, each of them was carrying a large, card-board box. The boxes were placed on the living room floor, and our father said, "O. K. Put them on and get back to school!" We children nearly danced at the sight, smell, and feel of our respective items as they were ex-tracted from the boxes.

That evening at supper, collectively, we children at-tempted to convince our father that, since we had been absent for more than five days, we would each need a note from him before we would be allowed to return to school. "You won't need a note this time," our father assured us. "Besides," he added, "your teachers are really going to be glad to see you!"

When Hank and I walked into the front hall of our school the next morning, he received a big smile and a hug from his teacher, Mrs. Stephens. Miss Bell smiled as though she had slept with a coat hanger in her mouth and hugged me and said she was really glad to see me. I wondered if she would be smiling that way when we were working on beginning fractions later in the day.

A few days after returning to school, we received our annual, large box of Christmas candy from our Aunt Annie in Indiana. Wow! New clothes, back in school, Miss Bell smiling, and a large box of candy—all in one week. In spite of the Depression, it was going to be a really good Christmas.

WE BROTHERS LEND A Hand

When we children all returned to school after the holi-days, our father continued to impress upon us how lucky we were because nearly half of the men in the country were unemployed. He also added that most of the men who were working were making less money than they had been a few years ago. That made it very difficult for them to buy food, clothes, and fuel for their families. He told us about a group of men in Detroit, Michigan, whose children were so hungry that the men smashed store front windows at night in order to obtain food for them. After the men did this, they then walked to the local police precinct and told the officers what they had done but they were not arrested.

In Chicago, Illinois, and Cleveland, Ohio, he added, groups of men stole clothing and fuel because their children were cold and they, too, were not arrested.

We were not cold or hungry, but our coal supply in the woodshed was nearly depleted, and Detective LaRance had not called in some time. Big brother Winston came up with a plan that he was sure would cause Detective LaRance to call our father and request that we boys bring our horse and wagon to the railroad tracks to pick up a load or two of hard coal. Our brother emphasized, however, that we were not to tell our father about our plan or we would be in for some serious punishment.

The original plan called for Winston and Lowell to sneak out of the house at 12:30 a.m., go to the barn and retrieve a container of axle grease and several applicators, walk along the cottonwoods to the railroad tracks, and conceal themselves in the adjacent ditch until the 1:20 a.m. Columbus-bound passenger train had passed. After much pleading, the plan was modified to include me, too, but only in the role of lookout.

A long line of unemployed welcome the arrival of the Golden Crust Bread truck.

After the passenger train passed by, my brothers jumped up onto the railroad bed, ran about a hundred yards east, and applied a generous amount of grease to each of the rails until the container was empty, and raced even faster back to where I was waiting in the ditch.

Our intended target was the 1:35 a.m. freight train which conventionally consisted of two or three engines and dozens of cars piled high with hard coal bound for industrial plants in Toledo, Ohio, and Detroit, Michigan. In just a few minutes we could see the beam of the locomotive's headlight and hear the whistle as it pulled out of the station and crossed Columbus Street. When the engines encountered the axle grease, they slowed to a crawl. Each of my brothers boarded a coal car and began pushing large chunks of coal toward our north fence as fast as they could. While they were doing this, I could hear the engineers calling for more sand to be sifted onto the rails as they cursed the unknown perpetrators.

During the early afternoon that same day, I stood proudly on top of the second wagon-load of coal and waved to our father as we drove toward the woodshed to off-load our Depression project. Our father smiled, removed an over-worked cud of tobacco from his cheek, and playfully tossed it onto the load of coal. After we had finished off-loading the coal, my brother Lowell commented that the whole plan came off "slicker than cow slobbers."

SLEEPING Lover

During the winter of 1932, my brother Winston was "sweet" on a young lady, Jenny, who lived on the city end of our road and was a classmate of his at the high school.

Following completion of his evening chores and with the approval of her parents, he had convinced our father that he should be permitted to visit her one evening a week. Our father reluctantly consented and the courtship appeared to be going very well. In fact, my brother often extolled the many attributes of Miss Jenny at our evening meal. He seemed to fancy himself as a local Rudolf Valentino.

Winston's early morning farm chores included feeding and watering the animals as well as milking. As the weeks went by he was spending even more time with Miss Jenny and we began to notice that he was consistently arriving late for breakfast.

One morning, following my brother's late- night return from Jenny's house the previous evening, our father went to the barn to determine why my brother needed extra time to complete his chores. He found the cow, also named Jenny, contentedly enjoying her ground corn in the manger. My brother was sitting on the milking stool, with his head on her flank, sleeping soundly. According to our brother Lowell, our father gently awakened Winston and said: "Boy! What kind of lover are you, anyway? Here you are, early in the morning with a contented lady, with a teat in each hand, and you are sleeping blissfully. What kind of lover is that?"

Sixteen

In March of 1932, Aunt Aline baked a large chocolate cake for my brother Winston's sixteenth birthday. During the past year, Grandpa Jim had taught my brother how to drive his Model T Ford sedan. For a long time after we finished our supper, we sat at the table and talked. It seemed to me in the last year, that my brother and his friends, who formerly played various types of games with us, now only participated in athletic games. Also, he and his friends spent a great deal of time talking about girls and automobiles. In fact, Grandpa Jim, without our father's endorsement, purchased a 1924 Star touring sedan for my brother from a gentleman who lived near him, Jerry Moore.

My brother and his friends tinkered with this jalopy for several weeks and were unsuccessful in getting it to operate properly. He and his friends eventually disassembled the auto and sold the parts for a small profit. Of course, our father approved very highly of the latter effort. My sister Rachel penned the following ode to the jalopy's demise:

If you buy an old twenty-four
You might buy it from ol' Jerry Moore,
Put it in the barn and the thing wouldn't start.
So, we pushed it behind the chicken house and tore it all apart.
Now, we've sold the parts for lotta junk
So, our father's out of his great big funk.

The failure of this auto venture meant that we brothers would still be driving our horse and wagon into the city occasionally to attend a Saturday night movie. A few weeks later, my brothers each invited a friend to ride along with us when we attended our next movie. Instead of sitting in the rear as they usually did, this time the older boys all took seats in the front row near the exit door which opened onto a poorly-lighted side street. Before the movie started, they bought a large bag of buttered popcorn and told me that I

Henry Cultice, Mildred Cultice, & Wendell Cultice, 1935.

could eat as much as I liked, but that I needed to watch the movie carefully while they were gone for a little while. They also told me that when I heard a knock on the exit door that I should get up out of my seat and open the door quietly.

I was nearly finished with the popcorn and the villain was about to be captured when I heard the knock on the door. As I let my brothers and their friends back into the theater, I was aware of a strong perfume odor. On the way home, after I had given them a small boy's interpretation of the action in the movie, I asked them where they had gone during the movie. This questioned prompted them to tell me that I was too young to know, and I would have to wait a few more years to find out. Since they told me not to tell our father what they did, I just guessed it was some place they didn't want our father to know about.

SPELLING Bee

As we were gathered around our kitchen table enjoying supper, we remembered our mother, ever the school teacher, who occasionally attempted to enhance our learning by engaging one, or more, of us in limited spelling challenges.

About a year after our mother's death, while our family was enjoying one of her favorite recipes—pork backbone, boiled potatoes, and sauerkraut—Aunt Aline, our father's youngest sister and our caregiver since our mother's death, suggested, that we share, in memory of our mother, our recent efforts to expand our spelling prowess.

Being of German descent, there was still a measure of primogeniture in our household, and our senior brother Winston invariably exercised this status during any sibling activities. He had turned sixteen the previous month, and, according to our father, he and his peers were "car crazy." He projected an impish grin as he proceeded to pronounce and spell "c-a-r-b-u-r-e-t-o-r," tipped his water glass, and glanced toward Lowell who was two- months-shy of his fourteenth birthday. He had recently suffered the embarrassment of being the first one in his class to go down in a spelling bee, when he spelled the word "posse," p-u-s-s-y. Winston, who knew of the incident, attempted to further embarrass Lowell by having him repeat his spelling bee disaster at the supper table. Lowell, sensing Winston's attempt at entrapment, pronounced the word "posse" and gave the correct spelling. As a last-ditch effort to gain the advantage, Winston remarked, "Well, brother, it was probably your pronunciation and not your spelling that sat you down in the spelling bee." My father leveled a piercing stare in Winston's direction and quickly redirected the conversation.

THE NEW Era

During the second half of my third grade year in Miss Bell's class, there were several significant events that stood out in our family and in the nation. Our father's romance with the widow at Jimtown appeared to be going very smoothly, and we children were aware that he was spending more time with us after supper before going to work at the slaughterhouse.

He particularly enjoyed having our sisters brush his hair as he listened to his favorite radio program, "Amos and Andy," at seven o'clock several weekday evenings. He very rarely attended a movie, and we children were all surprised and elated when he told us that he and the Jimtown widow had gone to see Cary Grant and Mae West

John Dillinger was Public Enemy #1 in 1934.

in the movie *I'm No Angel.* I didn't know what the movie was all about, but I surely had heard my older brothers and their friends tell a lot of jokes about Mae West. Maybe our father had heard some of these jokes, too, and that's why he wanted to find out if they might be true.

During our class celebration of President Washington's and President Lincoln's respective birthdays in February, my art class portrait of Washington was not selected to be displayed in our room's front windows. However, when we celebrated Lincoln's birthday, I won a measure of compensation by memorizing and reciting the following lines at "show and tell":

Meat on the Table
I sing this glorious land of ours,
Its motor cars and shows
Its little gardens gay with flowers,
Its phones and radios
From here your ambitious boy
May go to be our President if he's able
But what spells USA to me
Is meat upon the table.

Miss Bell asked me who wrote the verse, and I told her I couldn't remember, but my father would know. Then, she asked me if I thought I would be President someday, and I answered, "Yes!"

In March, a few days after we had celebrated our oldest brother's birthday, Franklin D. Roosevelt became President and gave a nationally broadcast "fireside chat" on Sunday night. Since we didn't have a fireplace, we children kept quiet near our living room stove as our father listened attentively to the President's words. After the President was finished, our father told us that the President was going to have a "New Deal" program that would probably help a lot of poor people and a couple programs that might help the farmers and his business.

Within months, a Civilian Conservation Corps (CCC) Camp, which provided work for unemployed and unmarried 18-25 year-old men was constructed just west of our town. Our father was the successful bidder on providing the meat products for the several hundred men in the new camp. Our brother Winston said that the Manning sisters and their mother, who had an established "house of entertainment" in the west end, would probably keep the young men from becoming too lonely on the weekends.

In April, our father told our sisters and Aunt Aline not to go out of the house alone after dark because of the increasing activities of gangsters in our area of the country. He told us that the new President had set up a special crime agency called the FBI in an effort to catch a man by the name of John Dillinger.

We children were excited to learn, a short time before Easter, that our father had invited the Jimtown widow and her children to our home for supper. After everyone had been introduced and we'd eaten, we children went into the living room while the adults remained at the table and conversed. We quickly satisfied our curiosity by asking them to repeat their names, tell us how old they were, and what grade they were in.

At about seven-thirty there was a knock on the front door, and Aunt Aline responded. When she opened the door, two men, each displaying a badge, told her they were United States Treasury agents and they had a warrant to search every area of our farm. They also told her that there were already agents at the other buildings on the farm. For more than an hour, our father accompanied them as they searched throughout the house, barn, and slaughterhouse.

Just before the two local agents left the house, our father retrieved a large jar of dill pickles from the larder and asked them if they would like a shot of "garden juice" before leaving. The agents laughed and thanked him for his time.

In the second week of May, the Agricultural Adjustment Act (AAA) was established to encourage farmers to voluntarily reduce their crop and animal production. Our father said that this program, too, would help the farmers because they would be paid for bringing their livestock, especially hogs, to his slaughterhouse when the animals were much smaller. By doing so, the farmers would also save a lot of money on feed.

When these animals, mostly hogs, were slaughtered, they were delivered to a relief agency located on Whiteman Street. The pork carcasses were so small that I could carry a whole carcass into the agency by myself. Our father referred to this process as the "parity program." Directly across the street from the produce relief agency was an agency which gave out clothing to people who lined up on the street waiting for clothes. We children did not visit this agency.

At the school district's annual "Field Day" contests just before school closed, I won both the fifty and one hundred yard dashes when I ran against the other fourth graders in the entire district and received a bright, new half-dollar for each event. Miss Bell seemed to be really happy that day. I couldn't tell whether she was happy because I won two races, or because I wouldn't be in her room the next year.

NATURE'S Laboratory

Our swimming hole at Shawnee Creek was not only a delightful recreational facility, but also a type of rural, coeducational learning laboratory.

While attending Sunday school, the first Sunday of June 1932, my brother Lowell invited one of his classmates, Leonard Starky, to come to the farm for a swim the following Saturday afternoon. Not knowing about Lowell's plans, the next day my sister Rachel invited our neighbor and her playmate neighbor, Bonnie Boysell, to come for a swim on that same Saturday afternoon. Since Rachel knew that Bonnie's cousin, Roberta "Bobby" Boots, was going to be coming from Hazard, Kentucky for a visit, she included "Bobby" in the invitation too. These invitations were the first two links in an interstitial chain of events during the week that would alter the traditional image of our nature's laboratory. On Tuesday, our Aunt Aline, who had served as our caretaker since our mother's death over a year before, had furtively implied to us that our practice of co-educational "skinny-dipping" might not meet with the approval of our present minister, Reverend Dowell. Reverend Dell Dowell had succeeded our previous parson, Solomon Simpson, when the church conference, yielding to his demands, reluctantly transferred him to a new congregation a few weeks after all six of us had individually "mooned" him in our family kitchen a few years before. At the time Rev. Simpson was transferred, my father voiced the theory that perhaps he was not properly trained at the seminary to cope with our particular type of congregation.

On Wednesday, very likely at the urging of our Aunt Aline, my father had informed Winston and Lowell that their days of coeducational "skinny-dipping" were over. Now that we were all getting older, he no longer felt it was appropriate for them to continue to go "skinny-dipping." Lowell and Winston were in agreement. They didn't believe that the issue was one of morality. Instead, they concluded it was merely a ploy to afford them more time in the slaughterhouse. At any rate, Lowell neglected to inform his friend Starky that his invitation had to be retracted. Therefore, Starky, heading east, walked the railroad tracks and arrived at the swimming hole at approximately one o'clock on Saturday.

When kid brother Hank and I learned that our older brothers would not be at the creek on Saturday, we hurriedly held a "pow-wow" with our sisters and devised a plan. We boys would meet Starky at the edge of the railroad tracks, swim for a couple of hours, walk him back to the tracks, and then hurry across the open alfalfa field toward the house. Our appearance at the north end of the field would be the signal for our sisters, Bonnie Boysell, and her cousin Bobbie Boots to head for the swimming hole. This plan would afford both parties, as my father had infrequently remarked, of swimming "suited or unsuited."

After the four girls arrived back at the pump house for a fresh glass of water, they exchanged goodbyes and Bonnie and Bobbie walked quickly up the dusty lane toward the Boysell house.

There was no "skinny dippin" at the swimming pool on Church Street.

While no mention was made of the day's swimming sessions at the supper table, our prevailing "can't wait to tell" facial expressions revealed that we had something to share and that we wouldn't be able to wait very long. After supper, the girls stalled when Aunt Aline indicated that it was time for their baths. As soon as we possibly could, we gathered in the woodshed where we exchanged the day's secrets behind a closed door.

My sisters had swum naked with Bonnie before but not with her tall, buxom, dark-haired cousin. Rachel, employing only the pronoun "she," spoke first. "Well, when she turns on her back and does the 'two cupcakes on the platter' act, it really looks like 'two angel food cakes on the platter.'" My sister Evelyn quickly gave her version of Bonnie's "double buns for sale" routine. "When she pushed her backside up, it looked more like a 'full moon on the top of the water' than 'a double loaf of bread.'" Evelyn went on, "Besides that, when she took her bloomers off, her sparrow's nest looked more like a crow's nest. It really did!"

My brother and I, with our limited vocabularies, were much less descriptive. However, he suggested, and I nodded in agreement, that when Starky did his back float and called out, "Last little wienie on the platter," it looked more like the "last jumbo frankfurter on the platter."

Maybe, just maybe, without the guidance of our older brothers, we four still had a whole lot to learn in nature's laboratory.

THE FULL House

In the middle of June our father married Merle, the Jimtown widow, and she and her brood of three children—Louise, 8; Beatrice, 5; and Gerald, 3—moved into our three-bedroom, farm house. Aunt Aline, who had been our caregiver for two years, accepted a private, live-in, nursing position in the city.

We younger children had heard many and varied stories, beginning with *Cinderella*, about stepmothers, and we believed it would be in our best interest if we held a council in the poultry house to determine our course of action, just in case our new stepmother ever attempted to physically punish one of us. We soon agreed we would collectively surround the intended victim and prohibit her from spanking the individual. Since girls at our home never seemed to receive spankings anyway, Hank and I felt that the agreement was heavily weighted in our favor.

There were now eleven individuals occupying our three-bedroom house. Of course, this would call for several adjustments. Our kitchen table, which formerly seated eight, was quickly extended to accommodate eleven by placing the kitchen table from our stepmother's house in a tandem position with the existing table. Sometimes when we were really hungry, it seemed to take a long time for the serving dish to be passed around to where we were seated.

Our father told us that we had relatives who had sixteen children in their family and when the children were called for a meal, they would all run as fast as they could. If one of them fell, he said, that child would not bother to get up because he knew that by the time he got up and reached the table, all of the food on the table would be gone. We all thought this was a pretty funny story.

Since our two upstairs bedrooms were already "genderized," the sleeping arrangements were adjusted by bringing a double bed from our stepmother's house and placing it in the girls' room where there had been only one double bed before. It was not possible to add another bed to the boys' bedroom because it already contained two double beds, one of which was occupied by our older brothers. Therefore, Hank and I made space for our stepbrother by sleeping crosswise with three rather than two in our bed. On many nights, especially when it was very warm, our older brothers would sleep in the large tree house. When they did this, Hank and I would sometimes sleep in their bed and try to audit the conversation in our parents' bedroom below. On one occasion, we heard our stepmother's query, "My god, Walter, don't you ever think of anything else?" "Not recently," our father responded.

A few weeks later, we guessed they were talking about religion, when we heard our father say, "If the good Lord created anything better than this, he must have kept it for himself."

It was necessary when we traveled as a family to employ two automobiles. The girls all rode in our sedan with our father and stepmother, and we five boys rode in a delivery truck, which our brother Winston drove.

Almost all of our Sunday school teachers had at least one of our gang in class, and our family now filled nearly two entire pews in our small church.

While all of these adjustments were taking place in our home, the National Recovery Administration (NRA) was establishing a partnership between government, business, and labor, which called for workers to work shorter hours and to receive higher wages, among other things.

Our father did not look favorably upon such a program and jokingly referred to the acronym (NRA) as standing for "No Ragged Asses."

ECONOMIC TURN Around

For some reason, unknown to me, Miss Bell was able to rationalize promoting me to her fourth grade in September, and we appeared to be having a very good beginning. Mr. Edwards, the janitor, was bootlegging unwrapped candy and gum to me and brother Hank after school. My idol, Babe Ruth, had hit a big home run in the World Series, and our father was enlarging the size of the slaughterhouse. Not only was he increasing the size of the slaughterhouse, but he was also having ammonia-operated machinery installed that would refrigerate three large rooms-chilling, hanging, and processing. As a result, he would be butchering year-round—not only hogs but also cattle, calves, and lambs. During the construction, he purchased a used truck and a Pontiac demonstration sedan from his nephew Dallas, who was a salesman for a local car dealer.

While we children didn't give a whole lot of thought to our father's apparent economic turn-around, I'm sure that it did not go unnoticed by his business associates and local denizens. There were no less than three other slaughterhouses in our area, and someone suggested to our father that he call his enlarged plant an "abattoir" which was a French word for slaughterhouse. This title, according to his advisor, would tend to give his slaughterhouse an air of sophistication and cause it to stand out over his competitors. I, for one, however, was not looking forward to being addressed as the "Abattoir Kid!"

The fall was alive with the pending Presidential election, the many facets of the Depression, and the call for the repeal of Prohibition. These weighty national concerns, of course, were being resolved by some of the best minds in this small town, especially at Del Johnstone's barbershop and Bart Bently's Barbeque, which was located about three blocks south of the barbershop, near Shawnee Creek.

Orval "Doc" Harness, a close friend of our late Grandpa Sandy, was getting his monthly trim in Del's shop when he was asked for his opinions on the upcoming election between President Herbert Hoover, a Re-

Front row, L to R: Louise Morris, Mildred Cultice, Gerald Morris, Rachel Cultice, & Henry Cultice. Back row, L to R: Wendell Cultice, Evelyn Cultice, Lowell Cultice, & Roger Cultice, 1935.

publican, and Franklin Roosevelt, a Democrat and the challenger. "Hell," he said, "it don't make a damn bit of difference who wins, 'cause they're all alike! Politicians are just like baby's diapers; they should be changed frequently and for exactly the same reasons." Having solicited room-wide laughter with his political assessment of the candidates, he confessed that he had never voted in his life. "I'm too damn smart to be a Democrat," he said, "and too damn poor to be a Republican."

City folks depended on local delivery for their dairy products.

Fred Fremont attempted to divert the conversation to the current status of the Depression by reading Will Rogers' comments from the previous evening's newspaper. "We got more wheat, more corn, more food, more cotton, more money in the banks, more everything in the world than any nation that ever lived ever had, yet we are starving to death. We are the first nation in the history of the world to go to the poorhouse in an automobile."

For several years, a few local Prohibition advocates had alleged that Bart Bently's delicious pork barbeque sandwiches were being served up in a "blind pig." These individuals also accused the local police of enjoying a free drink or two with their sandwiches when they ate there. Beyond this, a few thought the police might be taking "ice" which caused them to "look the other way." The Prohibition advocates, however, were convinced their's was a losing cause, when it was pointed out to them that Judge Gordon "drank" his lunch at Bart's Barbeque nearly every day that court was in session.

Looking Ahead

In the spring we planted another large garden, celebrated a couple more birthdays, and wiped the onion-flavored cow dung off our faces at milking time, after the cows had been turned out to pasture. Hank, our friends, and I would occasionally hitch Coli to the wagon, pack in a plentiful supply of stale cracklings, and drive east of our farm for an afternoon of excitement.

On one particular trip, we stopped just this side of the swamp, and utilizing some small tree branches, proceeded to engage in a condom contest we had learned from our older brothers a few years earlier. It was a very simple contest with few rules. The first person to locate, spear, and hang five condoms on the proximal barbed wire fence was unchallenged as the winner. Hal Hoop was

Borden's
MILK & MILK PRO
NO. 1

the winner. As the condom catch for the day fluttered in a light breeze, we piled back into the wagon and headed east again seeking more adventure.

About two miles from the farm we pulled off the gravel road into a small cemetery that was located near a covered bridge. While wading in the stream, we looked for frogs under the bridge and rested against tombstones while we ate our cracklings.

Then we checked the entire cemetery for a birth-date or death-date that was the same as this day. We were in the habit of gathering around such a grave marker and singing the individual a happy birthday or "deathday" song. On this day, somewhat to our disappointment, we did not locate such a headstone.

In mid-afternoon, we hitched Coli back to the wagon and headed west toward the farm. As we approached the wooded swamp area adjacent to our farm, it seemed that we all felt the need for additional adventure. Since we noticed that this area was free of gypsies, lovers, and even automobiles, we felt fairly safe when we pulled into the edge of the woods and tied Coli to a tree. As we investigated various, abandoned objects and assorted clumps of trash, Billy Brewer called for us to come quickly and look at what he had found. When we got to him we were stunned to see a newly-dead baby with the umbilical cord still attached, partially wrapped in several sheets of newspaper. We ran as fast as we could back to the wagon and headed toward the house at a gallop. Billy thought maybe he had found Lucky Lindy's baby who had been kidnapped several months before and he was hopeful that he might receive a big reward for discovering the baby in the swamp area. Hal told Billy to forget it since the baby had already been found. Hal did say, though, that the police were still looking for the guy who had kidnapped the baby.

Once we got home, our stepmother called the sheriff. Needless to say, we felt very important when he came to investigate and we responded to his questions. This event was, however, a little more excitement than we had planned on at the beginning of the day.

A TRUE FISH Story

In the summer, we and our visiting friends, all of us conventionally barefoot, spent a great deal of time in our swimming hole, carrying out our work assignments and listening to the adventures of the increasing number of hobos who visited our home for water, food, and rest.

The warm summer months were memorable because two or three times we hitched a horse to the spring wagon, tossed in our homemade fishing gear, and drove a few miles east of our place to a larger fishing and swimming hole alongside the New York Central Railroad tracks. Due to the depth of the water and the size of the fish, this site was our favorite place to swim and fish. In addition it afforded us a better opportunity to "moon" the diners on the passing trains.

I distinctly remember one day when Lowell was learning how to swim. As he "dog-paddled" we spotted a hobo walking along the railroad tracks. With his bindle securely tied to the stick that was over his shoulder, he called out, "Having trouble swimming, Sonny? Well, if you are, stick a cork up your ass and you'll float!" Needless to say Lowell didn't appreciate hearing that even if he was just learning how to swim.

Later, we fished, very successfully, from the railroad trestle. Before long we had approximately a dozen assorted fish on a stringer which Winston had tied securely to a tree root at the water level of the swimming hole. This practice kept the fish submerged and alive until such time as we departed for home. When that time came, we would put the stringer into a large container of water in the wagon. While some of the fish would usually die before we were all the way home, they would still be fresh enough for us to scale and gut upon arrival.

On one occasion, while we were still engaged in some frolicsome activities in the water, Lowell noticed a large blacksnake near our stringer of fish. He hurried out of the water, retrieved a small tree branch, and prepared to scare off the intruder. He was unable to scare off the snake because it had swallowed one of the smaller fish on the stringer. Winston said we could not take the snake home with the fish. If we did this, he contended, our parents wouldn't allow us to eat the fish.

We watched as the older boys untied the stringer, carried all of the critters out of the water and onto the bank, and cut the line in two places, a few inches beyond the snake's mouth. As the snake slithered away from them, my brothers quickly tied the line ends together and returned the fish to the water.

I surely hoped that the blacksnake was not headed for our house. Our older brothers frequently teased us about a snake named "Blackie" that allegedly lived in our outdoor jake.

Recitation

When my sisters were in Miss Bell's class they learned a poem entitled "The Mysteries of My Body." They learned it so well they even attempted to recite a couple of the lines backward. However, even after being kept after school, I was only able to get about halfway through the poem before Miss Bell threw up her hands and surrendered.

The Mysteries of My Body
Where can a man buy a cap for his knee
or the key to a lock of his hair?
Is the crown of your head where jewels are found?
Who travels the bridge of your nose?
If you wanted to shingle the roof of your mouth,
would you use the nails in your toes?
Can you sit in the shade of the palm of your hand
or beat the drum of your ear?
Can the crook in your elbow be sent to jail?
If so, just what did he do?
How can you sharpen your shoulder blades?
I'll be darned if I know—do you?

I didn't tell Miss Bell, but Grandpa Sandy had taught me lines that were similar to those she wanted me to learn.

You can't raise a cow from
the calf of your leg. Don't
try it; it cannot be done.
You can't get milk from a
gentleman cow. Don't try it, it
cannot be done.

I guessed, just maybe, that Miss Bell knew I could recite the words to my grandpa's poem and that's why she didn't ask me to recite the poem in class.

Hill Talk

Our stepmother grew up in the hills along the Ohio River and only attended school through the eighth grade. Her vocabulary seemed to be a combination of Pennsylvania Dutch and Appalachian Mountain.

I was already having enough trouble with the pronunciation and meaning of words in Miss Bell's class. How

My father and stepmother, 1937.

was I expected to learn a lot more? The definitions of most of my stepmother's expressions have faded from my memory. However, the following should offer some sense of the difficulty I faced in trying to understand what she was saying:

Poke—paper bag. "He put the chicken in a poke."

A-fixin—getting ready. "We're a fixin to go to the store."

You'ns—you or you all. "You'ns ain't gonna git no vittles."

Lollygag—to loaf or loiter. "Why's Orval always lolygagin' around?"

Smackdab—on the dot, exactly. "I hit him smackdab in his eye."

Smart—to hurt. "My bee sting shor' smarts."

Doin's—a function. "Are you'ns gonna go to the hogallin' doin's?"

Orta—ought to. "He orta take something for his croup."

Kranky—ill or sick. "Why is Orval so kranky all the time?"

Biggety—stuck up or acting snobbish. "He's been actin' biggety since he won the race."

Plumb—completely. "I'm plumb upset with his lack of manners."

Parts—area or neighborhood. "When did she move to these-here parts?"

Put Out—annoyed or angry. "She shore was put out 'bout her grocery bill."

Pizen—poison. "I seen lots of pizen boils on Grandpa's arms."

Hesh Up—stop talking. "Tom all of a sudden heshed up."

Askeered—frightened of or afraid of. "Joel's shor' askeered of them dogs."

Loud as how—to think about. "Fred loud as how he'd go to church next Sunday."

"HAIR" TODAY, GONE Tomorrow

A hometown is where the great are small and the small are great. It has been said that an old-timer is a local person who's had an immense amount of interesting experiences, some of which may be true. There was no place in town that depicted a better portrait of this scene than Delmar Johnstone's-B.S.-Barbershop. Located on the west side of Detroit Street between Second and Third Streets, the space was formerly occupied by Buck's Meat Market.

We purchased our half soles for 15 cents at Woolworth's.

Del Johnstone, the owner and head barber, had hit upon the idea of combining a men's barbershop with a ladies' hair salon. The hair salon, under the capable direction of his wife Gertrude, whom he affectionately referred to as "Pet," was frequented daily by ladies from the north and south sections of town.

Pet's hair, always meticulously groomed and brilliantly blonde, was much admired by all of the ladies and men who patronized the business. When Del was asked about his wife's nickname of "Pet," he gave a conventional response. "After we were married, I discovered that Gertrude couldn't cook so I asked her mother to take her back. When her mother refused, I decided to keep her for a pet."

The barbershop, with up-to-date equipment, featured four tilt-back chairs, shampoo sinks, and electric hair clippers. Sometimes, Pet would stroll into the men's shop and take a rolled up towel and clippers from Del, who held

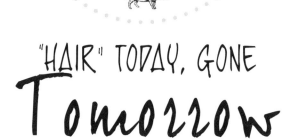

forth at the chair adjacent to the door leading into the salon. All three of the other barbers knew right away that Mrs. Davis, who was under the dryer in the salon, was going to have her legs shaved. The three of them were looking forward to the lucky fellow who would sit next in Del's chair and feel those clippers humming on the back of his neck.

While the barbering accessories in the shop were very much up-to-date, the waiting area, for the most part, profiled Del's former shop. Del referred to the bench, chairs, coat hooks, umbrella tree, personalized shaving cups, and spittoons as being "a touch of antiquity," although most of the men who occupied and used them weren't quite sure what he meant when he used that "foreign" word. The barbers, aside from Del, who was an incessant cigarette smoker, all exhibited the conventional characteristics and habits that were associated with their chosen vocation. They were conversational, chewed tobacco, enjoyed and recited jokes at the appropriate moment, and had a keen eye for Pet's patrons who passed through the shop. They did, however, differ in physical appearance.

Edward "Easy Ed" Leahy's chair was only a few feet inside the front window and his chair shared a ceramic cuspidor with the second chair. "Easy Ed" referred to himself as the "mane" barber in the shop. He was Catholic, ate seafood every Friday for supper, and usually told true stories.

Jim "Jaycee" Coates held forth in the second chair and professed to be styling the best pompadour haircuts in the county. He was a devout Methodist and recited jokes that were equally divided between truth and fiction and consistently received the most money in tips in the shop. He was able to do this by tilting his patrons to almost a horizontal level when he shaved them. Then, after they left the shop, he would pick up the loose change that had fallen into the hair he had designedly accumulated and swept under his chair.

The third chair, which shared a large brass spittoon with Del's chair, was managed by Mr. Brown H. Herr. With our father's permission, he was known to our family as "Brownee" Hair. Outside the shop, however, he was frequently referred to as "Herr Hairless Herr." He was our father's favorite barber. Ironically, he himself was devoid of any hairline and had a long, well-groomed beard which he occasionally referred to as "alfalfa." A few years earlier, when my brother Hank was about to be seated on the board across the arms of Brownee's chair, he cried and said that he didn't want "any man with hair on the bottom of his head" to cut his hair. Brownee never forgot the scene. Brownee was particularly adept at fashioning crock or bowl haircuts and fond of every type of wild game, especially baked 'possum stuffed with sweet potatoes. All of the other barbers, and some of the patrons, knew when Brownee had "cut a cheese." When he did this, he laughed the loudest, waved his towel the fastest, and told yet another "shop lie."

When a patron, new or known, would ask if this shop was formerly Buck's Meat Market, any one of the barbers would reply, "Yep! Same shop, same butchers, same tools, but cheaper prices. You're next."

A cast of characters—blue collar, white collar, and professional—frequented the shop for fun, insults, gossip, and other tonsorial treatments. With known "regs" the barbers were very astute with the application of "suds, goose grease, or panther piss." When a newcomer, seated in the first chair remarked that his hair was thinning, "Easy Ed" replied, "Well, who wants fat hair anyway?"

One Thursday afternoon, Jaycee was shaving Judge Don Thompson, who stopped in on every Fourth Circuit Court day for a shave and a haircut. Now, while Jaycee was somewhat known for having a little "homemade hair tonic" with his lunch, the judge was known for "drinking" his entire lunch at Bart's Corner Tavern before coming to the barbershop. When Jaycee nicked the judge's face with his razor and quickly apologized, the judge was said to remark, "Well, what do you expect when you've been drinking?" Jaycee, who apparently had predicted the incident replied, "Yeah! It sure does make your face tender."

When Brownee Herr asked Father Renniger how he would like his cut, the Father, a first-time patron but familiar with the barber's "shop prose," replied, "In silence, if you don't mind." Brownee, not to be upstaged before his colleagues and waiting patrons, pondered a few seconds, laughed, and said, "Father, your head's beginning to resemble heaven because there is no parting there."

The country was well into the Depression when Bill Garrison, who owned several houses in town, drove by the shop in his newly converted Hoover buggy. Everybody laughed and wondered what he'd do next to economize the situation.

When Sam Lloyd parked his leaning 1927 Model T Ford coupe in front of the shop, all activity ceased, as patrons and barbers alike, watched his wife attempt to unwrap herself from the vehicle. When she was backing out, Joe McNamara, seated in "Easy Ed's" chair said it "looked like two kids fighting under a blanket." Charlie Kemp ventured that Sam was "all breath and britches," and his wife had to be "at least six axe handles across the rear end." He had it on pretty good authority, he went on, that when Mrs. Lloyd made an appointment with Doc. Henderson, Doc. called Sam and suggested that he take his wife to the

Farmer's Exchange and have her weighed on the livestock scale before coming to his office.

Later, when the fire truck, with sirens blaring, sped past, three lathered faces simultaneously sat up in their respective chairs and shot a quick stream of tobacco juice into the designated cuspidors. "Easy Ed" assured them it wasn't the shop that was ablaze. He then laughed and quipped, "Those guys are the pride of this town. They haven't lost a damned basement in over a hundred years."

It was not openly discussed, but rather well-known by the regulars that if you were homebound, Del's barbers would call and dispense their services for the regular price of a shave for 10 cents and a haircut for 15 cents. Although Del didn't make it known, a select few could expect to get a free, full-service call just before they were "patted in the face with a spade."

On a bright July morning when the sun was shining through the large front window, Sally Chambers, a young widow, was walking from the salon to the front door of the shop. As she walked between the waiting men and the front door, the bright sun rays penetrated her light, print dress revealing her very shapely anatomy. When the door closed behind her, Joe Hurley wanted to know whether she was a grass widow or a sod widow. "Sod widow," Del replied. "According to Pet, she keeps her good looks and lean body by taking bubble baths daily." "Well," intoned Fred Schultz, "it don't matter to me what kind of 'wider' she is, but I sure would be interested in drinkin' some of her bath water."

HOLY Chittlin's

It seemed to us that there was always one or more characters, usually Negro, non-salaried, and funny, who frequently showed up on the killing floor of the slaughterhouse to engage in menial tasks for a reward of non-saleable items such as lights, stale cracklings, mountain oysters, or chitterlings. Due to a shortage of water, they were not permitted to clean the chitterlings on the premises. Some of these characters had constructed hand pushcarts from scrap materials which they pushed over a mile to and from the slaughterhouse so they would be able to take home more than they could otherwise carry.

It was the day before Halloween and Gus Ewing, probably the most humorous of all the characters, was filling

Looking south on Detroit Street, 1933. Right page: During the last months of President Hoover's administration, Adolph Hitler was capturing the headlines.

his hand-made pushcart to the fullest capacity with the chittlin' take from nearly a dozen butchered hogs. He had mentioned several times during the latter process of the butchering that this chittlin' haul might be the makings of the biggest chittlin' casserole that the ladies in his tiny church kitchen had ever cooked. It was, in his estimation, also going to be the makings of the biggest "chittlin' walk" that his church brothers and sisters had ever participated in. It was after dark when he loaded his cart at the west door of the slaughtering room, covered it carefully with a split burlap bag, pushed through the farm gate, and headed west toward the first north-south street which was located in the city. At this intersection, which was dimly lighted with a small street lamp, he would make a right turn, pass down a rather steep incline, and cross over a few sets of railroad tracks. There was a small church at the northeast corner of the intersection. The parishioners, familiar with the aroma of chittlin's and the passing time of the chittlin' carts, conveniently lighted incense candles in self-defense between six and six-thirty in the evening.

What Gus was not aware of was that my older brothers had departed on foot about twenty minutes before him with white sheets secreted out of our bedroom hidden under their winter coats. They walked behind the church and down to within thirty yards of the track, crouched in a ditch with their sheets folded under them, and patiently waited for the execution of their well-planned Halloween prank.

After about twenty minutes had passed, they saw Gus appear under the streetlight headed down the steep incline toward the tracks. Concurrently, they saw the crossing watchman with his lantern and stop sign walk across the tracks and station himself in the middle of the street. They could also see the powerful headlamps and hear the warning whistle of the engine. They waited for Gus to draw parallel with them in the street. Pulling the sheets over their heads, they stepped to the edge of the street

"All the News That's Fit to Print."

The New York Times.

LATE CITY EDITION
WEATHER—Fair and slightly warmer today and tomorrow.

Copyright, 1933, by The New York Times Company.

VOL. LXXXII....No. 27,401. Entered as Second-Class Matter. Postoffice, New York, N. Y. NEW YORK, TUESDAY, JANUARY 31, 1933. TWO CENTS In New York City. | THREE CENTS Within 200 Miles | FOUR CENTS Elsewhere Except in 7th and 8th Postal Zones

HITLER MADE CHANCELLOR OF GERMANY BUT COALITION CABINET LIMITS POWER; CENTRISTS HOLD BALANCE IN REICHSTAG

GROUP FORMED BY PAPEN

Nationalists to Dominate in Government Led by National Socialist.

HUGENBERG GETS POST

Frick In Interior Ministry to Control Police, but Army Has Non-Partisan Chief.

REDS URGE STRIKE TODAY

Cabinet Stresses That It Will Not Attempt Monetary or Economic Experiments.

By GUIDO ENDERIS.
Special Cable to THE NEW YORK TIMES.

BERLIN, Jan. 30.—Adolf Hitler, leader of the National Socialist party, today was appointed Chancellor of Germany after being twice rejected last year for that office.

Hitler Pledges Fight in Cabinet

By the Associated Press.

BERLIN, Jan. 30.—A proclamation emphasizing that the present Cabinet is not truly representative of Hitlerism and the nation was issued today by the new Chancellor, Adolf Hitler. In it the Nazi leader announced a determination to "carry on the fight within the government as tenaciously as we fought outside."

"After a thirteen-year struggle the National Socialist movement has succeeded in breaking through to the government; the struggle to win the German nation, however, is only beginning," the proclamation said.

"The National Socialist party knows that the new government is no National Socialist Government, but it is conscious that it bears the name of its leader, Adolf Hitler. He has advanced with his shock troops and has placed himself at the head of the government to lead the German people to liberty.

"Not only is the entire authority of State ready to be wielded, but in the background, prepared for action, is the National Socialist movement of millions of followers united unto death with its leaders. Our historic mission is now in the field of political economy."

Calling Herr Hitler's appointment "historic," the document lauded President von Hindenburg with these words:

"In this hour we wish to thank President von Hindenburg, whose immortal fame as a Field Marshal in the battlefields of the World War binds his name perpetually to that of young Germany, which is striving with burning heart to gain its liberty."

MODERATE CABINET PLANNED IN FRANCE

HOOVER SKEPTICAL OF SUCCESS ON DEBT

NEW BRITISH RATES AFFECT U. S. GOODS FINISHED IN CANADA

After April 1, 50 Per Cent 'Empire Content' Is Required for Preferential Duty.

1,000 PLANTS INVOLVED

Many Expected to Be Moved to England or Withdrawn to United States.

HUGE CAPITAL AT STAKE

$1,500,000,000 Invested in Factories in Dominion—Political Struggle There Foreseen.

Special Cable to THE NEW YORK TIMES.

LONDON, Jan. 30.—United States manufacturers who apply minor finishing touches on their goods in Canada and then send them to Great Britain under imperial tariff preferences as "empire goods" will lose that privilege under an order issued by the Board of Trade tonight.

"Certain classes of empire goods imported into Britain," the order says, "in order to qualify for the imperial preferences agreed upon at Ottawa, must contain in the future a minimum of 50 per cent of empire material and labor instead of 25 per cent as at present."

The regulation will go into effect April 1. The list of goods affected

MORTGAGEES STAY $200,000,000 DEBT OF IOWA'S FARMERS

Insurance Companies Here Act to Suspend Foreclosures Pending Legal Relief.

GOVERNOR'S PLEA HEEDED

Policy Announced by New York Life Followed by Other Eastern Organizations.

NEBRASKA NAMES BOARD

Bryan Appoints Seven Conciliators as Debtors' Resistance Drive Spreads Through West.

In the most extensive private effort to cooperate with the owners of mortgaged farms ever made, a number of the leading Eastern life insurance companies, with nearly $200,000,000 invested in Iowa farms, have decided to suspend foreclosure activities throughout that State until the Legislature can enact its program to improve the position of the debtors.

This decision became known yesterday after the publication of an announcement of such a policy in behalf of his own company only, by Thomas A. Buckner, president of the New York Life Insurance Company. This company has been the object of stormy criticism in

LEHMAN ASKS $84,000,000 IN NEW TAXES, 1% ON '33 GROSS INCOMES, 3/4% ON SALES; STATE BUDGET CUT 23% TO $234,998,531

Gov. Lehman's Revenue Proposals

Special to THE NEW YORK TIMES.

ALBANY, Jan. 30.—Governor Lehman's chief proposals on the budget included the following:

INCOME TAXES—Lowering of exemptions for a single person from $2,500 to $1,000 and a married person from $4,000 to $2,500, the $400 exemption for dependents to remain unchanged. Emergency rate to be continued. Establishment of a 1 per cent gross income tax, no personal exemption allowed, on every single person whose income is $1,000 or more and every married person whose income is $2,500 or more. Capital gains and losses excluded, and interest, bad debts, contributions and other actual losses subtracted. This tax, an emergency levy for one year, to be in addition to the regular State income tax. Both the lowered exemption and the emergency tax to be applicable on 1933 incomes, payable in April, 1934.

SALES TAX—Enactment of a three-quarter of 1 per cent levy on retail sales of all tangible personal property, exclusive of food products and motor fuel, effective from April 1, 1933, to June 30, 1934.

MOTOR FUEL TAX—emergency levy ef... making the tax p...

SALARIES—Reductio... $2,000 a year of ... per cent on that ...

FEES FOR PAMPHL... partments to be c... preparation and p...

PUBLIC SERVICE F... charge against a... such inquiry.

MACHADO SAYS

CENT ADDED ON GASOLINE

Sales Impost Proposed on All Retail Items Except Food.

FOR LOWER EXEMPTIONS

Governor Suggests Drop of $1,500—Pay Cut for State Employes Urged.

The Depression was worldwide, and brought grim changes elsewhere. Above is part of the front page of the *New York Times* for January 31, 1933; below, a demonstration against Hitler held in front of City Hall, Philadelphia, after he had begun his persecution of the Jews in Germany.

while simultaneously uttering ghostly sounds. To their delight, Gus released his firm grasp on the cart handle and broke into a gallop heading for the street to the west where a viaduct served the tracks. He had just gotten out of their view, when they heard this crunching noise at the crossing. On the steep grade, the unrestrained cart had rolled past the crossing guard and collided with the right, front edge of the engine's cowcatcher.

Frightened, my brothers crouched once again in the ditch as the engineer pushed the throttle closed and stopped the train. They dared to look and listen as the fireman, swinging his kerosene lantern, disembarked from the engine, looked with fright at what appeared to be the intestines on the cowcatcher, and proceeded to step gingerly over several more sets of intestines and cart remnants as he walked toward the crossing guard. He shouted, "Holy shit, what did we hit?" The crossing guard replied, "I don't know how holy it is, but there is shit on my clothes, my lantern, and my sign!" The guard then explained that he was sure that the cart was unattended. By this time, my brothers, with their sheets again tucked under their coats, were heading for the safety of home.

At the breakfast table my father explained that Fred LaRance, the railroad detective, had called at about six o'clock that morning to see if he knew anything about the accident. During the rest of the meal, my brothers grinned through their fried mush.

RITE OF Passage

In 1933, with all of the very young children in our family, Santa Claus enjoyed a major revival at Christmastime.

By early spring, our father had hired a young man, Jimmy Ernest, to work on the killing floor of the slaughterhouse. Jimmy was a very good baseball player and he and I became very good friends. He was very helpful when I was getting ready to take my "rite of passage" ritual shortly after my twelfth birthday. My older brothers had passed the ritual, and they appeared to be eager to see how I would conduct myself. They had also told me that both Grandpa Sandy and my father had passed the ritual when they were my age.

It was a simple event. While a stunned steer was hanging by its hind leg from an overhead hoist, one was required to slit the animal's throat with a sticking knife, cut the jugular vein, catch the blood in his cupped hands, and proceed to drink it.

Johnny had told me that every other week, an anemic young lady, as prescribed by her doctor, came to the killing room to drink a pint of warm beef blood.

I never told my brothers, but I had sipped beef blood before and knew it was tasteless. So, on my ritual day, I just closed my eyes, slurped it down, and offered my brothers and their friends a wide, crimson smile. They responded with only a furtive cheer because I'm sure they were really disappointed.

Johnny and I talked a lot about baseball, and he usually gave me a nickel or a dime each time I helped him. I told him that I had told my father that someday I was going to be a baseball player and make lots of money. Then my father would not have to work. He grinned and said that would be great. Shortly after that, on a Sunday, he and his wife took me to Cincinnati to see Babe Ruth play. During the game, my idol popped up once and struck out three times. I could hardly keep from crying on the way home.

When our father determined that all of the full-time employees at his slaughterhouse would eat dinner at our kitchen table, he also employed a bosomy Negro lady, Mrs. "Newie" Newsome, full time to assist our stepmother with all of the household chores. She was an excellent cook, and several of the workers confessed that they ate a lot better during the week than they did at home on the weekends.

"Newie" was also very nurturing and seemed to enjoy hugging us at every opportunity. Brother Hank, however, did not take too well to her affectionate hugs and said, "Everytime 'Newie' hugs me, it seems like somebody turned out the lights."

We brothers and our stepmother had another large garden to attend during the summer, and it helped us to get to know her much better. While we were working, she told us that she always enjoyed gardening except when she was pregnant. We brothers promised her that any spring she was pregnant we would plow, plant, and hoe the garden. This promise, unbeknownst to us at the time, would turn out to be a major "labor relations" mistake.

Before I entered Miss Crumley's fifth grade class at Spring Hill School in September, Public Enemy Number One, John Dillinger, was shot dead by FBI agents outside a Chicago movie theater.

Reynard

During the trapping season for at least three winters, we brothers had been unsuccessful in our attempts to catch a large red fox which we suspected was responsible for killing several of our chickens. It had probably also killed my brother Hank's kittens a couple of years prior to that. Grandpa Jim told us that since there were so few foxes in our area that we had probably seen the same fox several times. He also told us that we ought to name the fox Reynard since that was the name of a fox who was a hero in a play many years earlier. He also told us that many inexperienced trappers think that there are more foxes than there really are because they see the footprints of the same fox many times.

Since Grandpa knew Remus Mace, he suggested that we ask him about the best method of catching Reynard. Mr. Mace told us that since foxes travel during the coldest weather as well as at all other times, it would give us an opportunity to show our skill when other animals such as raccoon, opossum, and muskrat were "denned up." He added that fox skins are at their best when it's the coldest and therefore bring the highest prices then.

We already knew that foxes mostly lived on flesh—rabbits, squirrels, etc.—because we suspected that Reynard had raided some of these animals when they had been caught in our traps. Mr. Mace suggested that we should use some of the meat scraps from our father's slaughterhouse to bait our traps and said it would be more tempting to Reynard if we allowed the meat to become tainted first.

We knew how the pelt should be cased, that is, skinned without ripping and drawn upon a board. We knew how to tack the skin in place and to leave it on the board for three to five days depending on the weather. We also knew to turn the fur side out after the pelt was removed from the board. Finally, we were aware that in drying the pelt to keep the skin in a cool, shady place that was free from smoke. We had done all of these things correctly with raccoon furs several times previously. We knew what to do after we trapped an animal. What we didn't know was how to outfox Reynard.

When we suggested to Mr. Mace that he loan us one of his hunting dogs, he told us that his dogs would probably not respond to our commands. We guessed he didn't want to loan us a dog, anyway. During the winter, we employed several types of bait on our steel traps, fashioned nearly a half-dozen snares, and dreamed about shipping

Reynard's beautiful red coat off to St. Louis and receiving a big check in the mail.

In July, when he was out of season, Reynard was crossing the road about a half-mile from our farm when he was hit and killed by a livestock truck.

SLIM AND Frank

Between Remus Mace's place and the school where I would be attending fifth grade the next year, was a somewhat dilapidated house and several small outbuildings. According to neighbors and denizens of the town, the three residents of this property exhibited a somewhat unconventional lifestyle, especially the father and son. Both were tall and gangly, wore knee boots and knit caps year 'round, employed a single gallous to hold up their bib overalls, and were always accompanied by a large Airedale dog named "Lover."

Shortly after we moved to our small farm, we watched with extreme interest, as Frank, the father, or Slim, his son, periodically led a train of emaciated horses, tied tail

The sad state of the sharecroppers of the South was profiled in Jack Kirkland's play, "Tobacco Road," which opened on Broadway in 1933.

to head, past our house on the way to the county fertilizer plant which was three miles east of our farm. We understood that these lean "plugs" would bring two dollars a head if they arrived "on foot." Sometimes there would be as many as seven or eight of these worn-out creatures, and we children would attempt to determine the total amount they would bring. Our father would laugh as he explained to us that the nags were going to be made into baseballs, shoes, glue, and hog tankage. We were surprised to learn that hogs would eat cooked horses.

Our mother had been uneasy when our father hired Slim to stack several cords of wood next to the slaughterhouse for fifty cents. She was even more upset when he wandered away from his assigned task and seemed curious about the interior of the other outbuildings on the farm. Slim and Frank's main occupation was cleaning outdoor jakes and they were humorously referred to as the Orient Hill Honey Dippers. Their septic truck was a converted Model T coupe with a rear bed large enough to accommodate two fifty-five gallon barrels. The vehicle, loaded or unloaded, was seldom seen without Lover riding on the right running board.

As a result of their chosen occupation, Slim, Frank, and Lover were "persona non grata" in more than a few businesses in the community. Even without Lover, they had their admission refunded and were asked to leave the Orpheum Theater during a Saturday matinee, after a lady seated near them upchucked her popcorn and had to be given smelling salts.

Lighthiser's Grocery, which was only a block north of the railroad viaduct on Monroe Street, was a favorite lunch stop for the septic crew. However, they were obliged to comply with the following rules in order to frequent Mrs. Lighthiser's Grocery: they must park on the far side of the street, leave Lover on the running board, enter the rear door of the grocery, and once waited on, take their food outside to consume it. After going outside, they were prone to seat themselves on the steps of the side porch. Once when they were seated there, and Slim had eaten about half of his miniature, five-cent cherry pie, he complained to Frank that the crust was "tougher-than-hell." Frank explained to him that he had eaten the section of the cardboard plate that the pie was resting on so no wonder it tasted like that.

A few times we children watched Slim and Frank carrying unauthorized fruit out of the orchard which was just outside the northeast corner of our property. We discovered later that they set up a small stand, without Lover, and sold the fruit on Saturday morning at the Courthouse Market.

Just beyond our north fence line, Slim and Frank occasionally pilfered coal from the slow-moving freight trains pulling out of the depot. Such action, of course, caused railroad detective Fred LaRance to shadow them closely since they had, in fact, already been arrested several times. These arrests prompted young Slim to retaliate against the detective's family, especially his wife. Shortly after being released from the city's "Crossbar Hotel," Slim positioned himself on the bottom step of the front walk of the detective's home and proceeded to "cuff his carrot" at ten o'clock in the morning. When Mrs. LaRance opened the front door of the house and asked him what he was doing, he replied, "I'm f---ing you from fifty feet away, and you're lovin' it, ain't you?"

At his trial, Judge Joe Gowdy, in lieu of sentencing Slim to a ninety-day incarceration in the adjacent Montgomery County Workhouse, remanded Slim to a six-month rehabilitation period in the state's mental asylum.

Shortly after his release from the asylum, Slim and his father were passing over the viaduct on their way to Lighthiser's Grocery when a rear tire blew out on their "honey wagon." As a result, Lover and two barrels of septic spilled out all over the area. They wiped themselves off as best they could, walked to the grocery for their snack, and seated themselves on the side-porch steps. When they had nearly finished eating their bologna sandwiches, Slim turned to his father and said, "We got two barrels of shit in the street. Lover's covered with shit, and we got a flat tire. Ain't that hell, Frank?"

We last saw Slim when he again led a small train of horses past our house on his way to the county fertilizer. According to my brother Winston, Slim was set up by the county sheriff, and he never made it to the fertilizer with the horses. As the sheriff suspected he would, he evidently fell in love with a sleepy-eyed, aging Appaloosa mare early in the trip. He stopped at the stable behind our one-room school house to express his feelings. As the other tethered nags watched, he expressed his feelings toward the Appaloosa and was immediately arrested by a sheriff's deputy. According to the sheriff's deputy, "It must have been that dotted patch of white hair over the mare's rump and loins that set Slim off." Needless to say, Slim spent the rest of his life in the state insane asylum.

RIDING Shotgun

Our father's newly remodeled slaughterhouse included a steam boiler but not a tankage cooker. Therefore, the waste materials—bones, fat, and guts—had to be transported by truck to the county fertilizer plant, which was about three or four miles east of our farm.

The waste materials were deposited in designated fifty-five gallon steel barrels and stood unrefrigerated for several days before being hauled to the fertilizer. During this time, they would serve as an egg-laying base for hoards of large blow flies. Within eighteen to twenty hours, the eggs would hatch and there would be waves of maggots on top of each barrel. The stench from the barrels permeated the air for over a quarter mile in every direction. This of course, meant that it flowed freely throughout our home, both day and night.

We played basketball under the gooseneck light late at night.

Our "gut truck" was fashioned from a Model T Ford touring sedan and had a four-barrel capacity. Actually, it resembled Slim and Frank's "city honey wagon." My older brothers, Winston and Lowell, would alternate as drivers and "barrel wrestlers." Hank and I, and any playmates present, would plead to be permitted to stand on the running boards during the "gut runs" and pretend we were riding shotgun on a stagecoach that was carrying a large cache of gold.

The appearance and odor of the fertilizer plant were similar to that of our slaughterhouse. Here, however, the animals usually arrived dead. After they were skinned and fabricated, the fat was heated until it was reduced to oil. Mr. McGuiness, who was in charge of the operation, told us the fat was transported to Cincinnati and made into soap. He also told us that the guts, meat scraps, and bones were cooked and ground into hog feed, called tankage.

A large black and white sign over the unloading platform read, "A Pig Will Make a Hog of Himself on Hogmaker Tankage."

MIDNIGHT Lovers

The county gravel road leading out of the city toward our farm gate and the neighbor's farm gate, which was almost directly across the road from ours, was maintained reasonably well during most of the year. At reduced speed there was room to safely pass another wagon or vehicle. However, the remaining half-mile of the road was poorly maintained, infrequently utilized, yielded less than a half-a-dozen places to pass safely, and was locally referred to as "lover's lane." The final two hundred yards curved gently to the north around the unfenced and forbidden swamp and dense woods. With access and exit at either end, this road was a haven for lovers, day or night, whether they were traveling by horse and buggy or automobile.

White couples usually entered the west end of the road, passed our house, parked for their passion, and exited from the east end of the road. Negro couples, however, generally entered the east end of the road, enjoyed several pints of ice cream before their passion, moved on past our house, and exited the west end of the road. Due to the condition of the road and shoulders we brothers would frequently have an opportunity to earn a little spending money by extricating a mired auto out of the soft surface of the road's shoulders.

When my father responded to a midnight knock on our front door, he would gently ease into a litany of questions. "What is your name? How far back the road is your car stuck? How many people are in the car? What is the license number of the car?" and, finally, "Which direction is it facing?" While the man, almost always embarrassed, waited on the front porch, my father would walk to the foot of the stairs and call out these words, "Would you boys like to lend a helping hand to a needy gentleman, Mr. Jones?" Flashlight in hand, we would scan our list of previous emergency services. If the guy's name and license was on our MLSL, we responded in the negative. As far as we were concerned, he could walk home and get someone else to take care of his emergency in the morning. If the guy was not on our "midnight lover's shit list," we would quickly pull on our clothes, locate our three-cell flashlight, go to the stable, harness Coli with a single tree and chain, pass out the farm gate, and move down the road.

At the scene, we routinely and politely attempted to answer any questions that the mortified lady might have,

quickly extracted the mired vehicle, thanked the gentleman for the reward for our services, watched the waving couple drive off into the dark, returned Coli to her stall, and hurried back to the house.

The standard reward for our services was a half-dollar. Poor lovers gave us a quarter, and great lovers would give us a dollar bill. Almost without exception, if any member of our family knew one or the other of the lovers, we would receive a dollar for our midnight assistance.

We were still baffled by the fact that we couldn't frequent this area in the daytime, but we could go there at night to help these humiliated individuals.

BIG Discovery

Our summer activities were not significantly altered by the addition of our stepbrother and sisters, since, except for Louise, they were too young to engage in most of our outdoor activities. As younger brothers are prone to do, Hank and I attempted to improve on the home and away games that our older brothers had devised and initiated us into. This was especially true when our friends were visiting and our father and stepmother were not at home. More often than not, they took all of the stepmother's children with them when they were gone for an afternoon.

When the new brood was at home, Hank and I would frequently retreat to our swimming hole or tree house in an effort to maintain our independent play patterns. We innovated our Sunday afternoon, barnyard rodeo, away games by charging our visiting friends a fee to observe a bull breeding a young heifer or a milk cow giving birth to a calf. Sometimes all in attendance would wager a nickel or dime trying to be the closest to approximating the time the event would happen.

I spent quite a few hours working on the killing floor of the slaughterhouse during the summer learning as much as I could—mostly trimming offal and cleaning guts—in preparation for the next summer when I would be twelve years old and make my "rite of passage debut."

When I arrived at Spring Hill School in September, my fifth grade teacher, Miss Crumley, too referred to me as "the boy from the slaughterhouse," something I liked very much. She also told me how much she had enjoyed having my twin sisters Evelyn and Rachel in her room for

Interior of Davis Grocery, caddie-cornered from Spring Hill School. We bought our penny candy here.

two years. As she talked about what good students and nice young ladies they were, I wondered if she would say the same things about me in two years when my brother Hank entered her fifth grade room.

Miss Crumley, like all of my previous teachers, was really smart. I did have to help her out one time, though, when she told our class that all resting, farm animals get up on their front legs first. I put up my hand and she called on me! I said, "I don't know what all the other cows do, but the cows on our farm all get up on their hind legs first." I guessed she probably didn't live on a farm.

United States Treasury agents had visited our farm in the spring, looking for "John Barleycorn," and we were unable to accommodate them. However, it appeared by late fall that they failed to look in the right place.

In November, about one month before the repeal of Prohibition was passed by the federal government, we brothers, on a Saturday morning, hitched the horses to our snow sled. Accompanied by our dog, we headed up to the cornfield adjacent to the swamp area where we were getting our first load of fodder to be used for winter feed and bedding for the livestock. Per our established practice, when we reached the southeast corner of the field by the road entrance gate, we immediately pushed over a full shock of fodder. We did this in order to brush the snow off the shock and expose any critters, especially rabbits, the dog would try to catch.

We were dumbfounded when we pushed over the first shock and exposed several one-gallon, glass jugs filled with liquid. My brother Winston pulled the cork from one of the jugs, sniffed the opening, and said, "So, this is what the Feds were looking for last April." My brother Lowell hurried back to the house to tell our father what we had discovered. The deputy sheriff, accompanied by our father, soon arrived and authorized us to push over all of the shocks that we had planned to haul to the barn that day.

In all, that morning we found eight jugs in each of the seven shocks for a total of fifty-six gallons. It was necessary for the deputy to call for a second vehicle to haul the find back to his office. He thanked us. Then, just before he pulled away, we overheard him say to our father, "Hell, Walt, we got enough here for the whole department and all the damned city fathers."

Chicago

In the fall of 1934, Fred Irwin, owner and operator of a feed mill located next to the railroad track in the southeast corner of Xenia, invited my father to join him for a four-day trip to Chicago, where he intended to tour the country's largest stockyards and several large meat packing plants. Once in Chicago, in addition to the stockyards which held thousands of animals awaiting slaughter, he expected to be able to visit the Armour, Cudahy, and Swift meat packing plants. My father had heard and read about these assembly-line meat packing plants, and he accepted Mr. Irwin's invitation almost immediately.

Although my pleas to be included in the trip were unsuccessful, my father promised to tell me interesting details of his trip and even bring me some picture post cards if I promised to take good care of the livestock on our farm while he was gone. I assured him I would take good care of every animal. We shook hands and I sensed he knew I'd keep my word.

Over the course of several days after he returned, he told me about his many and varied experiences. These included watching a steer pass from the slaughtering floor to eventually appearing in a roast beef sandwich, seeing the preparation and loading of refrigerated rail cars, and even witnessing special drivers backing up large, livestock trucks through narrow alleys to the holding pens. He also told me about a "goat-worker" who would be sent into a holding pen of sheep. These sheep would follow the goat right into the slaughtering area. I told my father that my Sunday school teacher had mentioned something about that a couple of years ago—something about how a goat would lead lambs to slaughter.

My father indicated the companies he visited, especially Armour, manufactured a great variety of animal-based products, from bacon to glue. He said the tour guide mentioned two or three times that they prided themselves on using "every part of the hog except the squeal." When the guide mentioned this for the third time during the all-male tour, one of the men asked him, "What about the farts?" "Well, we don't really utilize them here in the plant; we send them out to sell the hog, and they like to call themselves salesmen." His answer, of course, drew a laugh and even applause from the group.

Since my father had installed an ammonia "refrigerating machine" about a year before and would be butchering more cattle, lambs, and calves, he was especially interested in the federal inspection of these carcasses at the plants he visited. He said the carcasses were graded as follows: prime, choice, good, commercial, cutter, and canner. I was familiar with the first four classifications so I only inquired about the last two. He explained to me that "cutter" meant the carcass had to be "cut up" before it could be shipped out of the plant and was mostly made into hamburger or sausage. "Canner," he explained, "had to be cut up, canned, and cooked before being sold."

Of the several picture postcards that he brought me, I found the one related to backbone splitting to be the most interesting because that was the major problem that I was encountering with hog butchering. Several times I would look at the photo and imagine that someday I might be standing in that line at Swift's, with that large clever in my hands, artistically splitting those "critters" as they moved along that assembly line. My father would be so proud of me!

My father said that he found the meat-packing plants to be reasonably clean and safe However, he went on to indicate that had not always been true. He said that when he was about ten years old they were not very clean. In fact, he said, they were so dirty and dangerous that a man wrote a book about them. President Teddy Roosevelt read it and invited him to the White House. After Roosevelt talked to the man, he asked Congress to pass a law that would force the owners to keep the plants clean and safe. Years later, I read Upton Sinclair's book, *The Jungle*, for one of my make-up book reports in Miss Marshall's English class. My brother Lowell, who helped me write the report, thought it needed significantly more manure, blood, and guts. Miss Marshall, according to the red marks on it, thought it needed significantly less gory adjectives and better narrative transitions.

Only then did I really understand why my father talked so much about how surprised he was that the meat packing plants were reasonably safe and clean.

A HEARTY Breakfast

Even though Miss Crumley had been our homeroom, English, math and social studies teacher last year, our

class went to other teachers' rooms for art, music, and science. I liked Miss Crumley, but I also liked going to other rooms during the school day. When Miss Crumley asked me how I liked Mrs. Burke's music class, I told her, "It was real good," and she just smiled. I'm sure she smiled because she was glad she didn't teach music, especially the two years that I was in Spring Hill School. Another thing that I liked about Spring Hill School was Mr. Davis' grocery store, which was caddy-corner from the school. Mr. Davis was a very friendly man, and his store was known as the "Penny Candy" store by all the students going and coming from school.

Returning from the watermelon patch astride Coli.

By January 1935, I was frequenting Mr. Davis' store whenever I had a few pennies, finishing up the second half of Miss Crumley's sixth grade class, and looking forward to being in junior high school in the fall.

Upon my return from school, before I went to the livestock barn to attend to my regular chores, I would sometimes go to the abattoir killing floor to visit with Johnny and Ed. They would usually allow me to help hang up the offal, clean the equipment, or salt down beef hides. In fact, by this time, I had my own trimming knife and it was secured in the knife cabinet with my older brothers' knives.

Dan Brewer and Will Whetstone lived near the school, and sometimes I would stop at their homes after school to look at their pigeon coops. Their pigeons were much fancier than mine and, when we traded, they always wanted two or more of my "barnyard birds" for one of theirs. My Uncle Will said it was fine to trade like that because they probably paid for their pigeons. He said as long as I caught mine in barns and sold them, it was alright to have a few fancy birds that didn't end up on a kitchen table.

Two years earlier, when I was only eleven, I became very interested in a radio program, "Jack Armstrong, the All-American Boy." This program, an adventure serial, was sponsored by Wheaties cereal. The sponsor gave out pedometers, whistling rings, secret decoders, etc., which I sent for. I also encouraged our stepmother to buy Wheaties when she went grocery shopping. I memorized the show's theme song and would sing it while I was doing my farm chores:

Wave the flag for Hudson High, boys,
Show them how we stand!
Ever shall our team be champion,
Known throughout the land!
Rah, Rah; Boola, Boola; Boola, Boola
Boola,Boola, Boola, Boola; Rah, Rah, Rah
Have you tried Wheaties!
They're whole wheat with all of the bran.
Won't you try Wheaties?
For wheat is the best food of man!
They're crispy and crunchy the whole year through,
Jack Armstrong never tires of them
And neither will you
So just buy Wheaties
The best breakfast food in the land!

The Wheaties Company also featured profiles of nationally known personalities, mostly athletes, on each box of Wheaties, and I was sometimes scolded for cutting them out with the scissors before the boxes were totally empty. I guess I was starting to believe that someday I might play athletics for a living and maybe even be a champion.

ON THE Platform

By late winter, our father's abattoir was slaughtering a dozen or more government pigs every workday in addition to meeting his regular customer's needs.

During our school winter vacation, I worked on the killing floor several days, and my father was present for a time each day to observe my progress. My brothers told me that our father chose this time to slaughter the government pigs because the hogs were small and the dressed carcasses were not going to be processed at the abattoir but rather at the relief agency in the city.

My father's major concern, as I recall, was directed toward my ability to man the sticking platform. Here, after the animals had been shackled by one hind leg and hoisted onto an overhead track, they were conveyed along the railing over a platform in order for their throats to be penetrated with a special "pig-sticker" knife.

My father was still my hero and I always wanted to please him when I was working. So, as he observed me, I was somewhat nervous hoping I would not make a major mistake. However, as the first dozen animals passed in front of me, I inserted the "pig-sticker" into each one's throat, rotated my wrist a few degrees, and quickly withdrew the head of the knife. My apron and face spattered with blood, I descended the platform ladder and enjoyed my father's approbation, as he assured me that I was "going to be a good butcher just like Grandpa Sandy." Love has no equal like a father's approval of his son's achievement.

According to my brother Winston, our father was very charitable and had canceled the debts on his books of at least three grocery stores in the city, one in the west end and two in the east end. Later, when one of the grocers offered to pay him, he refused and said he believed in forgiving and forgetting. "He believed," my brother said, "that the Depression had been hitting some folks very hard, and he was just lucky to pull out of it before some other folks."

Toward the end of winter, our father purchased a new Crosley radio and our family spent time listening to more of our favorite programs. Our father usually listened to Walter Winchell's news commentary on Sunday evening and thought Winchell talked too fast sometimes to be understood. The entire family laughed on Tuesday evening as Fibber McGee and Molly wrested with their household closet full of junk. Hank and I regularly tuned in to a classic western, "Death Valley Days" on Friday evenings and then would attempt to re-enact some of the scenes during the weekend.

Spring

It was not necessary in March for our stepmother to announce at breakfast that she was expecting the stork to visit our home in May. Hank and I had concluded several weeks before her announcement that our labor-relations, garden agreement with her was in jeopardy. So we were resigned to plowing, planting, and attending the pending garden.

We guessed our stepmother must have told our father about the expected stork's visit because he announced that the house was going to be remodeled in April. The remodeling plans called for the large back porch to be converted to a modern kitchen and a smaller back porch to be constructed on the east side of the present porch. The present kitchen was to be converted into two small bedrooms and a full bath.

March was always the harbinger of spring and the maple syrup season in our area. We boys, in an effort to get an extra jump on the finished product, prowled the woods, removing buckets from the trees, and drinking our fill of sweet water. Also, we anticipated that during this season our father would again barter custom slaughtering for several gallon cans of maple syrup.

About the third week in March, our five-year-old stepsister Beatrice fell while attempting to climb a tree in our front yard and suffered a fatal seizure. The doctor said that she had pulmonary stenosis, which meant that not enough blood was getting from her heart to her lungs. After she died, we learned that her brother Donald and her sister Dorothy also had died when they were infants from a similar affliction. While it was a sad time for all of us, it was especially so for our stepmother. Our sisters told us that being pregnant probably helped her get through this difficult time.

Around April Fool's Day, I was walking home after school with Marjorie Jackson, and we started talking about how much fun it was to ride our horses. She told me that sometimes when she was riding her horse King, especially when he galloped a certain way, that she got this funny feeling in her lower stomach and upper legs. She asked me if I got that kind of funny feeling when I rode our horse at a gallop. I told her that I wasn't sure what caused her to get such a feeling. I wondered, however, if I should tell her what I did about getting a feeling like that when I finally got back to the barn and got off the horse. I decided not to tell her that part since I was afraid that she would go home and tell her mother who would then tell my father. I remembered that we had gone through a similar situation when we were in Miss Bell's room at Orient Hill a couple of years before. Like my older brothers reminded me, Marjorie was probably too young to know what was happening to her as she rode King, and she would just have to wait until she was older to learn about it.

Step and a Half

In April at my father's request, Johnny saved a slunk calf from a pregnant cow that he had butchered that day. That evening, under the watchful eye of my brother Lowell, who was already an accomplished skinner, I successfully butchered the entire animal except for a few hide punctures. On Saturday of that week my brother and I delivered the carcass to Brownie Herr's house, and he gave each of us free haircuts.

A week or two later, Johnny showed me how to open up a hanging hog carcass, remove the intestines and offal, and pull the leaf fat away from the rib cage before it hardened. After working my way through these phases of the process, I was confronted with the most difficult task of the butchering process, aside from side-skinning a beef carcass, that of splitting the hog's backbone evenly with a large cleaver. I did not fare well with this step of the process for a prolonged period of time. Johnny said it didn't matter anyway because the critters were "parity pigs, and my father understood that I was trying to learn.

Hampshire and Chester Whites enjoy their last meal, 1938.

By the end of April, my oldest brother Winston was engaged to be married in November to a very nice girl who lived on a farm near ours. He said it was a really easy courtship because he only had to hop over three fences when he was calling on her. However, he also said it was much more difficult to climb over the same fences when he was returning home. Whenever he said this, all of the grown-ups would laugh. I guessed I would just have to wait a while longer to understand why what he said was funny.

The first week in May, our half-brother Roger was born at the local hospital, but he was not delivered by Doc Harris since he had died the previous year. Roger's arrival afforded our parents an opportunity to someday employ this line, "Your kids and my kids are out in the yard beating the hell out of our kid."

During the second half of fifth grade, I only had to help Miss Crumley once with her lack of knowledge of farm life. She told the class that a pig's tail is always curly, and we would probably never see a pig's tail hanging straight down. I told her that a pig's tail will sometimes hang straight down for one or two days right after it has been "castrated." She wanted to know how I knew that big word. I guess she also didn't understand that the punishment the pigs received would mean that they would never be daddies.

Summer Fun

Shortly after school was out in 1935, my cousin Dallas, a graduate of Ohio State University, took me to Columbus to see one of my idols, Jesse Owens, participate in a track and field meet. Owens was the star of the team and eventually established a half dozen world records. I already knew that I could run faster than most of my playmates, but after watching him, I wondered if I would ever be able to fun as fast as he could.

I had been to the ice house with my father and older brothers a number of times to purchase ice for our ice box, but had never seen or swum in the large, outdoor pool which was adjacent to the ice house. So I was really curious that summer when my brother Lowell told me about a "big flap" at the city's only outdoor pool. My brother told me that several high school girls showed up one afternoon at the pool wearing two-piece suits with bra tops in bold prints. According to one local minister, the town would never be the same. I was sure it wasn't our minister who was upset because he had probably already heard what had happened to one of his predecessors at our farm several years earlier.

Sometime during the summer, our parents and another couple drove to Cincinnati to attend a night baseball game. When they arrived at the ballpark, my father discovered that he had left their four tickets on the bureau at home. Every time our stepmother told someone how our father convinced the officials at the ballpark to admit them on the promise that he would send them the tickets upon his return home, she would laugh. She'd go on to explain that he had done just that!

Cozy DeWine, who was a member of that evening's foursome, said that our father "would probably be able to talk his way right past St. Peter if it was necessary." Cozy said our father was so convincing at times that "he could piss on your leg and convince you that it was raining."

I had worked on the killing floor during the last two weeks of July, and the first week of August our parents drove Hank and me to Indiana for a ten-day visit on our Aunt Annie's farm. It was during the harvest season, and we served as water boys for the threshing crew in her farm area. She was an excellent cook and the men frequently congratulated her when they finished their noon meal.

There was a girl, Carolyn Rowe, who lived on a nearby farm, helping our aunt. Since she spent quite a bit of time at our aunt's house while we were vacationing there, Carolyn and I became very good friends during our stay. During this time, she seemed to take an unusual interest in my appearance. She told me why I should brush my hair and not just comb it and why I should scrub my face with a rough wash cloth rather than just wash it with soap and water.

One evening when Carolyn and I were sitting in the porch swing, she got up, went into the house, and returned with a jar of my aunt's facial cream. While she was applying this treatment, a first for me, she told me that her older sister had spent time with my older brother Winston when he was visiting there a few years ago, and her sister thought he was real nice. Carolyn said her sister wanted to know about my brother so I told her that he was going to get married in November.

When I returned home, I told Winston what Carolyn's sister had said about him. He smiled and said that she was nice, too. My brother then asked me if I thought Carolyn was as cute as her sister Martha. I told him I didn't know because I didn't see Martha while I was visiting our aunt's farm. So then he asked me if I liked Carolyn. I told him that when she was giving me my first facial that her hands smelled real good and she made bulges in my underwear, so I guessed I must have liked her more than most of the other girls I knew.

A Favorite Teacher

In September of 1935, I would be attending the combined junior-senior Central High School located near the center of the city. I had been warned, of course, by my brothers and sisters of all of the dire things that can happen to a neophyte seventh grader upon entry. They told me that there would be over two hundred and fifty kids in the junior high school and that the kids coming from the west-end elementary school were bigger, smarter, and tougher than we kids from Spring Hill Elementary. In addition, I was warned that a lot of teachers were men. While the male teachers were really nice to the girls, they sometimes punished the boys, especially boys who had "smart mouths" or ones who forgot to treat the girls with respect. Finally, there were consequences when it was obvious that you weren't paying attention in class. I wasn't quite sure what they meant by "consequences," but it sure sounded like punishment to me.

College students initiated goldfish swallowing contests in 1935.

I was assigned to Mrs. Dean's homeroom, and she was also going to be my arithmetic teacher. She was tall, wore glasses, and looked a great deal like my Grandma Delie who had died when I was in the second grade.

My geography teacher was Pat Patterson, and I was really glad because he had been the favorite teacher of all my brothers, sisters, and their friends. Mr. Patterson was a rather short man who tended to stammer more than a little when he became emphatic or excited. When this happened, it was difficult to keep from laughing even if his words were directed to you.

Mr. Patterson addressed me not as the "slaughterhouse kid" but rather as "bull-knocker," which made me feel very proud. Besides, when he referred to me this way, the other kids in the room laughed, even the kids from the other elementary school who mostly lived in the north end of town.

Soon after I arrived at school one morning early in the year, I discovered that I had cow dung on my shoe, and I asked Mr. Patterson what I should do. He sent me to the main office to see Mr. Benner, our newly appointed principal. Once I arrived at the office, I was embarrassed to explain to the secretary what had happened. Before Mr. Benner did anything else, he had me go to the lavatory, wash my shoe, and return to his office. Then we talked for a while about the slaughterhouse, school, and Mr. Patterson. I told him that I really liked Mr. Patterson and since he was the junior high basketball coach, I hoped that maybe someday I might be able to play on his team. Mr. Benner laughed and told me that if I played basketball, to be sure not to wear my basketball shoes when I was milking the cows. I promised not to do that.

Learning Every Day

During the first half of my seventh-grade year I enjoyed being in Mr. Blackburn's physical education and health classes. It was also his first year at our school, and he was going to be the varsity football and basketball coach.

When I was wearing my cast and could not actively participate in physical education class, he gave me several related tasks – equipment check, scoring, timing, etc. – and I learned that he also taught the high school history classes.

I was in Mr. Patterson's geography class at this time, and he had already told us that Mr. Blackburn was an excellent history teacher so I was sure I would enjoy learning about history when I got to high school. Besides, my brother Lowell who was currently in Mr. Blackburn's history class said he was a very popular teacher. Lowell was not always receptive to adult directions and supervision so I guessed if he liked Mr. Blackburn, he must really be a good guy.

About this time, our horse Coli broke her left foreleg, had to be "put down," and hauled to the county fertilizer. Her replacement was a skittish mare with a brand on her hip. When she arrived, our father told us that she was very nervous and we should not fire our pistols while she was saddled. He also suggested we name the new sorrel mare "Nervous Nellie" and we did! Within a couple of weeks, on a late Saturday afternoon, Mr. Grooms drove into our driveway with our brother Lowell in the rear of his automobile. Lowell was unconscious. Our father helped Mr. Grooms carry him into the house and place him on the sofa in the living room. Lowell had a huge knot above his right eye. While my sister Evelyn applied a cold wash cloth to the knot on my brother's head, Mr. Grooms went to his auto and returned with my brother's .38 caliber pistol which he gave to our father.

Before Mr. Grooms departed, "Nervous Nellie," with stirrups swinging at her sides, raced past the house toward the barn. When my brother finally opened his eyes and mumbled a few words asking about where he was and what had happened, our father asked, "Well, boy, did you learn anything today?"

Hide and Shoes

In the fall, in addition to my regular chores, I was spending my school vacation days working on the killing floor of the abattoir. I was under the tutelage of my brother Lowell who was only nineteen years of age but nearly as adept at slaughtering as Ed Schmidt and Johnny Ernest.

I was progressing with respect to sticking and knocking out the front feet and heads of the cattle passing across the floor. However, even though I was anxious to move to the next level, my brother, Johnny, and Smitty did not seem anxious to have me try my hand at siding the animals after they were placed on their backs between the floor prick plates. This process, which called for a special skinning knife with a wide, curved blade, was considered the most difficult aspect of slaughtering cattle. Not only was it difficult to remove the hide from the carcass, but there was the possibility of perforating the hide as well. When a hide was perforated, especially on the back or rump area, it would fall into the cull sales category. Butchers evaluated and prided themselves on being able to remove scores of hides without creating a single cull.

Aside from the pleasant aromas of the smokehouse and the lard kettle, all others were very offensive to anyone who was not affiliated with the slaughterhouse. Nothing else equaled the stench that permeated hair, clothes, and even underwear when the animal hides were removed from the basement in preparation for sale. This was a six-hour, ten-man job. They unfolded the pack, shook the salt off the hides, refolded and bundled them, and carried them to the waiting truck.

As soon as the men had processed 100 hides, they each enjoyed a "job perk" of Ripple or Sweet Luci with an encore at 200 and 300. In addition to their five-dollar-a-day salary, they enjoyed another perk of a sauerkraut-and-feet lunch at Scottie's Restaurant. According to the workers, the odor of the hides was somewhat subdued in the afternoon due to the men's frequent release of "nature's wind."

That same fall, when the purchasing agent was present and carefully inspecting each laid-out hide for perforations, he told me that a hide from a nine hundred pound steer would yield forty pairs of shoes. He also said that the highest quality shoes were made from the back and rump areas of the hide. Finally, while laughing, he asked, "You wouldn't want to buy a shoe or football with a hole in it, would you?"

In the newly-constructed, refrigerated processing room, I had caught on fairly well to the established cleaver and knife cuts, including those of the drawknife, which were involved in converting the pork carcasses into the various wholesale products. As such, I was looking forward at this time to working in the Saturday retail section of the processing room that our father had recently added. Both my older brothers were already working there, and they seemed to be having a lot of fun.

Toward the end of October, our father was the successful bidder on a contract to supply retail cuts of pork products to Wilberforce University. The university was four miles east of our farm. This contract would eventually afford an opportunity to interact with several highly-cultured Negroes, who would have a significant influence on my life.

'TIS THE Season(ing)

Shortly after the abattoir began selling meat products to Wilberforce University and other public institutions, it came under the scrutiny of public health officials. As a result, our father's plant was required to submit to random, carcass inspections by a licensed veterinarian. Dr. Ayers, who had cared for our farm livestock since we moved to the farm nearly a dozen years before, was appointed to carry out the carcass inspections.

Our father, however, said he might have to go to court because he was not going to tell the city health department how he made "good German sausage." Eventually, the Board of Public Service revoked the abattoir's wholesale permit for this particular sausage because our father refused to give them his secret family recipe. Our father retained Joe Finney, his personal lawyer, to appeal the health board's decision, and again stated that he was not going to give away family secrets on the art of sausage making. When our father discussed the board's decision at the supper table, he laughed and said, "These guys on the health board wouldn't know a good sausage if they ate one."

Xenia Abattoir, Birch Road, Xenia, Ohio, 1936.

When I asked my brother Winston about the "Sausage War," he told me that our father would tell the health board that he used beef, pork, and spices in our sausage and would even tell the amount of spices per 100 pounds, but we would not say how we make it. My brother indicated even he didn't know the plant's sausage formula. "Only our dad and our sausage maker Joe Downs knew," he explained.

After a couple of weeks, when our father's appeal was upheld by the court, each customer who offered "congratulations" to one of the clerks during our Saturday sales received a free pound of this great sausage.

When Doc Ayers received his free pound of sausage, he thanked our father and said, "Walter, those damned health officials probably wouldn't know the difference between a castrated pig and a pocketed pork chop."

The enlarged abattoir in 1933.

A GOOD Break

Knowing our parents were not going to be home the Saturday before Thanksgiving, Hank and I had invited several of our friends from school to the farm for an "away game" of football. We boys well understood that our father was adverse to our participation in the sport. Consequently, my older brothers didn't bother to request permission to try out for the team in junior or senior high school.

It was beginning to grow dark and we would be concluding our game within a few minutes when I bent over to pick up the football and a tackler landed with his full weight on my back, twisting my left leg under me. As I crumpled to the ground I heard a snapping noise, and my lower, left leg immediately began to ache. I hobbled to the adjacent farrowing box, leaned against it, and cried from the pain. Hank ran to the house to tell my brother Winston what had happened, and he drove me to the local hospital.

An X-ray confirmed that my leg was broken, and the doctor applied a plaster cast from my toes to within a few inches of my knee. The doctor told me that I would be wearing the cast for about eight weeks, gave me a pair of crutches, and told me to have all my classmates sign the cast when I returned to school.

I was still crying on the way home, afraid that my father would find out how I had broken my leg. My brother told me if I would stop crying, he would tell my father how it happened. That sounded like a very good deal to me, so I stopped. The cast was too tight. That evening, about the time our parents returned, the doctor came to our house and adjusted it for me. While he was making the adjustment, he and our father joked about a couple of the town's characters. Then, when he was finished, he accompanied my father to the abattoir to pick up a beef roast in exchange for his services.

When I returned to school the Monday following Thanksgiving, I was swamped by classmates who wanted to sign their names on my cast. Many of them were classmates whose names I didn't even know. Even Mrs. Dean and Mr. Patterson signed it without my asking them if they would like to put their names on it.

Marceille Storer, a girl who signed my cast, told me the next day that her mother knew my father. She said her mother really loved pork cracklings and my father's cracklings were always fresh.

My oldest brother, Winston, was married during the holidays, and I was happy to occupy his half of the other double bed in our room. It was nice to sleep lengthwise after several years.

Citizenship

During the year-end holidays the year I broke my leg, I was spared my share of the farm's chores. My younger brother Hank reluctantly filled in for me. While my activity was mostly sedentary, several other happenings left footprints on my mind.

During this period my sister Rachel brought home a couple of Mark Twain's books from the county library for me to read. It sure seemed to me that Tom and Huck had a lot of fun playing every day along the Mississippi River. I tried to imagine how big it really was.

At about this same time, I saw pictures in our newspaper of the huge Hoover Dam that was being built on the

Colorado River and hoped someday I would get a chance to see it.

Several times during this period when I was physically restricted, I got a large book, *A Pictorial History of World War I*, out of our attic. While looking at the pictures and reading the captions, I was curious. When I asked our father if he had been in the war and had his picture taken, he told me that he did not have to go to Europe and fight because my two older brothers were very small at that time.

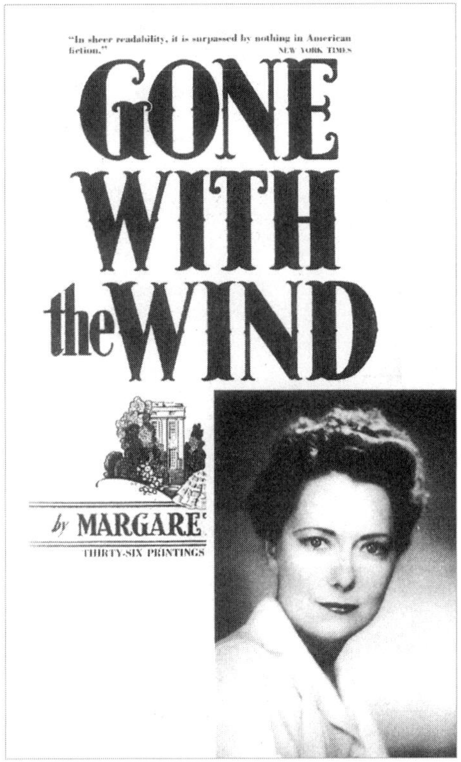

Our Aunt Grace visited with us at Christmas-time from Chicago, and she did not appear to be too disappointed that we were having a large, hickory-smoked ham rather than Rocky Mountain oysters for dinner. Since the sight of my leg in a cast had already warranted a bright half-dollar, it wasn't necessary for me to throw a snit in her presence.

Shortly after New Year's, a young man from our area was shot and killed while playing at the site of a saw mill after dark. When the owner of the sawmill was not charged for shooting the young man, my brother Lowell told our father that it didn't seem fair. Our father explained to him that over several years there had been quite a number of thefts at the saw mill and the owner, Mr. Troy, had asked the sheriff's department for assistance with the problem. According to our father, Mr. Troy was advised by the sheriff's department to post nearly a half-dozen "No Trespassing" signs on and about his saw mill site before he confronted any unauthorized person with a weapon. Since Mr. Troy had complied with the sheriff's request and the young man had disregarded the "No Trespassing" signs, Mr. Troy was only protecting his property and therefore had not broken the law. It was sad, but "Being a good citizen," our father said, "means respecting all of the laws, even if you are only playing."

The fiction hit of hits during the 1930's was Margaret Mitchell's Gone with the Wind, which first appeared in 1936.

KEEP 'EM Smiling

By early March, I had convinced our father that I was old enough to perform "flunky work" in the Saturday morning retail sales section. This was a lot of fun. Even though I did not deal directly with the customers, I could overhear the conversations and learn their names.

My oldest brother Winston was really good at retail sales and he frequently caused the customers to laugh when he answered their questions. One Saturday morning he printed and posted a large sign above the main butcher's block which read, "Prices are born here and raised elsewhere."

Mr. Byrd, a Negro man and a regular customer, worked for the railroad. He had three sons who were sometimes our playmates on Saturday afternoons. When he entered the market, he would say that he had to get some birdseed for all of his little birds. When my brother would ask what kind of birds they were, he would project a wide, toothy grin and say, "De all blackbirds! De all blackbirds! De eat all the time and de never seem to get filled up!"

When Mrs. Crawford, an established "pita" would enter the market, my brother seemed to be the only clerk who was not hesitant to wait on her. She seemed to be a self-appointed advocate for lower prices not only in our market but also in the local groceries, department stores, in fact, any place she spent money. One morning she asked Winston about the price of a pound of beef tenderloin. After my brother replied, she blurted out, in her usual plaintive voice, "My God, Winston, was there ever a time in history, when beef was any higher?" "Just one time that I know of," my brother answered. "Well," she continued, "I just wish you would tell me when that was." "When the cow jumped over the moon," my brother responded. A titter of laughter ran through the market as all present enjoyed the moment.

Since our father had experienced a short, economic struggle during the Depression, he was prone to recognize that some folks were still hard-pressed to make ends meet. When he was working in the market, he would always adhere to the posted prices, but he would silently recognize the customer's plight by under-reading the scale weight of the item purchased.

On a few occasions, when he learned that one of his long-time customers was ill or had been injured, he would have my older brothers deliver their orders without charging the usual delivery fee.

SPRING HAS Sprung

By spring, about a dozen girls in our class had formed a kind of social club and named it the "Worry Warts." Marceille Storer was a member of the club, and she invited me to attend one of the club's Friday evening events. I was glad she had invited me and was really excited about meeting her parents. I remembered that her mother liked fresh cracklings. So when I called for her at home that evening, the cracklings became a big joke because Marceille thought I had brought them for her.

I was not aware of it at the time, but the girls and boys present, and their respective parents, would all have a profound influence on my life during my remaining school years.

One morning in April, while we were enjoying breakfast, our stepmother drank a glass of orange juice and accidentally let forth a large belch. As she was excusing herself, my sister, Rachel, whispered to me. "You'd better get the plow sharpened because you and Hank are going to have to make the garden again this year." This, as we would unfortunately learn, would not be the last time Hank and I would lament that dreadful "labor relations" contract we agreed to shortly after our parents were married.

A CCC worker fighting a forest fire in Colorado, 1935.

At school, it seemed that several boys, myself among them, in Miss Zepher's music class were becoming infatuated with her. She was a beauty and had a great personality. We were extremely curious about the remainder of her anatomy, too. One of our group, Dave Adair, said that she lived near his house. According to Dave, there was a garage across the alley from her rented room, and from there we could probably satisfy our curiosity by climbing onto the roof and peering over the ridgepole into her window. I recall that we spent considerable time planning our escape route and our excuse in case were caught, but I do not recall a single one of us climbing onto the roof that evening.

During Thursday's music class when Miss Zepher told us how much she had enjoyed a music program at a Dayton theater on Tuesday evening, we just figured she was not only really pretty, but she was also very smart. Since she could look into our faces and tell right away what was happening in our pants, she was real nice and did not ask us to stand before the class when it was happening.

SHOW AND DON'T Tell

Among the many characters in our small town were a couple of queers named George Grippe and Bruce Skinner. George was employed as a clerk at McDorman's Men's Store and Bruce held a similar job at the Criterion Men's Store. According to my brother Lowell and his friends, George and Bruce were very adept at guessing a customer's waistline measurement, but they were never sure about the gentleman's inseam length, even after they had measured it two or more times, especially if the customer was a young man.

When not working in the stores, they were easily recognized because they were the only two men in town who were wearing printed shirts, open collars, and gold necklaces. They would frequently be seen cruisin' the city's streets in Bruce's baby-blue, Chevrolet sedan. The interior of the sedan sported two small felt hearts suspended on a gold lanyard from the base of the rearview mirror. On the rear seat of the car rested a large, heart-shaped pillow embroidered with white yarn which read, "A Hard Man Is Good to Find."

Bruce's sedan would sometimes be parked near the courthouse late at night. According to my brother, they would be in the basement men's room of the courthouse waiting for the movie directly across the street to let out. Sometimes they would even bring their own brooms and dustpans with them and pretend they were employees trying to finish up a hard day's work. My brother and his friends usually referred to George and Bruce as "peckerheads."

I didn't sense anything unusual in mid-summer when Lowell, who for a couple of years had appeared to be more interested in girls than movies, suggested that we once again attend a Saturday night movie at the Orpheum Theater, where we brothers used to go. He told me that his friend Beans Harrison and younger brother Jake, who was my age, would also be going with us.

When we entered the theater, Beans and Lowell went to the front of the theater, and we all sat in the front row near the side exit door. I reminded Lowell that we hadn't purchased any popcorn, and he laughed and told me I wouldn't have time to eat it anyway. As soon as the theater lights went out, Jake and I were quickly escorted out the exit door and down the dimly-lighted side street about a hundred feet, where Beans opened the street door. Once inside, we climbed two sets of steep stairs to the third floor, hurried to the end of a long hall where my brother knocked on a red door and spoke to a lady wearing a housecoat who answered. The lady seated us in a parlor and asked if we would like to have some pop. While we were drinking our pop, Beans and Lowell handed the lady who answered the door some paper money and she thanked them. After I had finished my pop, a lady came out of another room, sat down beside me, and wanted to know if I knew why I was there. I told her that I was there because my brother told me on the way up the stairs that I would have a lot of fun and it wouldn't cost me any money. She then told me that I seemed to be a very nice young man, and she had known my older brothers for several years. By this time, I recognized the aroma of the perfume she was wearing, and I had no doubt that she knew both of my older brothers really well.

When we were down on the side street again, we walked around the corner to the theater entrance and read the posters for the current movies and coming attractions. For some unknown reason, I had forgotten that we had not purchased any popcorn when we originally entered the theater.

BIG Brother

By now, the additional bedrooms and indoor toilet facilities that were created in 1935 were being utilized, for the most part, by the newly arrived step-siblings. We older boys, in an effort to avoid waiting in line, frequently utilized the toilet and shower facilities that had been part of the last slaughterhouse renovation.

This room was also good entertainment, since the interior of the locker doors conventionally displayed cartoons, pin-ups, and "cuss words" that the workers thought they would like to share. I could always tell when our father had paid a recent visit to this room. I would notice right away that the cartoons and pin-ups were new and the cuss words, again, creatively spelled.

Sometimes the male customers who frequented our Saturday morning market would use this room, but we always told the female customers that we did not have a lavatory available. Winston used to joke about this room. Once he said that if Mrs. Dodge didn't sweeten up, he was going to lock her in this room until she died.

Winston was always making his customers laugh. He put a penny box beside the cash register one Saturday morning that read, "Need a penny, take one! Need two pennies, go get a job!" It was the topic of conversation that morning until my father told him to remove it.

At least once, however, my brother seemed to carry his humor too far. On this occasion, when a lady had finished her produce purchases, she purchased several additional items—sanitary napkins, Ex-lax, and toilet paper. While she was paying at the cash register, my brother told her he was sorry that she wasn't going to have a very enjoyable weekend.

While I still idolized my oldest brother, he was still responsible for getting me into mischief. I was called into our father's office in the middle of a Saturday morning. Mrs. Clark, a high school teacher, whom I had waited on the previous Saturday, was talking with my father. "Did Mrs. Clark pay for a dozen wieners last Saturday?" my father asked. "Yes," I replied. "How many did you give her?" "Eleven!" I answered. Then I went on to explain that Winston had told me that while a baker's dozen contained thirteen, a butcher's dozen only contained eleven. I don't know what my father said to my brother about the incident, but my sisters told me that they were in Mrs. Clark's algebra class, and she never mentioned it to them. I guessed she would probably wait until I was in her algebra class, and then she would get even.

LAUGH AND Play

At the beginning of my second year of junior high, I was assigned to Mr. Patterson's homeroom and geography class. Even though I was confident that I was going to enjoy the school year, I still thought of myself as being somewhat of a Reuben.

Mr. Patterson's disciplinary practices were a little different from the conventional methods of his faculty colleagues, and we students were always ready to be entertained by them. When Mr. Patterson called on Jack Burton to answer a question, Jack answered that he did not know the answer because he had not read his homework assignment the previous evening. Jack's reply caused Mr. Patterson's face to grow red, and he began to stutter. Finally, he put Jack under his desk and told him that he was going to stay there until he could remember to do his homework.

A few minutes before dismissal, Mr. Patterson pushed his chair back from his desk and instructed Jack

Going for a dip in Shawnee Creek, 1939.

to come out. After Mr. Patterson had repeated his request two more times and Jack had not done so, he looked under his desk and discovered that Jack was curled up and sleeping very soundly. Mr. Patterson pulled Jack out from under his desk by his left ear and explained to him that his desk was not a hotel. Additionally he reminded Jack that he should sleep at home but only after he had finished his geography homework assignment.

Several weeks later, Mr. Patterson called on Bob Hazelbaker to answer a question. Bob did not reply, but it appeared that Bob had heard Mr. Patterson's question because he stood up and was looking right at Mr. Patterson. Mr. Patterson repeated his question. When Bob still did not respond, he called Bob to the front of the room, opened the supply closet door, ushered him inside, and closed the door. A few minutes before lunch period, Mr. Patterson opened the closet door and discovered that Bob's breakfast was all over his clothing and the closet floor. When Mr. Patterson had called on him, Bob was afraid to open his mouth to answer because he had a small cud of chewing tobacco in his mouth.

Our high school athletic program had not been very successful from the standpoint of winning contests, and Mr. Blackburn was attempting to create interest in athletics by initiating a Saturday morning, touch football program for seventh and eighth graders. He encouraged me to participate in the program, and I told him I would ask my father's permission to do so. My father gave me a contingent approval to participate. That was, after the contests were finished, I had to come straight home and assist with Saturday morning sales' cleanup. I guess he still did not know how I sustained my broken leg just one year before. In my team's first Saturday morning game, I caught a touchdown pass and our team won by a rather lopsided score.

I was late to school the following Monday morning and had to report to Mr. Benner's office. While he was signing my admit slip, we talked about the Saturday morning football program, and he told me that he was glad that my father had allowed me to play. Just before I left his office, he mentioned something about responsibility. Then he said that Miss Quentin, at the county library, had notified him that I needed to return an overdue book and when I did, to bring twenty-two cents with me.

BUTCHER Boy

By the first week in October 1936, the New York Yankees had defeated the New York Giants in the World Series and our father had purchased a new four-door Plymouth sedan. Previously, when my older brothers went courting in our family auto, our father would sometimes have a heated discussion with them the next morning relative to the amount of gasoline that was consumed. If I recall, gasoline was about eleven, or twelve, cents a gallon at that time. Anyway, our father seldom argued so loudly, so I was sure it was very important to him. At this point in my young life, my father was still my greatest idol, and I began to entertain the thought that I might never learn to drive if it meant that I could avoid making him angry.

Business at the abattoir was growing and Winston, who had married last November, was employed there full time. By the end of October, Grandpa Jim, according to my brother, "had fooled some lonely widow into marriage" and was relocating to Indiana. My brother purchased Grandpa Jim's property of more than two acres, attached a bathroom to the east side of the house, closed down the smokehouse, and converted the horse stable into a large garage and workshop.

At school, I seemed to be really enjoying all of my classes, and my teachers were almost always friendly and helpful, even though I probably didn't ask for assistance as often as I should have. My favorite class by this time, as with most of my male classmates, was Mr. Blackburn's physical education and health class. I discovered that I could outrun all of my classmates in a fifty, or one-hundred-yard dash, and, in addition, that I probably should not share my toothbrush with my younger brother Hank.

When Coach Blackburn was giving me a ride out to our farm following one of our Saturday football games, I told him that I was not sure that many of the city kids really liked me. He told me that when the city kids discovered that I could play athletics as well as they, they would all like me. "Besides," he said, "you and I already know that you can outrun them." By the time we arrived at the farm, I was feeling a little better about my peer status. When he said, "I'll see you at school, Butcher Boy," and drove off, I was grinning broadly.

On the 29th of October, I returned home to discover that I had another baby brother, Wayne, and it occurred to me that he might be the last one I would ever have.

The Big Dumbs, L to R: Jim Leach, Roy Leach, Williard Bath, Wendell Cultice, & Dave Adair, 1937.

POLITICS AND Practice

Just prior to Election Day, several of my classmates were collecting and wearing campaign buttons. Most of us, especially me, knew very little about the candidate whose profile appeared on the button we were wearing. It seemed to me if your button was big and brightly colored that your classmates tended to listen when you bragged about the candidate's abilities.

After I had accumulated more than a dozen small and medium buttons, I traded them all for a large button of President Roosevelt and one of Governor Landon. When Miss Reeder, my English teacher, asked me if I was "bi-partisan," I told her I didn't know what the word meant. She said she was not surprised and someday, if I paid really close attention in school, I would probably learn what it meant.

After the harvest season had passed, our Uncle Will gave us a real basketball hoop and braces. We made a backboard from scrap lumber and using binder twine, fashioned a net. This unit was assembled and attached to the southwest corner of the main barn, directly under a gooseneck light. We boys, when our work assignments were caught up, sometimes would shoot baskets at night until our father turned the light out from a switch inside the kitchen.

One night when our father was returning to the house from the abattoir, he watched us practice for a short time and then joined in the fracas. While he was participating, he proceeded to tell us about his high school basketball team. When he had talked for a while, I asked him what had happened the night his team got into a fight with their opponents and the officials had to call the sheriff. He said he wasn't quite sure what had happened. I asked him if he was one of the players who had been arrested, and he said "NO!" By this time, he was laughing, and he told us that our Uncle Will had a tendency to exaggerate once in a while, and "we should take some of his stories 'with a grain of salt.'"

When the football season was over, I tried out for the junior high basketball team, and survived two of Mr. Patterson's roster cuts. I had worked very hard toward this

XENIA
10
XENIA
5
XENIA
3
XENIA
6

My first love, Roberta "Bobbie" Knight, 1939.

objective. Since a really "slick chick," Roberta "Bobbie" Knight, had entered our class from Indiana and had already been accepted into the Worry Warts, I had an additional incentive to make the team. I was just absolutely sure that she would be attracted to a guy who played basketball.

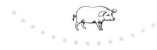

SQUIRREL Fever

The last month of the year seemed to be replete with work, school, basketball, radio and romance. I was spending more of my time at the abattoir after supper. By this time, I was permitted to dress a veal calf unassisted. My father, however, was always in the plant when I was doing this, and he was prone to look in on me during the process. When I was finished, he would inspect the hide very carefully and make certain it was free of holes, salted thoroughly, and properly folded into the hide pack in the basement.

My twin sisters were in the high school section of the building at the time. Sometimes I would go for a whole week without seeing them in school. I was enjoying the small measure of independence, especially not having to justify my school actions at the supper table.

Mr. Patterson kept five seventh graders and ten eighth graders on the junior high basketball team. He divided the eighth graders into two teams. One team consisted of the five smallest boys, who for the most part, were faster. The other team, of which I was a member, was made up of the five largest boys on the squad. Mr. Patterson would platoon us in and out of each game and would affectionately refer to our respective teams as "Little Dumbs" and "Big Dumbs," before, during, and after each game.

He once told my team, after we had not executed a play properly "that the only way we could be dumber was to be bigger, and he was afraid we would grow during the Christmas vacation and our team wouldn't win a single game during the second half of the season."

Stuttering, shouting, and pacing in front of our bench, our coach, according to nearly everyone who attended our games, "was the best show in town."

Sometimes, when we "Big Dumbs" had played up to Mr. Patterson's expectations, he would say that we were better than "Gangbusters." We all knew what he meant because this was a very popular radio program. However, it aired late on a school night, and we didn't want him to know that we stayed up late to listen to it.

Just before Christmas, I learned that the Worry Worts were going to have a holiday party at Doris Lowe's house. She was Bobbie Knight's cousin, and she told me that Bobbie was going to invite me to the party. She did. The night of the party, I called at Bobbie's house, met her mother and little sister, and walked her to Doris' house.

At the party we ate a lot of food, laughed at every opportunity, and played several games. One of the games was "Spin the Milk Bottle." This was the first time I had ever played this game, and the first time I had ever kissed more than one "babe" in the same evening. Even though it was fun, I was not able to have the spinning milk bottle point at Bobbie a single time when it stopped so I knew that I was going to need to get a bottle and practice before the next party.

On Saturday morning, my father asked me if I had had a good time at the party, and I replied, "It was the cat's meow." He laughed because he frequently used that expression. I also told my father that Bobbie was "cuter than a bug's ear" and that she might teach me how to dance some time. My father, again, laughed, and said that I sounded like I was getting a mild case of "squirrel fever" and that maybe we should talk more about it before too long.

HISTORIC Words

In the early months of 1937, in addition to the colorful, local characters in our town, the newspaper comics, radio broadcasting, and an occasional movie constituted our main sources of entertainment. The Sunday newspaper edition, of course, was replete with several pages of the best-loved comics of the day.

Our father was a regular reader of "Blondie," "Bringing Up Father," and "Tillie, the Toiler." In addition to the aforementioned comics, my twin sisters enjoyed "Little Orphan Annie," and they were good about reading her many adventures to our little brother Hank.

Hank and I, almost weekly, engaged in a verbal confrontation in an effort to gain first reading rights to the exploits of "Dick Tracy," "Joe Palooka," "Li'l Abner," and "Popeye." Hank was certain at this time that he was going to be a detective when he grew up, and he would sometimes ask our sisters to help him with words that he did not understand.

At our house, when the radio was turned on, it was generally broadcasting music or news. However, our stepmother sometimes listened to soap operas in the morning or afternoon. In the evenings, we children, sometimes to the agitation of our father, listened to a variety of crime shows, comedies, and mysteries that were being aired. While I enjoyed these programs, I was not prone to allow any variety of them to interfere with an opportunity to listen to a baseball game. I still believed that I would be a major leaguer someday.

In February, Miss Reeder, our civics teacher, kept us after school because we were unable to recite the full Gettysburg Address during our regular class period earlier in the day. She kept telling us how important it was for us to learn this historical document, and reiterated that we weren't going to be dismissed until we had mastered the entire address. At about four o'clock, while I was standing before a half-dozen of my classmates and struggling with the fourth or fifth line, Miss Reeder's fiancé entered the room, approached her desk, and whispered something into her ear that we children couldn't hear. Miss Reeder smiled, nodded her head, and asked me to sit down. She then told us that we were excused, and we would talk about the Gettysburg Address at some other time.

While walking home, I thought to myself, I probably can't even guess what it was that her fiancé whispered into her ear, but whatever he said must have been more important than Lincoln's Gettysburg Address. So, maybe, I should just wait until her fiancé comes to our room next time and ask him what it was that he whispered into our teacher's ear. It might be more important to me later on in school.

STANDING Tall

For almost a year, we had been finding eggs in our poultry house that were not crushed but rather had the contents

I drove my step- and half-siblings to school in a Model A Ford.

sucked out of them through a small hole in the shell. Although he had never seen the culprit, our father who had hunted and trapped when he was a boy, told us that it was probably a weasel.

Toward the end of the hunting and trapping season, I was finally successful in trapping the predator, and it was, as our father had said, a white weasel. After I had skinned, stretched, and cured the pelt, I took it to school to show my classmates. Mr. Bales, the high school biology teacher, asked if he could borrow the pelt for a couple of days to show to his students. Later, when he returned the pelt, he told me that a girl in his class said that she didn't know that we butchered weasels at the abattoir.

I asked Mr. Bales if he saw any holes in the pelt and he said that he didn't. "I guess you learn that in the slaughterhouse," he said. "Yes, sir," I answered. Anyhow, I was glad that a high school teacher would be interested in something that I was able to do.

At about the same time, my twin sisters, Evelyn and Rachel, had their photographs in our local newspaper. Someone had discovered that in a combined junior-senior enrollment of 650 students, there were eight sets of twins. Since the newspaper was distributed throughout the county, my sisters received several telephone calls from boys who were not in their high school.

When our father asked Rachel who had taken the photograph at school, she told him it was "Tiny" Matson, and that she had stood on a ladder when she took the picture because she was less than four feet tall. Our father answered that he knew "Tiny" very well and she drove an English Austin automobile. While grinning broadly he then asked, "Did you know that 'Tiny' is going to sue the city?" "Why?" my sister wanted to know. "Because they built the sidewalks in town too close to her rear end," our father said. All present howled with laughter.

Early in March, our basketball season had ended, and we had recorded eight wins in ten games. Our coach, Pat Patterson, gave a party for the team at his house, and we received our small monograms at a junior high assembly.

When I returned home from school, I went directly to the abattoir to show the monogram to my father and asked him if I could buy a new blue sweater. He shook my hand and said, "Yes." My sister Evelyn sewed the letter on my new sweater on the weekend, and I strutted around school in it on Monday. Much to my disappointment, Bobbie Knight was absent. I thought about calling her that evening and telling her what she had missed, but then I decided not to.

Change

In the spring, Mr. Boxwell, the varsity track coach, invited the eighth grade boys to practice with the high school track team. He told us that we were not eligible to participate in varsity competition, but he wanted to get an idea of our individual interests and ability.

After experimenting with each of the track and field events for a few weeks, I chose to concentrate on the dashes, hurdles, discus throw, and high jump. While I was unable to surpass any of the upperclassmen in these events, I did manage to surpass all of the freshmen in the dashes and hurdles.

When the track season ended, Mr. Boxwell encouraged me to try out for the track team in my freshman year. He also loaned me three hurdles to take home in order that I might work on my skills during the summer. I told Mr. Blackburn that Mr. Boxwell had given me the hurdles for the summer, and he said that was good, and that, he, too, wanted to give me a well-used football and basketball. I didn't want to tell them that when I wasn't working at the abattoir during the summer, I preferred to play baseball as much as possible.

The first week in May our family listened several times to the live radio broadcast of the Hindenburg dirigible exploding and burning in New Jersey. On that day, Hank and I had started to prepare the garden and were speculating as to whether or not we would still be indentured the following spring. Our garden preparation was well along when it occurred to us that we didn't have a confirmation that our stepmother was pregnant. We discussed the possibility for a short period and considered asking our father if he could help us. We finally concluded, however, that while we both loved him very much, we probably didn't know him that well.

The progress of air dirigibles was set back when the Hindenburg exploded at Lake Hurst, New Jersey, in 1937.

Toward the end of the month, our father took Hank and me to Cincinnati to watch a night baseball game. It was a combined birthday gift, since Hank's birthday was only a couple of weeks away. On May 22, I was fifteen years of age, weighed one hundred and forty-five pounds, and stood five feet and nine inches tall. I had three brothers, twin sisters, one stepbrother, one stepsister, and two small half-brothers.

Even though our house had been remodeled and my brother Winston had married, we still seemed to have a full house. At this time, a new and very popular game, miniature golf, was being promoted in our area, and a friend of our father had constructed a course at the north edge of the city. We children wondered if there was a possible chance that our father might enjoy an outdoor activity of this nature for a change.

County Fair

By mid-summer, there was a prolonged drought and several neighbors were hauling water from our well to maintain the health of their registered livestock. The drought is easy for me to recall because some of our leghorn hens and a few of my pigeons died of heat exhaustion.

During this time, Hank and I expanded our conventional sales of cattle horns and head pieces to include bull penises. We discovered that by stretching and drying a bull's penis that one could fashion an unusual walking stick. This idea caught on in the community rather quickly, and a few of our friends referred to Hank and me as the "Birch Road Pecker Packers."

As in many county seats across the nation, the major event in our area each summer was the Greene County Fair. The midway with over-cooked bullburgers, hairless dogs, and pretzels; games of chance; hucksters of snake oil and passion creams; and a full complement of unusual and exciting rides was generally frequented by the younger set.

The grandstand was replete with men who believed they were authorities on fast horses, good chewing tobacco, and the few young women who dared to intrude on their "fair domain."

The women could generally be found in the home economics area, where they competed for prizes each year in baking, food preservation, stitchery, etc. In addition, they cooked and staffed the main dining hall, which rightfully boasted of the "best fare at the Fair" title each year.

Many members of a 4-H club could be found in the livestock exhibit pavilion, day or night, attending their potential club champion. These animals, of course, merited very high sale prices and were almost always purchased by local supermarkets and slaughtered at the abattoir. It was not unusual for the animals' owners to cry when their pets were sold and destined for slaughter.

Since the fair, at its inception over a hundred years before, was agricultural in nature, there was always a giant display of new farm implements and a representative from the respective displaying company to demonstrate and respond to questions relating to the various machines. Each year, it was conventional for one or more visiting farmer to ask, "Do you stand behind all of the machines you sell?" And each time the question was asked, that salesman would answer, "Yes! All of them, except the manure spreader." And every year, it seemed, the joke was just as funny as ever.

Another accompanying fair joke, true or not true, had to do with a farmer who yearly brought his twenty-two hundred pound Hereford bull, Sampson, to the fair and charged an admission price of fifty cents to view Sampson. According to legend, a man with fourteen children told the ticket booth operator that he and his children wanted very much to see Sampson, but he couldn't afford to pay the admission cost of seven dollars and fifty cents. The operator told him to wait while he consulted the bull's owner inside the tent. When the operator returned, he gave the father seven dollars and fifty cents and told him to wait right where he was standing with his children. When the father asked him what the money was for and why he should wait, the operator said, "The owner's going to bring the bull out to see you!"

Subject at hand, Grandpa Jim, much to the embarrassment of our mother when she was living, always enjoyed telling about her visit to the county fair when she was six years old. It seems that our mother, attended by her mother, Grandma Delie, was visiting the livestock pavilion, when she stopped, pointed to the rear of a large Holstein bull, and asked, "Mother, what kind of cow is that with the heart-shaped bag?"

School's Open

During my summer vacation, there were a number of major news stories that kept us tuned to our radios at home and at work. In the Far East, the Japanese began a war against the Chinese and in San Francisco the Golden Gate Bridge was dedicated. In July, Amelia Earhart vanished during an around-the-world flight in her plane, the Flying Laboratory. Likewise, in that same month, Joe Louis knocked out James "Jimmy" Braddock for the World Heavyweight Boxing title.

Shortly after school opened, I heard about Bessie Smith, a Blues singer, who was hurt in an automobile accident in Mississippi. When I learned that she was denied admission to a local hospital because she was Negro and later died, I felt very sad.

An example of the way the "Okies" traveled West during the Depression, 1938.

I continued to participate in football, and a week before school opened, I was excused from my work at the abattoir to attend practice sessions at the high school athletic field.

Even though I was hesitant to do so, several of my classmates encouraged me to become a candidate for class treasurer. I enjoyed making posters with my friends and was very proud when the election results were announced over the school's public address system. It seemed that all four winning candidates were on the football team.

By the time that the New York Yankees defeated the New York Giants in the World Series, my classmates and I had survived the non-sanctioned ritual of carrying baby dolls and being dunked in the school's water fountain, and were very busy with our assigned subjects and creating nicknames for our respective teachers. Although I was not in her class, Miss Stout, an unusually tall and thin Latin teacher was a prime subject for much of our fun. Bob Crawford, who was in her class, said that she was so tall that one time when she was walking in the woods, a squirrel ran up her back and hid a nut in her ear. She was also affectionately known as "Miss High Pockets," "Miss Weeping Willow," and "Miss Peanut"—but never to her face.

THE WRONG Letters

For the first time in more than a dozen years, our high school football team experienced a winning season during my freshman year. In fact, we had tied for the league championship, and I was really happy that my father attended our annual banquet. He seemed to enjoy talking with the parents of my teammates, even though he wasn't able to chew his favorite tobacco until we were riding home.

About this time in the year, I was encountering more than a little difficulty in Mrs. Cavanaugh's algebra class. We students referred to her as "Prune Face," and she was frequently "hounding" me about my homework assignments, which of course I hadn't completed. She didn't think it was funny, when I suggested to her that I was probably having more trouble with algebra because I was using the wrong letters. One of the reasons I wasn't doing my homework was because I was enjoying riding around the city with my friend Bob Lighthiser. Bob frequently delivered groceries for his father in the evenings, and I would ride with him.

On other evenings, I would go to the abattoir and butcher calves or lambs while visiting with my father. He and Bob's father were good friends and business associates, so he never questioned where we had gone the previous evening as long as I was home before ten o'clock. Some evenings we just rode around the city for an hour with a couple of the girls who were usually members of the Worry Worts.

Just prior to Thanksgiving, my father permitted me to skin a deer and a bear, which Herman Cruse had shot in Pennsylvania and brought to the abattoir to be custom butchered. At our Thanksgiving dinner, most of the family members enjoyed smoked ham, while my father and I bragged about the great taste of the bear meat.

During the first half of the school year, there was a devastating flood in the Cincinnati area, and our coach, Mr. Blackburn, and two senior boys who were members of the National Guard, were summoned for duty in that city for more than a week. Upon their return, we were fascinated with their stories and photos of the flood. I was particularly caught up with a photo of Crosley Field, the home of the Red's baseball team, which depicted one of their pitchers in a rowboat twenty feet above the pitcher's mound. A few of us discussed the idea of joining the National Guard when we were old enough.

GEORGIA Peach

Multiple dances, including the Big Apple, were introduced in 1937-38.

By the end of the calendar year, a new student from Georgia had enrolled at school, my aunt died, and Adolph Hitler was becoming a household name.

Not only had our football team, for the first time in nearly two decades, won a share of the league championship in the fall, but later in the year, our basketball team won the league title and went on to compete and lose its initial game in the state tournament in Columbus. I, and several other members of the reserve varsity, attended this game. When it was over, I promised Coach Blackburn that when we were seniors we would return to the state tournament and win the title.

In early October, Cindy Gibbons, a senior from Atlanta, Georgia, enrolled in our school. This "blonde bombshell" had a "classy chassis" and wore a little more make-up than the rest of the senior girls. She instantly became known as the "Georgia Peach," was "date bait" for more than a few boys in her new school, and accompanied Joe Haller, an above-average "hoofer," to a post-game dance.

At the dance, while Cindy and Joe were going all-out with their version of the "Big Apple," including the steps of "the shag," "the Susie Q," and the "truck," several faculty members furtively objected to the dance because it

appeared to be immodest and lacking in grace. Miss Cavanaugh, my former algebra teacher, shook her head until her glasses nearly fell off her nose. She allegedly told Mr. Benner that she would resign as senior class advisor if he permitted another such dance.

According to Joe Haller, Miss Cavanaugh told her calculus class the following Monday, that the dance didn't appear to be based on "natural and harmless rhythm, but on a craving for abnormal excitement." We fellows guessed she had missed the point of the dance. We were there seeking excitement.

Our father's brother, Uncle Charlie, had been in poor health for several years, but we were caught off-guard when he telephoned early a few days before Christmas and informed us that Aunt Edna had passed away during the previous night. While it was understandable that Uncle Charlie would notify his brother of his wife's death, it was not uncommon for relatives and friends to initially contact our father when they were confronted with emergencies. My father was an excellent listener. Although he had no formal training, he was also unusually adept at non-directive guidance. These qualities appeared to be very compatible with his extroverted personality and consciously, or unconsciously, they did not go unnoticed by me. I was glad that he was my father and that he enjoyed helping people when they seemed to need it the most.

By the close of the year, Germany had annexed Austria, the number of out-of-work Americans had dropped considerably from the previous year, an East coast storm killed more than seven hundred people, the first Superman comic was published, and German Chancellor Adolph Hitler was *Time Magazine's* Man of the Year.

Bonding

As winter waned into March, the focus of my life continued to be on school activities and the abattoir. With respect to my academic subjects, I was not disciplined when it came to long hours of study or homework. At home, it seemed that any discussion of school conveniently focused on decorum and not on academic achievement.

This lack of academic achievement, however, did not dampen my enthusiasm for attending school. There was never a day to the best of my recollection that I did not look forward to being in the presence of my teachers, friends, and coaches. This enthusiasm, however, did not extend to the county library which was across the street from the school. This was where Miss McVain ruled with a glassy stare, an iron fist, and two-cents-a-day overdue book fees. We students were grateful that she reigned across the street in the county library and not in our school library.

At the abattoir, I continued to hone my butchering and sales skills, and my father always seemed to be pleased when I was able to do so. I was sure that he knew how much I idolized him and how important it was for me to meet his expectations in the industry of his choosing.

At about this time my father reminded me that in a couple of months I would be eligible for my automobile driver's license. By design, I did not respond to his remark. As indicated earlier, I had made up my mind that I did not want to go through the hassle that my older brothers experienced when they received their respective licenses. I hoped that he would have enough confidence in me to permit me to utilize the family automobile minus the hassle.

Often when we were discussing a particular facet of my father's business, my father would relate the situation to an earlier experience that was imprinted on his mind, and name the character or characters who were involved. I soon learned to ask him about his youth and adult associates because he seemed to always enjoy the conversations. In fact, he nearly always knew one or both of the parents of my classmates.

STILL Growing

By the end of April, Hank and I were aware for the third time that our garden relations contract with our stepmother was to encumber a sizeable share of our summer vacation time. While preparing and maintaining that garden was not as interesting as working in the abattoir, there was, however, always a sense of satisfaction in knowing that we had contributed to the economy of the household.

Again, as we had two years before, Hank and I entertained the possibility of discussing with our father these methodical, even-year additions to our growing family. Hank suggested that maybe we should have our minister talk with our father about the situation. I told him that our minister already seemed to have a son or daughter in each of our church's Sunday school classes, and his wife was presently pregnant so I thought he would not be any help to our cause. With a little luck, we concluded that the pending addition might just be the last one.

At school, I continued my interest in track and field by participating in two or three meets during the spring. While it was becoming more evident that I was somewhat gifted with speed, I still needed a great deal of refinement with respect to fundamentals. I was confident that I would be much more competent by next spring.

My classroom performance was still mediocre. Mr. Benner, our principal, called me to his office to inform me that even though I was going to fail algebra, I would still be promoted to the tenth grade at the close of the school year. He attempted to have me understand that I needed to balance my out-of-school time so that I could complete my homework assignments. I acknowledged that sometimes I had time to do them and I just didn't follow through. I was aware at this juncture of my schooling that my twin sisters would graduate the following month. Since my little brother Hank was only a seventh grader that year, I would be the only member of our family in high school the following year.

During summer vacation, my father had me accompany him to several livestock sales. He explained to me that while this is the easiest part of the packing industry, it is also the most important. Before making a purchase bid, it is necessary to compute the live weight, carcass-percentage weight, and eventual sale price of the animal.

Although our school did not sponsor a baseball team, the sport still held a lot of interest for those in my age group, and we sometimes scheduled games with nearby teams on Sunday afternoons. I usually played first base, or pitched, and was always happy when my father attended our games. I guess he wanted to find out how soon he could retire since I had earlier promised him he could, when I became a major leaguer.

Humiliation

During August of 1938, several athletic boosters in our town financed and organized a ten-day, outdoor, physical training program for under-privileged boys. This title was very misleading because all of the boys, including myself, were members of last year's football team. Since the program was held before football practice could officially begin, school personnel, including coaches, could not be affiliated with the program.

I was competitive and reasonably successful, with the exception of boxing, with the upperclassmen in most of the

"All the News That's Fit to Print."

The New York Times.

LATE CITY EDITION
Generally fair, slowly rising temperatures today. Tomorrow fair, temperatures unchanged.
Temperatures Yesterday—Max., 64; Min., 56

Copyright, 1938, by The New York Times Company.

VOL. LXXXVIII...No. 29,461. Entered as Second-Class Matter, Postoffice, New York, N. Y. NEW YORK, THURSDAY, SEPTEMBER 22, 1938. P THREE CENTS NEW YORK CITY and Vicinity | FOUR CENTS Elsewhere Except in 7th and 8th Postal Zones.

HURRICANE SWEEPS COAST; 9 ARE KILLED ON LONG ISLAND; 51 DIE IN NEW ENGLAND FLOOD

CITY IS HARD HIT

Storm Batters All New England; Providence Hit by Tidal Wave

GEN. WESTOVER DIES IN FLAMING PLANE; HEADED AIR CORPS

Officer Burned With Sergeant in Crash as He Attempts to Land in California

EXPLOSION IGNITES HOUSE

CZECHOSLOVAKIA DECIDES TO GIVE UP; CROWDS PROTEST, CABINET IN PERIL; CHAMBERLAIN TO DEMAND GUARANTEES

PREMIER OFF TODAY

Stalwart Czech Men Sob in Prague; People Tear Up Papers in Disgust

CZECHS ARE BITTER

"All the News That's Fit to Print."

The New York Times.

LATE CITY EDITION
Rain and cooler today. Tomorrow generally fair with little change in temperature.
Temperatures Yesterday—Max., 72; Min., 58

Copyright, 1938, by The New York Times Company.

VOL. LXXXVIII...No. 29,469. Entered as Second-Class Matter, Postoffice, New York, N. Y. NEW YORK, FRIDAY, SEPTEMBER 30, 1938. THREE CENTS NEW YORK CITY and Vicinity | FOUR CENTS Elsewhere Except in 7th and 8th Postal Zones.

DEWEY NOMINATED BY REPUBLICANS; ATTACKS TAMMANY

HAILED IN OVATION

Rainstorm and Winds Due to Hit City Today

TORNADOES KILL 26 IN CHARLESTON; HUNDREDS INJURED

Storms Strike City Without Warning, Causing Loss Estimated Up to $5,000,000

OLD LANDMARKS DAMAGED

FOUR POWERS REACH A PEACEABLE AGREEMENT; GERMANS TO ENTER SUDETEN AREA TOMORROW AND WILL COMPLETE OCCUPATION IN TEN DAYS

Flight to Ireland Goes On Despite New Peace Hope

CZECHS DEPRESSED

Text of 4-Power Accord

NAZI DEMANDS MET

"All the News That's Fit to Print."

The New York Times.

LATE CITY EDITION
Generally fair, continued cool today. Tomorrow fair, slowly rising temperature.
Temperatures Yesterday—Max., 64; Min., 52

Copyright, 1938, by The New York Times Company.

VOL. LXXXVIII...No. 29,470. Entered as Second-Class Matter, Postoffice, New York, N. Y. NEW YORK, SATURDAY, OCTOBER 1, 1938. THREE CENTS NEW YORK CITY and Vicinity | FOUR CENTS Elsewhere Except in 7th and 8th Postal Zones.

LEHMAN IS DRAFTED FOR FOURTH TERM; HE ATTACKS DEWEY

NEW DEAL A PERIL, SAYS GEN. MOSELEY; SHARPLY REBUKED

Retiring Atlanta Commander

BRITAIN AND GERMANY MAKE ANTI-WAR PACT; HITLER GETS LESS THAN HIS SUDETEN DEMANDS; POLISH ULTIMATUM THREATENS ACTION TODAY

activities that we engaged in during the ten-day session. A couple of my campmates and I were the "Joe Palooka's" of the camp. That is, we were knocked on the broadest part of our pants a few times when we were matched with experienced boxers. For me, it was a most humiliating experience.

When my father authorized me to attend this camp, he told me that my brother Hank would assume full responsibility for all of the chores at the livestock barn—milking, feeding, bedding, etc.

By the end of the first week of October, the Yankees had defeated the Cubs in the World Series, and I had another baby brother, Russell. When Mr. Mathews, the head janitor at school asked me if I thought this would be the last baby born at our house, I told him that his guess would probably be as good as mine. I thought, maybe, just maybe, he would like to discuss the matter with our father, since Hank and I couldn't bring ourselves to do it.

About the middle of October, I was late for school and reported to the main office to obtain my admission slip. When Mr. Benner, the principal, heard my voice, he opened his office door and motioned for me to enter. This time, he was not smiling and said that he had some very bad news for me. He told me that I had failed two of my classes during the first month of school, and I would be ineligible to play football until such time as I brought one, or both, of the course marks up to a passing grade. I promised him that I would work really hard to correct the situation.

Before I left, I told Mr. Benner that I thought the eligibility rule was always based on my grade-point average throughout high school. Then I asked him what my GPA currently was. He began laughing and said that he wasn't sure, but the last time he looked it up, it was so low that I owed the school one and a half points.

Coach Blackburn allowed me to practice with the team, but did not permit me to suit up for our Friday night games during the two weeks I was bringing up my grades. I felt I had let my teammates down, and it was a truly humiliating experience for me.

The New York Times *keeps us abreast of Hitler's demands, 1938.*

MORE SQUIRREL Fever

Shortly after Christmas my father, as he had indicated earlier he would, had a short conversation with me relative to "squirrel fever." He spoke about the need to respect the girl that you were spending special time with. "This respect," he said, "also included her parents." He told me that when I went calling on a young lady, that I should always take her a gift of flowers, candy, etc. I guess he remembered that on my first date I had only taken pork cracklings to Marceille's house. He also told me that I should be prepared to visit a short time with the girl's parents and listen carefully if they were inclined to set forth the "courting rules" for their daughter and home. Finally, he told me that "romance was a special secret between two people" and I should never discuss with anyone any aspect of a relationship that might be embarrassing to the young lady, her friends, or her parents.

A couple of weeks after our "squirrel fever" discussion, I invited Bobbie to see the movie *Captains Courageous*. Afterwards we walked a block and a half to Geyer's restaurant for a ten-cent steak sandwich and chocolate malt. This restaurant was a local, post-movie and post-game hangout for many of the high school students. While we were enjoying our treats, she told me how much she enjoyed watching our basketball games and that she would miss seeing them next year. She told me that in the spring her family was moving back to Evansville, Indiana. I had already worked my way up to starting center on the junior varsity team in order to impress her, and now she was leaving. Would I be able to concentrate on my school subjects, athletic endeavors, and life in general without her? I wasn't really sure!

We mutually agreed to keep in touch after her relocation, and I promised to come and visit her when I finished high school.

DIRECT Counseling

When we returned to school after the holidays, the remainder of our basketball practices and games would be held at the large, tabernacle building located on Third Street, very close to where my Aunt Sarah lived. This relocation, according to Coach Blackburn, would afford our team a regulation-sized playing floor, and, in addition, nearly three times the spectator space for the increasing numbers of fans who were attending our games.

In addition, it was announced that our school district was scheduled to begin construction of a modern, field house that would jointly serve the voc-ag and athletic programs.

I had been suiting up for the varsity games since the beginning of the basketball season and had substituted in nearly every game. However, my father had not attended any of the games. We had only practiced on the tabernacle floor a few days, when Coach Blackburn called me into his office on a Thursday and told me that I would be starting at the center position the next night. I was anxious to get home after practice and invite my father to attend this special event. He seemed very pleased when I told him and said he would also bring my stepmother to the game. He also cautioned me not to cut myself while I was butchering the large six-point, buck deer that Fred Langston had dropped off about an hour before I arrived home. Knife and related equipment cuts in the meat packing industry were somewhat common, and my father was a "stickler" for the safe handling of equipment in every area of the plant. As I was skinning the deer, I was very concerned that I might cut myself and not be able to play in the game that my father was going to attend the next night.

My contribution to the team's win in our first game at the tabernacle was not memorable. However, the introduction of Coach Blackburn to my parents was very memorable. My parents were waiting with Coach Blackburn outside our locker room when I exited so I introduced them to one another. Coach shook their respective hands and said, "Ole Butch is going to make a pretty fair, country basketball player if he pays attention and keeps working hard." Grinning, my father shifted his cud of tobacco to the other cheek and said, "If he don't, just

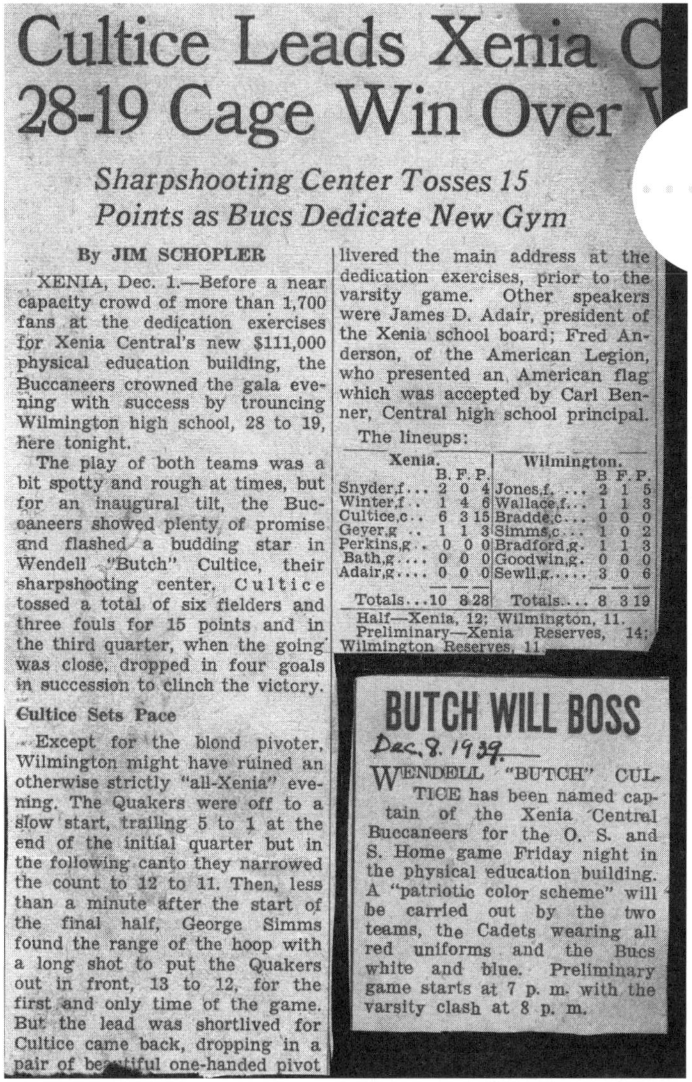

Cultice Leads Xenia C
28-19 Cage Win Over V

Sharpshooting Center Tosses 15 Points as Bucs Dedicate New Gym

By JIM SCHOPLER

XENIA, Dec. 1.—Before a near capacity crowd of more than 1,700 fans at the dedication exercises for Xenia Central's new $111,000 physical education building, the Buccaneers crowned the gala evening with success by trouncing Wilmington high school, 28 to 19, here tonight.

The play of both teams was a bit spotty and rough at times, but for an inaugural tilt, the Buccaneers showed plenty of promise and flashed a budding star in Wendell "Butch" Cultice, their sharpshooting center. Cultice tossed a total of six fielders and three fouls for 15 points and in the third quarter, when the going was close, dropped in four goals in succession to clinch the victory.

Cultice Sets Pace

Except for the blond pivoter, Wilmington might have ruined an otherwise strictly "all-Xenia" evening. The Quakers were off to a slow start, trailing 5 to 1 at the end of the initial quarter but in the following canto they narrowed the count to 12 to 11. Then, less than a minute after the start of the final half, George Simms found the range of the hoop with a long shot to put the Quakers out in front, 13 to 12, for the first and only time of the game. But the lead was shortlived for Cultice came back, dropping in a pair of beautiful one-handed pivot

livered the main address at the dedication exercises, prior to the varsity game. Other speakers were James D. Adair, president of the Xenia school board; Fred Anderson, of the American Legion, who presented an American flag which was accepted by Carl Benner, Central high school principal.

The lineups:

Xenia.	B.	F.	P.	Wilmington.	B	F.	P.
Snyder,f...	2	0	4	Jones,f. ...	2	1	5
Winter,f .	1	4	6	Wallace,f...	1	1	3
Cultice,c . .	6	3	15	Bradde,c...	0	0	0
Geyer,g ..	1	1	3	Simms,c ...	1	0	2
Perkins,g . .	0	0	0	Bradford,g.	1	1	3
Bath,g....	0	0	0	Goodwin,g.	0	0	0
Adair,g....	0	0	0	Sewll,g.....	3	0	6
Totals...	10	8	28	Totals...	8	3	19

Half—Xenia, 12; Wilmington, 11.
Preliminary—Xenia Reserves, 14; Wilmington Reserves, 11.

BUTCH WILL BOSS

Dec. 8. 1939.

WENDELL "BUTCH" CULTICE has been named captain of the Xenia Central Buccaneers for the O. S. and S. Home game Friday night in the physical education building. A "patriotic color scheme" will be carried out by the two teams, the Cadets wearing all red uniforms and the Bucs white and blue. Preliminary game starts at 7 p. m. with the varsity clash at 8 p. m.

We won our first game in the new field house.

kick his rear end." For a moment, I thought I was hearing Grandpa Sandy's voice.

Girls

Even though I was concentrating and participating on the track team in the spring of 1939, it was almost impossible not to notice how the former brace-wearing, giggling, scrawny girls, especially those who were members of the Worry Warts Club, had become very grown- up.

During the years we were in high school, hemlines rose from twelve inches to sixteen, and nearly all of the girls attained another fashionable look by wearing bras designed to uplift and accentuate their breasts. Less of a distraction were the babushkas that the girls frequently wore over their hair and tied under their chin. However, when three of the Worry Warts flaunted their new nylon stockings at a Saturday evening party, we boys were saddened to learn that their mothers would not let the girls wear them to school.

Unbeknownst to many of their parents, and much to the chagrin of more than a few of their teachers, rouge, lipstick, and mascara became very fashionable at this time in our high school. Following the example of the fashionable "Georgia Peach," the girls were wearing lipstick that was deep red and was put on after they arrived at school. It was applied "bee-sting" style, with the lips made full and pouty in the middle and left bare at the ends. It was made less pronounced before the girls arrived home after school.

It seemed that many of the things that girls wore, talked about, and did were designed to infect the boys with "squirrel fever." And I succumbed to this "fever" just before our class was scheduled to put on our Sophomore Dance at the end of April.

My brother Winston and his wife lived in an upstairs apartment in the west side of the city and they were going to be out of the apartment over the weekend. My brother asked me if I would stop at the apartment on Saturday evening and feed and water their two cats. I told him that even though I had a movie date that evening, I would be glad to accommodate them since their apartment was only a short distance from where my "hot patootie," Joan Hulsey lived.

When the movie *The Grapes of Wrath* was finished, we went to Geyer's for a small steak sandwich and Coke and walked to my brother's apartment. After I had fed the cats, we sat on the sofa with the radio on and the lights out and enjoyed an extended period of cuddling.

Joan excused herself and went through the dark bedroom to the bathroom. Shortly, she called to me and said she was lying on the bed and asked me if I would like to join her. She was on the far side of the bed near the bathroom. As I felt for the edge of the bed on the near side, I sensed that a pair of shoes was on the floor and several pieces of clothing, including undergarments, were on the edge of the bed. I quickly disrobed to my "birthday suit" and moved softly across the bed, where I discovered Joan fully dressed and demanding an answer to her question, "What kind of girl do you think I am, anyway?"

The clothing on the edge of the bed, of course, belonged to my sister-in-law. How was I supposed to know? Like my father frequently would say, "Life is about making mistakes and learning from them."

Americans grasped the scope of the Depression when John Steinbeck wrote The Grapes of Wrath *in 1939.*

Peers

International unrest, athletics, vocational agriculture, and socialization occupied much of my attention during the first half of my junior year. Shortly after school opened, while we were busy preparing for our first football game, the world, especially Europe, seemed to be turning upside down. In the first week of September, Germany invaded Poland. France and Great Britain declared war on Germany, and a German submarine torpedoed a British passenger ship killing nearly three dozen Americans.

Coach Blackburn, our American history teacher, told us that even though this international turmoil would stimulate our economy, he feared that we boys, like our fathers before us, might be called upon to "leave your footprints on European soil." In response to his inquiry, a show of hands indicated there were two girls in our class whose fathers had served in Europe during World War I.

During the previous summer, utilizing a football that Coach Blackburn had given me, I worked diligently at place-kicking. When the season started, I was awarded the left-end starting position and the place-kicking duties.

Since 1935, when Coach Blackburn arrived at our school, the last home football game of the season was designated "Dad's Night." My father, with my jersey number 22 attached to the back of his coat, attended our 6 to 6 tie game with Sidney. He said he "nearly choked on his chewing tobacco" when I caught a pass and broke into the open, only to stumble and fall within a few yards from where he was seated.

We tied for the league championship, and even though I had invited both of my parents to our Awards Dinner at Geyer's Restaurant, only my father attended since my stepmother was not feeling well. I just hoped it wasn't "morning sickness" that prohibited her from attending.

Our school chapter of the Future Farmers of America was chartered at the beginning of my freshman year, 1937, and Bob McClelland invited me to join each year since it had been in existence. He said Mr. Wickline, the instructor, was a good teacher and he didn't fail students who paid attention in class and completed their field-work assignments. Jokingly, Bob said, "You can pass the Voc Ag course if you only know which end of the horse the hay goes in. Beyond that," he went on, "if you only cut one ear off a lamb at its first shearing, you'll probably get a C-."

So, in my third year, I joined the organization and selected a home project for the year. I planned to purchase a Poland-China gilt from my father, have her bred at maturity, and raise a litter of marketable hogs. However, this project did not materialize because the gilt, named Gilta, did not conceive after having been serviced three times by Mr. Eavey's prize boar Boxer. She seemed to think of my project in terms of romance rather than economics.

We boys in FFA had our finest day(s) each year when we were excused from school for a day or two to shoot rabbits for our chapter's "Annual Rabbit Banquet." We were required to hunt the "critters" with a .22 rifle because our teacher did not want the many guests at our dinner chipping their teeth or dental plates on rabbit containing shotgun pellets. So, it logically followed, at our age, that we were never able to bag enough "critters" the first day for our dinner. However, on the second day, the rabbits were always very cooperative.

Socially, although I did not think it inordinate, I seemed to be in attendance at each athletic event, party, etc. that was affiliated with my class. In short, I felt I had earned the approbation and respect of my peers.

A Favorite Subject

By the end of April, our garden, labor-relations contract showed some promise. I became the senior male sibling at our home, reached an agreement with my father, and decided biology was my favorite school subject.

After the garden had been plowed and cultivated, our stepmother, who still had a full-time resident housekeeper, took over the planting and weeding for the remainder of the summer. Hank and I did not know at the time, but it would be little more than a year before our "contract" would put our hands back into the soil.

My brother Lowell and sister Evelyn were married by this time, and I was enjoying my status as the senior male sibling at our family home.

Around the first of May, my father and I had a rather prolonged discussion relative to my reluctance to obtain a driver's license. He explained to me that I would be of much more help to him if I could sometimes substitute for one of the drivers of the abattoir's delivery trucks, when I was not working in the plant.

Again, as I had over a year before, I equated learning to drive with driving the family sedan and told him I did not want to argue with him about where I went and when I returned home. At first he seemed rather agitated, and then he laughed and said, "Boy, we are never going to do that as long as you use a lot of horse sense!"

In about a week, when I told my father that I was ready to take the test for my driver's license, he seemed very surprised. He went with me to take the test and after I had passed, he wanted to know how I learned to drive so fast. I told him that my friend Bob Lighthiser had taught me to drive almost a year earlier. He didn't respond to my confession, but I was reasonably certain that he was aware that his admiring son had "hoodwinked" him.

Driver's Ed

Mr. Bales' biology class was my favorite subject in school. He was personable, dedicated to his students, and always had well-organized and interesting lab classes.

At one lab session, when he was demonstrating the effects of alcohol on the brain, he put two goldfish in a small, glass bowl and added alcohol until they eventually could not swim and turned upside down in the water. We students thought this was hilarious, but he surely made his point.

During our study of ornithology, he wrote on the chalkboard the names of 28 birds that were native to Ohio, and we dutifully copied them into our notebooks. The next day when we entered class, we noticed that someone had changed the number 28 to 30 and added "stool pigeon" and "jailbird" to the list. Mr. Bales never admitted to it, but we concluded that the additions were also in his handwriting. We always enjoyed his sense of humor.

Our biology room was a kind of an abattoir museum. That is, there were many specimens that my older brothers had brought to class before I was enrolled. I did uphold the tradition, however, when Mr. Bales gave me a large, glass jar half-filled with a preservative solution that I later returned, complete with a sow's placenta and nine piglets.

When I told Mr. Bales how we made walking sticks from bull penises, he seemed very curious and asked me to carefully wrap one in newspaper and bring it to his room before school started, which I did. He didn't mention it in class, but I knew from some of the comments of the other male teachers, that he had showed it to them. I hoped he hadn't shown it to the principal, Mr. Benner, because he might have questioned its presence in the school as a "teaching tool."

BADGE OF Innocence

During the final month of the school year, my father purchased a new Plymouth sedan, our class held a Sadie Hawkins' Day, and organized an end-of-the-year picnic at John Bryan State Park in Yellow Springs.

Just before I departed for school one Monday morning, my father handed me a check in the amount of three hundred dollars and asked me to pick up the new auto after track practice. The sedan was gun-metal gray in color and had a Motorola "Chatterbox." I felt an unusual sense of importance and independence as I drove in an easterly direction toward our farm.

On the next-to-last-day of school, I, with several classmates as passengers, drove our new sedan to John Bryan Park for a variety of co-educational activities and multiple hotdogs during our annual class picnic.

My fielding, throwing, and running skills remained competitive with those of my baseball peers. However, I was attempting to increase my ambidexterity by becoming a switch hitter, and my batting average was reflecting this attempted goal. In short, I was able to hit the ball more consistently from the right side of the plate, but had considerably more power from the left side.

For several years, this facility was the "Madison Square Garden" of Greene County, Ohio.

When school was out, I spent most of my working hours on the slaughtering floor of the abattoir and my recreational time playing baseball and swimming at the city pool.

My father and I agreed that there was still a need for improvement in my knife-siding skill and cleaver-carcass splitting. However, a few times during the summer, I attended livestock sales with my father and he seemed to be pleased with my progress.

Even though I was not a good swimmer or diver, I spent several evenings at the city park pool with my athletic friends. As I recall, we seemed to spend more than a little time entertaining the local girls and their visiting cousins with as much "horseplay" as the pool rules would permit.

On July 4th, I had introduced myself to a tall, well-tanned, strawberry blond, Ann Jeanette Tiernan, from Cincinnati, who was visiting her grandparents for approximately a month. Shortly into our conversation, I discovered that I knew her grandfather because he had the best coop of pigeons in the area, and I had purchased a pair of "white king" birds from him about a year earlier.

During the course of the evening, I explained to Ann that I had learned to swim in our swimming hole, and sometimes it was more fun than swimming in the city pool. I also told her that sometimes we even went skinny dippin' in our swimming hole. She said that she had never swum anyplace other than in a municipal pool, but it sounded like a lot of fun. I offered to drive her home, with a stop at the drive-in for a chocolate malt, and she accepted. While at the drive-in, I asked her if she would like to go for a swim in the farm pool the following Friday evening, and she accepted.

I called for her about eight o'clock Friday evening and spent nearly a half-hour "visiting" with her parents and grandparents. Her grandparents told me they had known my father for many years, and her grandfather recalled the sale of the "white king" pigeons a year ago.

We took a circuitous route to the farm pool in order to avoid driving past the house. With the auto lights out, we entered the east end of our road, drove past the swamp area, and passed through a gateway to a wagon-wheel path that ran alongside the west edge of the swamp to the remote area of the swimming hole.

During the time that we were at the swimming hole, we frolicked in the creek, compared high schools, exchanged humorous stories about our parents, shared our dreams for the future, listened to music on the auto radio, and studied the stars.

Just before we left, I took our dry, bathing suits to the creek, swirled them in the water, wrung them out about half dry, carried them back to the auto, and tied them securely to the side mirrors. When Ann asked me why I was doing this with the suits, I told her that these wet suits represented our "respective badges of innocence" for the evening's activities, and she gave me another hug.

When we stopped at the drive-in on our return to her house, the carhop noticed the suits dangling from the side mirrors and asked if we had enjoyed our swim. Ann responded, "It was the best swim that I ever had," and I said, "Me, too!" Ann put her hand on my arm and whispered, "Butch, it's I, too!" She had indicated at the swimming hole that she thought she might like to teach school. I guess she figured this was a good time to launch her career.

DON'T Ask

Besides the prophecy of our history teacher, there were many other events in the fall of 1939 to recollect. My favorite baseball team, the Cincinnati Reds, lost to the New York Yankees in the World Series; the World's Fair closed in Flushing, New York; scientists invented the helicopter and split the atom, and college students were caught up in the fad of swallowing live goldfish by the dozen.

Since I was a first-year vocational agriculture student, I was assigned to waiting tables on the evening of our Rabbit Banquet. Many of the parents and nearly all of the students knew me and I was "chit-chatting" with them and, in general, just having a fun evening. However, as I was serving the final few guests at my tables, I tilted a serving plate and spilled several gobs of rabbit gravy down the front of a sophomore girl's blouse. Her name was Jane Smith, and she sat across from me in our large, fifth-period study hall. I apologized profusely to her, and called her home on Saturday and offered to pay for the dry-cleaning of the blouse.

A broad smile following my first-place win in the Ohio FFA Meat Judging Contest.

The day before school dismissed for Thanksgiving weekend, I attended my Aunt Lizzie's funeral in Cedarville. When I returned to school, Jane asked me if I had been sick. I told her why I was not in school and she told me she was very sorry. She also told me that her mother thought "it was real gentlemanly" of me to offer to pay for the dry-cleaning of her blouse.

A few days later, I made a late Saturday afternoon and evening date with her to see *Gone with the Wind.* I promised her that, following the movie, we would not go to a restaurant for a rabbit dinner, and she laughed. She said her mother was looking forward to meeting me.

Early Saturday afternoon, I vacuumed the interior of the family auto and carefully scrubbed the tobacco stains off the entire left side. While I was in the process, my father passed by, grinned, and said, "She must really be something, boy!" I playfully squirted water from the hose over his head and said, "I'll keep you posted on this special evening!"

On Sunday, after church and without him asking, I filled my father in on the great movie and young lady. When I told him her name, he said that her mother transported "bloomer bootleg" during the Prohibition, and her father had died in the State penitentiary.

During our first date, I was glad I had not asked her the question,"What does your father do for a living?"

HAPPY Holidays

The last month of the calendar year was replete with school-related events. Early in the month, a former club, Varsity X, was reinstated; our newly-constructed field house was dedicated; our class sponsored the first alumni dance; our basketball team enjoyed a holiday tour, and I received Christmas gifts from several caring individuals. The purpose of the Varsity X Club was to promote good sportsmanship through athletics. The club was reorganized by the senior lettermen who had established standards for membership. Any letterman in football or anyone with two letters in the other school athletic sports was eligible to become a member. Since I already had a monogram in basketball and football, I joined and was voted President-elect for the year. Mr. Blackburn was our club advisor. We sponsored several significant activities, including the inauguration of the Alumni Dance during the Christmas holidays.

On the first day of December dedication exercises for our school's modern physical education building were held

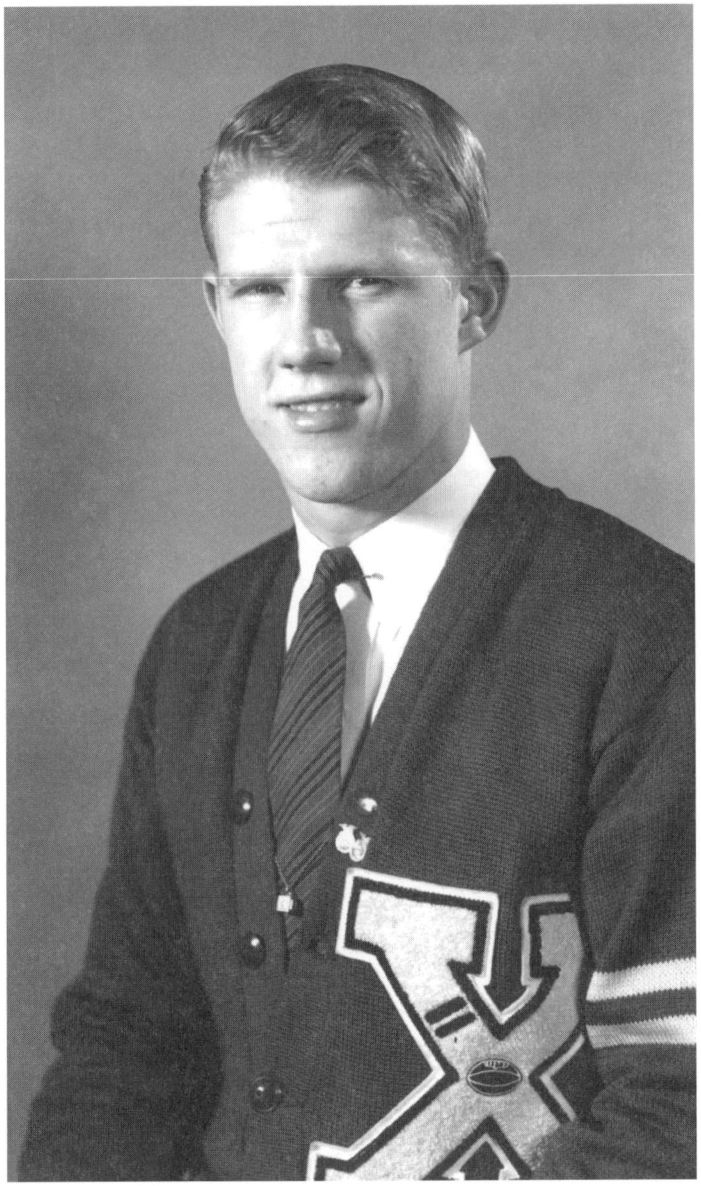

before our opening basketball game with Wilmington. The playing floor was one of the largest in the state, and it had a seating capacity of about 2000. There were numerous sports reporters and photographers present from throughout the state of Ohio, and I had my photo taken with the Commissioner of the State Athletic Association. My father posted the photographs on the wall of his abattoir office.

Sporting my new varsity sweater. I lettered in football.

It was a very memorable evening for me. In addition to winning the game, I scored the first varsity field goal in the new field house and more than half of our team's points during the game.

During the Christmas-New Year's interim, our basketball team made a four-day tour of the central part of the state and we won all of our games. When we returned, Jane and I attended our newly-sponsored Alumni Dance. Then after the dance, we went to Geyer's to visit with our friends and enjoy hot fudge sundaes.

The following day, along with several classmates and teachers, I spent several hours removing decorations, sweeping, and returning equipment to merchants who always seemed willing to support our school projects. Toward the end of the clean-up session, Miss Wilton with whom I had danced a couple of times the previous evening asked me if I could give her a ride home. I told her I would be very happy to do so.

Miss Wilton told me that while I was at her house I could pick up my Christmas gift that her mother had already wrapped. The situation did not sound inordinate to me since several adults, including Miss Wilton's widowed mother, had previously given me gifts. Little did I know what was in store later that evening.

When we arrived at Miss Wilton's home, she invited me to stay for supper, and I accepted. While we were eating supper, she told me that her sister in Toledo, Ohio, was expecting her first baby and her mother had gone to assist with the pending event.

Our advisor, Mr. Blackburn, had his hands full with this group of energetic young men. Front row, left to right: Coach Blackburn, Robert Lighthiser, Ray Snyder, Thomas Adair, Lawrence Davis, Willard Bath, David Adair, Wendell Cultice, Robert Winter, Robert Mickle, Robert Jones, Robert Geyer. Back row: Roger Thomas, Neil Shaw, Allan Miller, Hubert Mahaffey, James Jones, Jack Wilson, Winston Bahns, Paul Huston, Eugene Mercer, Conrad Leslie.

After we had cleared the table, washed and dried the dishes, we sat in the living room and talked about the previous evening's dance. I again apologized for having stepped on her toes and told her I would like to be a better dancer.

During the next two hours to the soft notes and words of several songs, including "Indian Summer" and "Deep Purple," I received my first dancing lessons. It was approaching ten o'clock when I told Miss Wilton that I probably should be going home. When I said this, she told me that her mother had probably left my gift upstairs and I was welcome to accompany her upstairs to look for it. I accepted the invitation, and remembered to thank her for the supper, lessons, and gift when I left at approximately midnight.

Many years later during the filming of the movie *The Graduate* I was disappointed that I was not asked to serve as a consultant.

Conspiracy?

In the final three months of the school year—March, April and May—athletics, social activities, vocational training, and international events were all shaping my future.

When basketball season ended in the first week of March, our team had tied for the league championship, and we won our first two games of the district tournament. I was the league's leading scorer and honorary captain of the all-star team. I did not fare as well, however, in dramatics. When our class play, *The Patsy*, first displayed the dramatic talent of our class, I was unable to gain a part.

In April, our class sponsored a bigger and better "Sadie Hawkins' Day Dance." I was chairman of the Door Prize Committee and was successful in obtaining a live Hampshire piglet, wearing pink rubber pants, for the winner. Many of our "Dogpatch" characters were later featured in the magazine section of the *Dayton Daily News*.

In contrast to the old clothes and carnival spirit of "Sadie Hawkins," our Junior Prom had a sunken-garden effect, which gave the illusion of a moonlit garden in the springtime. The night, so short, was most memorable. We closed the social year with our annual class picnic at John Bryan Park in nearby Yellow Springs.

My rural background, including my slaughterhouse experiences, was very compatible with my vocational agriculture studies. I enjoyed working with other members of the class during the judging of livestock, meat, dairy cows, poultry, and sheep. I was confident that I would improve

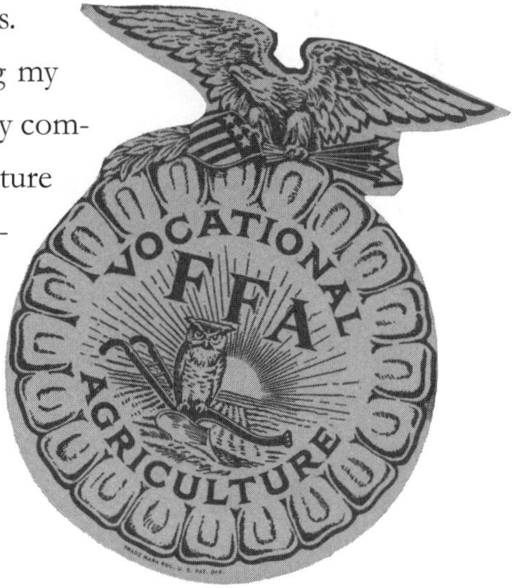

I was a proud member of the FFA.

my judging skills when I attended additional livestock sales with my father during the approaching summer. In addition, I was looking forward to taking my apprentice meat-cutter's examination in June.

Our history teacher's prophecy of pending war was fulfilled when Germany occupied Denmark and Norway in April, and invaded Luxembourg, Belgium, and the Netherlands in May.

Jane Williamson won the door prize, a piglet wearing rubber pants.

In addition to the aforementioned social events, I failed to include that Hank and I again prepared and planted the garden. Our father and stepmother were expecting their fourth child in August. Our stepmother told us that the pending event was her birthday gift to our father. It just seemed to Hank and me, that there was a "playpen conspiracy" at our house that was determined to defeat our garden, labor-relations agreement with our stepmother.

ROOM FOR ONE More

In June, war clouds continued to gather over Europe when Italy joined Germany and declared war on Great Britain and France. France was rapidly defeated and surrendered to Germany on June 21st.

A few days before the fall of France, I became an uncle for the third time. Sondra Jean was my first niece, and there was an unidentifiable pride in this event. Our

father always said, "No day is complete until you've heard the laughter of a child." I guessed my sister Evelyn was planning for many complete days because this was her second child in about fifteen months.

A few days after the fall of France, I took the apprentice meat cutter's exam at the Focke Packing Company in Dayton. My father and Mr. Walter Focke, one of the co-owners, were fellow livestock buyers and he arranged for me to take the exam at his plant. It was necessary to do this because my father's abattoir was not a union shop. I received a very high rating on the exam, and my father was very pleased with my effort.

By mid-summer, unemployment continued to decline and the employees at the abattoir were all enjoying a forty-hour work week. Their allegiance to my father's standards of customer service, punctuality, safety, and sanitation was a daily reminder of my father's expectations.

The International Olympic Games had been cancelled due to the war in Europe, and I was playing baseball on the weekends. I was also umpiring an occasional game and found it to be very satisfying. It occurred to me that if I wasn't able to get to the "bigs," I might enjoy a career as a professional umpire.

Jane was working at the box office of the theater during the summer, and when she finished at about nine o'clock, we would occasionally go for a ride in the country, smooch for a while, and enjoy a snack and drink at the dairy bar with our friends.

During my remaining years in high school, I faithfully continued to correspond with Bobbie.

My stepmother's birthday gift to my father, Patricia Gayle, arrived five days early on August 13th. Folks in the area had never quite been able to figure out whose children belonged to whom at our farm. And when this blessed event was announced in the local *Evening Gazette,*

My half sister, Patricia Gayle, was 16 months of age when she died in 1941.

they appeared to stop trying. They just seemed to conclude that our parents were either good Catholics or careless Protestants.

By the end of August, Germany attacked Great Britain by air in preparation for a later invasion, and we were purchasing our first M & M candies at Lighthiser's Corner Grocery.

HORSING Around

The county fair was many things to many people. However, for my father, it was all about harness racing. In addition to attending the races at the local fair, he would occasionally attend these events in contiguous counties when he was purchasing livestock. In fact, although it was economically beyond his means until the late '30's, he had always aspired to owning one or more of these beautiful creatures. By the late '30's, a local driver and trainer, Joe Hagler, owned a horse named Ray Henley who was establishing track records with regularity.

In 1939, my father had purchased two harness horses and stabled them for training with Mr. Hagler. One of them, Ramble Song, was fairly successful. Unfortunately, the other one, named Merle Rose, in honor of my stepmother, failed either to win or place during her career. They were, however, a most pleasurable activity for my father, and he fulfilled his life-long dream when he "sulkied-up" for their early morning workouts at the fairgrounds.

My father taking Ramble Song for an early morning workout.

My father's friend, Cozy DeVoe, frequently attended the harness races with him. During a summer evening in 1940, I had driven them to Hilliard, Ohio, to enjoy the trotters and pacers. After the program concluded, we stopped at a restaurant for a piece of pie and a cup of coffee. We each ordered a different flavor of pie for dessert, and when the waitress, an attractive university student, approached our table with the tray, she said to Cozy, "Is your's raisin, Sir?" "Well, now," he responded, "Honey, I hadn't thought a thing about it until you just mentioned it!"

HE'S MY Brother

Just before school opened in September of 1940, ably assisted by our father, Hank and I purchased a 1931 Model "A" Ford sedan for school transportation only. In the morning, we would deliver our step-siblings to their respective schools, and Hank and I would drive on to the high school. The step-siblings walked home after school, and Hank and I drove home after football practice. This was very economical transportation since gasoline was only 13 cents a gallon, or two for 25 cents. In short, we could fill the eight-gallon tank for just one dollar, which would last for nearly a full two weeks.

PRELIMINARY
1940
General Program

Thirteenth National Convention
of Future Farmers of America

and

National Contests for Students
of Vocational Agriculture

at

KANSAS CITY, MISSOURI
November 9 to 16, 1940

★ ★ ★ ★

HEADQUARTERS
MUNICIPAL AUDITORIUM
Wyandotte at 13th Street

Hank had suffered a severe bout with rheumatic fever when he was twelve years of age, and he showed a great deal of courage by attempting to participate in athletics during his first two years of high school. I always encouraged him to "hang-in-there" and would frequently tell him that I was proud of him. I guess he appreciated my support because

his junior varsity football and basketball jersey numerals were always the same as mine.

During the middle of September, the entire high school was wrapped in sadness by the sudden death of Mary Lou Martin. Our class was deeply touched since she was an outstanding student and a member of the Worry Warts. Several of us were excused from school to attend her funeral.

For several weeks, our FFA-Vocational Agriculture Meat Judging Team had spent many hours in preparation for the upcoming state contest to be held in Columbus during the last week of September. When the contest was over, our three-man team had won first place, and I also won the individual title with a near perfect score. Our win qualified our team for the national contest in Kansas City, Missouri in late November.

By the end of October, the Reds had beaten the Tigers in the World Series, our father had worn double 22's during our Annual Dad's Night Football Game, the first peacetime military draft had been conducted, and "Birddog" Cavanaugh was having another "snit" over our ability to "cut a rug," including jitterbugging, at the Senior Dance.

Practice Makes Perfect

By the middle of November, Franklin D. Roosevelt had been elected to an unprecedented third term as our country's President; Germany, Italy, and Japan had formed an economic and military alliance and became known as the Axis powers; and our FFA meat judging team was in Kansas City, Missouri, competing in the National Convention of Future Farmers of America.

Victorious Meat Judging Team. Left to right: Wendell Cultice, Albert Black, FFA Advisor P.D. Wickline, & Harold Petersen.

In addition to his persuasive personality, President Roosevelt's victory over the Republican candidate Wendell Willkie appeared to be the result of accelerating conflicts in Europe and Asia, which caused unemployment to fall in our country due to increasing factory orders spurred by the war.

The threat of a pending war, however, did not go unnoticed by our teachers and individually and collectively, they conveyed the seriousness of the situation to us as the school year progressed.

I sustained a back injury in our final football game at Sidney. Following a protracted automobile ride to Kansas

City, I encountered difficulty in walking immediately after the contest. I was able, however, to participate in the contest. The event was held at the Cudahy Packing Company in Kansas City, Kansas. I remembered that my father had visited there a few years ago.

This was my first national competition, and I wanted very much to be successful. Our three-man team finished in tenth place, and I finished sixth individually. In addition to participating in the meat judging contest, I had an opportunity to watch the National Livestock Show and Sale at the American Royal Building. I knew my father would be very interested in hearing about this part of my trip, too.

When I returned from the trip, the workers in the abattoir began to refer to me as "P. P. & J." This was an acronym for Pappy's Pride and Joy. On the surface, I found this to be somewhat embarrassing, but inwardly I was glad that the workers sensed that my father was proud of my accomplishments.

Shortly after my return from Kansas City, we were excused from school to hunt rabbits for our FFA Rabbit Banquet. Again, we were unable to bag the necessary critters for dinner on the first day. So, we were excused from school for another day. Our instructor was unhappy with us when he learned that on the first day we had flushed and shot several pheasants, instead of enough rabbits.

I was a contestant at the American Royal Livestock Show.

I escorted Jane to the Junior Class Dance and afterwards I drove slowly through several covered bridges in the area while we listened to a variety of "hit" songs, including "When You Wish upon a Star" and "Practice Makes Perfect."

POINT OF Prayer?

During the remainder of the first semester, including the holidays, I engaged in several school activities, a joyful Christmas gathering, and a nearly-devastating basketball moment.

I sat with my parents at our annual football banquet, and they seemed very pleased when I received my third varsity monogram and it was announced that I had been named to a first team position on the League's All-Star Team.

I had enjoyed spending most of Thanksgiving Day with Jane, her mother, and grandparents. I especially en-

BASKETBALL RESULTS 1940-41

Xenia	20	Spring Valley	31	Here
Xenia	28	O. S. & S. O. Home	22	Here
Xenia	38	Bexley	21	There
Xenia	28	Hamilton	21	Here
Xenia	22	Fairview	16	Here
Xenia	21	Middletown	30	Here
Xenia	21	Miamisburg	30	There
Xenia	48	Fairmont	22	Here
Xenia	21	Troy	16	There
Xenia	43	Piqua	29	Here
Xenia	39	Wilmington	13	Here
Xenia	35	Greenville	22	There
Xenia	50	Sidney	31	Here
Xenia	31	O. S. & S. O. Home	20	Here
Xenia	40	Ironton	31	There

DISTRICT TOURNAMENT, Dayton

Xenia	35	Hamilton	30
Xenia	37	Dayton Co-op	25
Xenia	34	Bellefontaine	25
Xenia	23	Roosevelt	21

STATE TOURNAMENT, Columbus

Xenia	47	Toledo Libbey	38
Xenia	47	Newark	38
Xenia	34	Martins Ferry (semi-finals)	36

Basketball Team of 1940-41

First Row—Willard Bath, Ray Snyder, Thomas Adair, Wendell Cultice, Robert Winter, Paul Huston, Lawrence Davis.

Second Row—Eugene Mercer, William Patterson, Bob Geyer, Jack Wilson, Roger Thomas, Rhey Feeley, Robert Shaw.

Third Row—Ralph Bullock, Kenneth Boxwell, Everett Sheets, Fred Blair, Henry Cultice, Bud Luttrell, Kenneth White, Harold Smith.

Fourth Row—Conrad Leslie (manager), Carlton Smith, Coach L. T. Blackburn, Paul Long (manager).

We were the first Xenia team to win a game in the State Tournament at Columbus.

joyed talking with her grandfather who was a recognized authority with respect to city, county, and state history. When the adults completed their entrée, they retired to the living room to enjoy their dessert—English Plum Pudding! After they had gone from the kitchen, Jane's sister Florence and her boyfriend Turkey Ferrell took our respective slices of the dessert into the backyard and fed it to the neighbor's dog.

About the middle of December, due to my previous back injury, I saw limited action in our team's basketball game at Bexley. However, I recovered in time to escort Jane to our Varsity X Alumni Dance the following Saturday evening.

On Christmas Day our family gathered at the farm house for an exchange of gifts, touch football, and a huge, roast pork dinner. That year it seemed that almost every interior corner of the house contained some type of baby accessory. In fact, my half-sister Patricia Gayle was several months younger than her niece and two nephews. I recall that my oldest brother Winston referred to our place a couple of times that day as the "fertile farm."

In the first month of the next year, our FFA Parliamentary Procedure Team won first place over sixteen other teams in the state finals at Columbus. A few days later, I experienced my first dramatic success when I appeared in our Senior Class Play.

On the final day of January, while playing basketball against Troy, a formidable league opponent, I was rebuked by Coach Blackburn at half-time for not rebounding more aggressively during the first half of the basketball game.

Shortly into the second half, I shook several players off a rebound and took the ball back to the basket. The ball rolled almost completely around the rim and back into my outstretched hands a second time. By this time I realized that I had come very close to scoring a basket for our opponent, and I quickly passed the ball off to one of our guards. When I raced past our team bench toward our end of the floor, Coach Blackburn was on his knees with his hands in a position of prayer and looking at the ceiling of the gym. We eventually won the game by four or five points.

Whenever we athletes were riding in Coach Blackburn's car and we were entering the south edge of Columbus, Ohio, he would ask for our attention. We soon learned that he was going to draw our attention to the State Insane Asylum on the right and a large cemetery on the left. He would point to the asylum and say, "There's where the coaches go when they retire." Then, he would point to the cemetery and say, "There's where they bury the ball carriers who don't follow their interference." Even though we anticipated his comments, they were always good for a giant laugh!

CAST IN Bronze

At the beginning of the second semester, a book entitled *One Hundred of the World's Best Short Stories* was being circulated among several boys who were enrolled in Miss Etta Marshall's English class. There was an inscription inside the front cover of the book which read, "This book is for football players only!" Several of us, all of whom were in love with Miss Marshall, were in arrears with our monthly book reports, and we found this book to be exceedingly helpful.

In the parlance of the times, Miss Marshall was a "slick chick" with gorgeous "gams," exuded oodles of "oomph," and was "built like a country, brick outhouse." She conventionally wore high heels, close-fitting sweaters, and long slender skirts. While standing before the class and holding her textbook just above her waist, she would rise up on her toes and then drop her heels to the floor. When she did this, we boys found our imaginations drifting beyond the classroom and the term "homework" took on a totally different meaning, one completely unrelated to school. It appeared that almost every girl in our class knew why we boys frequently referred to her as "Miss Etta Toes and Woes!"

During a unit on poetry, in recognition of Miss Marshall's attributes, several of us boys put together the following lines:

There was a nice teacher named Etta
Who bought herself a new sweatta
Three reasons she had
One to keep warm wasn't bad
But the other two were much betta.

When we completed our tribute to Miss Marshall, I was designated to turn our work in to her, but I could not bring myself to do it.

Sometime in February, when I arrived home from basketball practice and was eating supper, my father informed me that Mr. Bird had died, and he would like for me to call on Mrs. Bird and express our condolences.

When I had completed supper, I went to the abattoir and my father gave me a fresh pork shoulder and smoked ham to take to Mr. Bird's family. As I parked across the street from the Bird house, I recall seeing the kerosene lamp glowing through the front window. I knocked on the door and a lady opened the door and called my name to Mrs. Bird. Mrs. Bird approached and I expressed our family's condolences. She took my arm and walked me to manitarian attributes of my father. Finally, she led all the attendees in a prayer session in which she likened my fa-

I will always be indebted to these teachers and surrogate parents. Left to right, first row: M. Need, E. Stout, J. Frazer, V. Free, F. Cavanaugh, S. Williams, H. Miller, V. Forsyth, R. J. Warner, P. D. Wickline; second row: F. Marshall, O. Nybladh, M. Frank, F. Foust, J. Myers, A. Ballantyne, A. Hardy, D. Anderson, Z. Clark, R. Dean, E. J. Neff; third row: R. Seilhamer, C. Duckwall, R. Sultzbach, Z. Zerkle, B. F. Cranor, H. Bales, L. T. Blackburn, P. H. Boxwell, H. G. Patterson, C. D. Benner.

the end of the small living room where Mr. Bird rested in an open casket.

She then introduced me to all of the "wakers" in the dimly lighted room and proceeded to extol the many hu-

ther to one of Christ's disciples. I was moved to tears as she did this, and it would cast my father's image as my hero in bronze for all of his posterity.

Reality

Early in February, through our FFA instructor, I received an invitation from Dr. Ralph Stunkel, Chairman of the Animal Husbandry Department at The Ohio State University, to visit the university for a couple of days.

During the two days, I sat in on two or three classroom lectures, participated in laboratory sessions at a local meat packing plant, and worked with the University's meat judging team. In the late afternoon of the second day, during our closing discussion, Dr. Stunkel encouraged me, following graduation from high school, to attend Ohio State University and pursue a degree in Veterinary Medicine. He also told me that if I scored well on the Vet-Med entrance exam that I would be eligible for a scholarship.

About ten days later I drove to Columbus, completed the exam, and was immediately aware that I had not scored well on it. I had not taken advanced chemistry, Latin, or physics, which were pivotal to scoring well on the exam. I probably had not taken these subjects for two reasons: one, none of my older siblings had ever entertained the idea of pursuing a higher education; two, it was probably assumed that I, similar to my two older brothers Winston and Lowell, would pursue a career in the meat packing industry.

Our team traveled to Ironton, Ohio, on the Ohio River to win the final game of our basketball schedule. As was sometimes our practice after an away game, we stopped at a local restaurant for a celebratory meal. The euphoria of the win was dampened, however, when we witnessed an accident that later proved fatal to the pedestrian who was hit a few yards away from the window table where we were seated.

We completed our regular season with a record of twelve wins and three losses and shared the league title with Miamisburg. In the next two weeks, our team won all four of its games in the District Tournament at Dayton and qualified for the State Tournament at Columbus the following week.

At Columbus, our team won its first two games by identical scores of 47 to 38, and lost our semi-final game to Martin's Ferry (34 to 36) on two foul throws that were actually made after the final gun had sounded.

I apologized to Coach Blackburn after the loss because I had promised him three years earlier that we would win the State Tournament for him in our senior year. He told

Our FFA teams finished first in twelve state contests.

First Row—Edwin Wolf (treasurer), Leroy Donovan (secretary), Robert McClelland (president), Joe Eavey (vice president), Paul Watkins (watch dog).

Second Row—P. D. Wickline (adviser), Wendell Cultice (recreational leader), Kenneth Haines, Norwood Knick, Robert Harner, Junior Patton, Robert Short.

Third Row—Maynard Neff, Cecil Smalley, Eugene Randall, Robert Beason, Robert Turner, Eugene Devoe, William Robinette, James Strong, Dowell Thomas, Harley Hilderbrandt, Charles Thomas, Morris Storer.

Fourth Row—Winston Bahns, Don Huston, Henry Cultice, Charles Whittington, Dean Babb, Russell Randall, John Van Eaton (honorary recorder), Robert Ballard, Neil Jones, Joe Haines (social leader), Darrel Herdman, David Bickett, Paul Gultice, Paul Ford, Leon Haas, William Shaw, Vernon Smalley, James Whittington.

Not in Picture—James Armentrout, Carl Hetsel, Morris Shaw, Kenneth Coffman (reporter).

me that it was not necessary to apologize for our efforts and that he, the school, and the entire community were all extremely proud of what we boys had accomplished.

At our Basketball Banquet on the last day of March, I was proud to have my father and stepmother present when I received my monogram and it was announced that the coaches and sports reporters associated with the State Tournament had voted me to a First Team position on the All-Tourney Team.

Potential?

A few weeks after my visit to Ohio State University, Dr. James Ransom, a regular Saturday morning customer at the abattoir, invited me to visit him at Wilberforce University, an all-Negro school located about four miles north of our farm. I had spoken with Bishop Ransom a number of times and was aware that he was an admirer of my father. I also knew that he was the only remaining regent of the African Methodist Church serving on its Board of Regents. Bishop Ransom was tall, articulate, neatly attired, possessed a magnetic personality, and projected a fatherly image.

The walls of Bishop Ransom's office were replete with photographs of university graduates who, following many and varied struggles, had found their calling in life and were contributing to our country's success. He

I was required to wear my freshman "beanie" on campus.

was extremely proud of each one. During our discussion, Bishop Ransom commended me on my success in athletics and vocational agriculture in addition to my dedication to my father's business and spoke these words, "Butch, your father is an honorable and successful businessman, and you have several brothers who are capable of carrying on the business he has labored to establish; however, you have a higher calling—if not in medicine then perhaps in the ministry or in education. God is not unaware of your potential."

During the first semester of my senior year, I had received a few inquiries relative to participating in athletics at the college level. However, following the State Basketball Tournament, via correspondence, telephone, and personal visitations, I received nearly two dozen partial or full scholarship offers to attend colleges in Indiana, Kentucky, Ohio, Pennsylvania, and Virginia. After visiting a half dozen of these colleges, I accepted a delayed, athletic—football and basketball—full scholarship at the University of Dayton (Ohio). That meant that I would

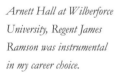

Arnett Hall at Wilberforce University, Regent James Ramson was instrumental in my career choice.

work for a year and enter the university in the fall of 1942. This approach afforded me an opportunity to establish a savings account and explore additional career opportunities. It was also possible that I opted for this delayed entry approach because I was not confident that I could cope successfully with college-level work.

HEAVEN, HOMINY, HISTORY, AND HIGHER Learning

This entry is third-person in nature since it was passed down from my father to my brother Winston and a few years later to me

It appeared that the ghost scare that my older brothers had perpetrated on Gus Ewing and his chittlin' garden cart sometime earlier had nearly worked a hardship upon a Baptist church located near the standpipe in the East End.

According to Booker Bass, a long-time and dependable utility man in the slaughtering room, those chittlins' had been promised to Deacon Abraham Lincoln Cunningham at the church and would constitute the main entrée at their pending church supper. They were very fortunate, according to Booker, that there were three other slaughterhouses near the edge of town, and the church was spared a significant loss of revenue by the donation of a similar garden-cart load from one of the other slaughterhouses.

According to Booker, who was a member of the church, it was constructed a few years before the Great Depression and enjoyed modern facilities including in-door jakes and old-fashioned moral values. According to my brother Winston, Booker also told my father that the foyer and sanctuary always appeared to be in competition with the basement which housed the kitchen, narthex, and utility rooms. Some members of the congregation, Booker said, thought it might be because they seemed to frequently get new parsons upstairs, but the same lady, Kassie "Casserole" Newsome, whose sister-in-law Newie, had been our caretaker following our mother's death, had been in charge of the basement ever since the suffragettes were trying to get the vote and Carry Nation was "takin a hammer" to all the glass bottles behind the bars in almost every city in the country.

When any individuals (s) regardless of title, stepped off the last tread of the basement stairs, they were in the

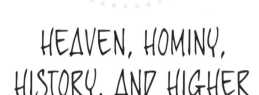

18-years of age, 6 feet tall, and 185 pounds.

eminent domain of Kassie "Casserole" Newsome. Here, at their own risk, they were welcome to challenge her on any aspect of life, love, learnin', or life hereafter and that included any newly appointed parson, fresh out of seminary.

When Ross Cowan, a church elder and owner of a very successful fruit and vegetable farm suggested to Kassie that those suffragettes ought to keep their powdered noses out of politics, she responded, "Now, you listen up, Elder. If your wife is good enough to be your baby's mother, then she's good enough to vote with you."

It just seemed, as Newie related the church's business to my father, that every time a new parson arrived he would get upset because the members of the congregation seemed to be more interested in Kassie's heavenly chittlin' casseroles than in his heavenly, long-winded sermons.

Newie said that several former Reverends—Spriggs, Crumley, Mills, and Walker—had tried to talk with Kassie about how she might also be telling the children something that the Almighty might not approve of. She would be quick, Newie also said, to respond with the following: "Parson, you take care of passin' the plate upstairs, and I'll take care of passin' the platter downstairs."

Deacon A. L. Cunningham, who held a catalogue divinity degree, was only prohibited from serving communion, but otherwise could serve any other function of the church including preaching. His favorite activity was teaching Sunday school to the children in the combined utility-pantry room in the basement. He knew that with every new class, the children would be in awe and ask, "Are you really related to President Lincoln?" "With my name, why wouldn't I be?" he'd reply. Then he would enter into dialogue about his famous ancestors. He would tell the children that his father told him that his grandfather was one of the slaves that General Zachary Taylor brought to Washington, D.C. when he was elected president in 1849. Because he wasn't allowed to have slaves then, he hid all of them in the attic. A year later, when President Taylor died, President Fillmore found them in the attic and made them free. He said President Fillmore gave him a job in the president's livery barn where he fed and watered the horses and cleaned the horse apples out of the stables. He said his grandfather worked the same job while Mr. Pierce and Mr. Buck'nan were in office, but when Lincoln was elected he got to saddle and harness the horses and sometimes drive Mrs. Lincoln and her boys shoppin'. Finally, President Lincoln even allowed his grandpa and father to borrow his name. So his grandpa passed it right along to him.

On Sunday morning while Deacon A. L. Cunningham was teaching in the utility pantry room, Kassie Newsome was simultaneously teaching another group which gathered around a work table with a rack of kitchen utensils overhead, about her famous ancestors. According to Kassie, her mother had told her that she had been named after her grandmother who had worked in the White House kitchen while several United States Presidents were living there, including Abraham Lincoln. Any reference to the obedience of Abraham in the bible would be apt to cause her to turn several pages of her grandma's historical contribution to our nation.

President Buck'an wasn't married and his pretty niece, Harriet, used to come into the kitchen where she would help them plan for a special dinner for some king or queen who was coming from the other side of the ocean for a visit. And she was workin' there when Abraham Lincoln was president and his wife, Mary, was telling them what to cook and how to serve it. Kassie said that Mrs. Lincoln would sometimes apologize for the mischief that her sons got into. Like the time when they drove their goats Nanny and Nanko right through the kitchen when they was cookin' one of those special dinners. President Lincoln, she said, always laughed when the kids got into trouble and seldom punished them. Kassie said her grandma thought Mrs. Lincoln spent too much money on new clothes, especially gloves, from New York, when her husband's soldiers were fightin', hungry for hominy, and nearly naked as jay birds.

"Well, that one son, Tad, was full of ginger and vinegar and was real smart, too. One time his folks received a big Tom turkey for their Thanksgiving dinner. Ted played with that "yardbird" for a couple of days. When he found out his pet was going to be cooked right in our kitchen, he went as fast he could go to his daddy. Before long he come running back carrying a piece of paper his daddy done wrote yellin' 'Tom's got a pardon; he's free to play with me.'"

She said her grandma told her that President Andrew Johnson had a lot of trouble when he lived there because he couldn't read very well and seemed to drink a lot of Barley Corn between his meals. One time, when her grandma was trying to get rid of the mice in the kitchen, he started feeding them flour and water by the fireplace in his bedroom at night. And, sure enough, them mice started making babies faster than the tomcats in the kitchen could catch them.

Finally, there was General Grant's wife Julia, who always walked like a crab and talked to me when she was facing somebody else or looking out the window. It took me over a year to tell that she was very cross-eyed and had been looking right at me all the time.

Kassie was never inclined to think very highly of those professors at the college four miles east of the city. She believed they just strutted around the college in three-piece suits like peacocks, carrying genuine, calf-skin satchels, wearing a lot of gold—tie tacks, cufflinks, and watch fobs—trying to make folks believe that they knew everything there was to know in the world. If that was not bad enough, she went on, some of them even tried to claim that they were the first ones to think of or to discover whatever it was they were talkin' about.

Kassie's kitchen, where the term "stovin'" was frequently employed to mean cookin', was a learning laboratory for all who labored there, especially young ladies from the nearby college who, according to her, might be spending too much time studying home economics, instead of stovin'. She was disappointed that more than a few of these young ladies did not know how to burn the pin feathers off a chicken, make red-eye gravy, or bake any type of chittlin' casserole. She would sometimes attempt to advance a young lady's love for cookin' knowledge with these words, "Now, listen up, honey, good looks might get you a man, but good stovin' will keep him from rovin'."

Another time a young lady was telling Kassie about a novel she had recently read about romance. When she had finished, Kassie responded, "Listen up, honey, you can buy all them dime novels at Gallager's Drug, read 'em, get gussied up, and an' go for his heart. It ain't true, honey; get to his stomach and his head and his heart will both find you."

Finally she professed, "If you don't want your man to still have an eye for other women, honey, then you better know how to make red-eye gravy that will keep him home." Kassie's black bean, noodle, rice, and potato chittlin' casseroles were well-known in every corner of Greene County. In fact, they became so popular that she hit upon the idea of sponsoring a county-wide Common Casserole Chittlin' Supper at her church in November and February every winter. This supper would also feature a chittlin' walk which was open only to single ladies in the participating churches. While Kassie would tell people that the chittlin' walk was intended to gain more disciples for Christ, it seemed to a few folks that it might be aimed more at getting young ladies and gentlemen into matrimony.

The last person to attempt to invade Kassie's territory was Reverend Lorenzo Robeson, who was wearing a pink coat, white pants, white shoes, and a yellow hat with a pink feather tucked into the band. When he arrived at the church for his ministry interview by the trustees, he was driving a 1930 Model A Ford sedan with white sidewall tires, a fifty-dollar radio, and a five dollar rearview mirror fastened under the dashboard on the passenger side. Newie said her sister-in-law was sure he would soon be coming down to the kitchen to impress her with all that heavenly learning he had received at the seminary and how to teach kids and operate her kitchen.

When Parson Robeson entered Kassie's kitchen a few days after his arrival, he sat down at a small table, opened his bible, and invited Cassie to join him. She listened for a long time, and then interrupted him. "Parson, I'm going to save you some time. I understand that you think you know everything there is to know about life, learning, love, and the life hereafter, but let me tell you that I'm old enough to be your mother and I know more about what you're talkin about than you do. In fact, Parson, I know it all from the erection to the resurrection. Now, Parson, I'm going to fetch you a piece of my lattice apple pie from the ice box and pour you a cup of my egg-shell coffee from the pot on the back of the stove. Then, when you finish, you can get back to the sanctuary upstairs and make sure those folks don't fall off the Holy Wagon on their way to the Pearly Gates, Parson!"

THIRTY Days

During the final week of April, a local man, Rolland Conners, who had just received his draft induction notice to report for his physical examination, attempted to commit suicide in the woods just east of our house. After he had shot himself and fallen backward into a bed of hot coals, he walked nearly a half-mile to our front porch. When we heard his cries for assistance, my father and I got out of bed, gave him a cup of cool water, and called the sheriff's department. Several weeks later we learned that he had survived his self-inflicted trauma, and he had been institutionalized at a mental hospital located in the central area of the state.

The final four weeks of my senior year were a whirlwind of athletic, social and graduation activities. Not the least of these was our annual Miami Valley League Track Meet during the third week in May. Our track team had won the league title in 1939 and 1940, but we finished a few points behind Greenville in 1941. I climaxed my scholastic career in sports by finishing second in all four events in which I competed. In a measure, I felt I had let my team down. If I had finished first in three of them, our team would have repeated as champions.

I escorted Jane to our Gingham Formal the second week of May. We had shared numerous social events for over a year, and I had grown extremely fond of her. Following the dance, about a dozen couples, mostly the Worry Warts "gang" exchanged our formal attire for casual "duds" and enjoyed a sunrise breakfast at Miss Wilton's home. As anticipated, I was more than a little anxious before the event, but was soon comfortable in her presence since I was in the company of my classmates.

A few days before my birthday, at our school's Annual Recognition Banquet, the guests were reminded that during our class' four-year scholastic career, our athletic teams—football, basketball, and track—had competed for a total of twelve league championships and had won outright, or co-won, eight titles.

Following the banquet, even though I had received half a dozen individual awards in vocational agriculture and athletics, I became aware that I had not distinguished myself in a single academic subject.

The boys and girls in our school's graduation classes had traditionally worn blue suits and white dresses. How-

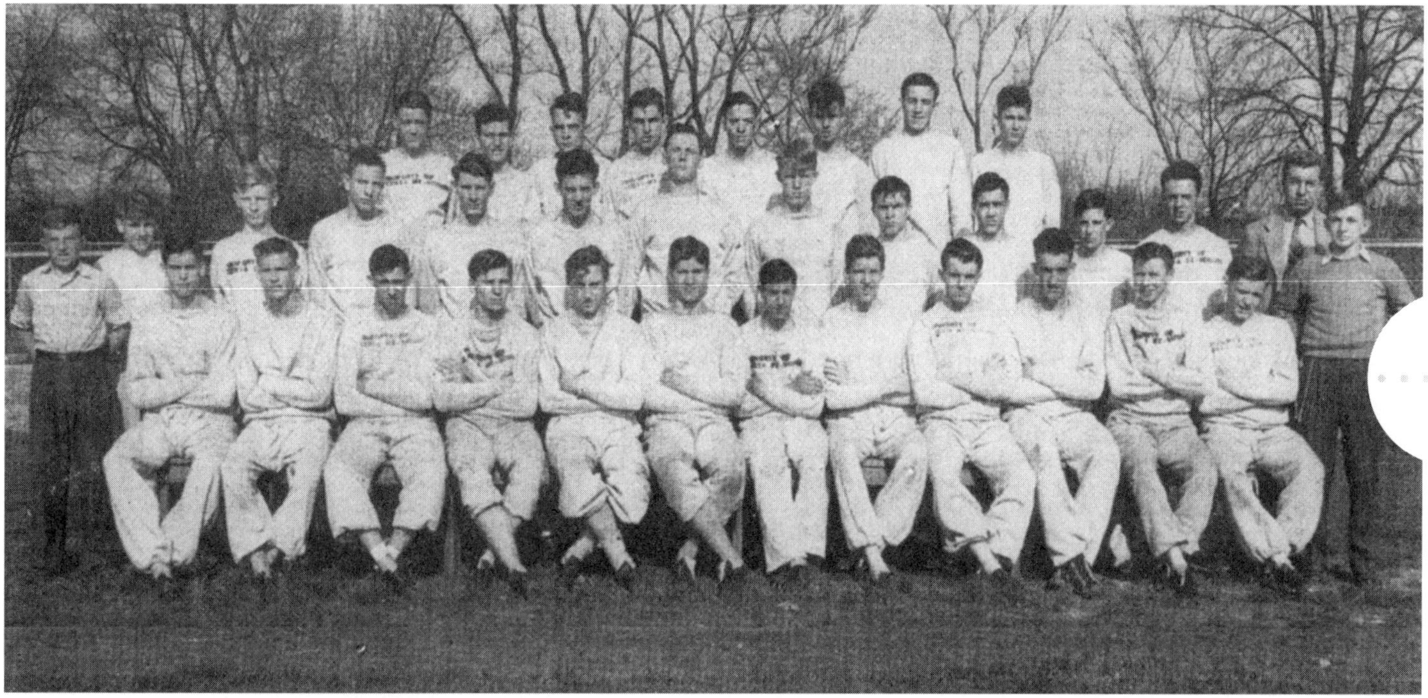

We were four points short of winning our third consecutive Miami Valley League Track Title.

TRACK RESULTS 1941

April 21
Xenia 50 Oakwood 68 Here

April 25
Xenia 90 Fairmont 19 There

April 29
Xenia 74 Wilmington 35 There

May 2
M. V. L. Track Meet, night Here
Xenia finished in second place

May 9-10
Miami Relays at Oxford

May 16-17
South Western District Meet at Springfield

May 23-24
State Meet at Columbus

Track Team of 1941

First Row—Robert Downing (assistant manager), Robert Winter, Mathew Turner, Joe Eavey, Harold Willett, Ray Snyder, David Adair, Clifford Bower, Rhey Feeley, Tom Adair, Allan Miller, Wilfred Jones, Leroy Donovan, Robert Geyer (manager).

Second Row—Robert Turner, Thomas Whittington, Carlton Smith, William Heather, Roger Thomas, Jack Wilson, Wendell Cultice, Jim Jones, Schuyler McClellan, Russell Duerstine, Robert Landaker, Coach Paul Boxwell.

Third Row—Everett Sheets, Harold Smith, Charles Kemp, Vernon Thomas, Paul Ford, Kenneth Boxwell, Ralph Bullock, Kenneth White.

ever, our class, the largest to date to graduate from the school, sought to wear caps and gowns. When I, and several classmates, approached our Principal, Mr. Benner, in early April, about changing this tradition, he told us that we would need a majority of our classmates to approve the request. I was asked to chair the polling committee for the change, and we received a simple majority approval. However, when we reported the results to Mr. Benner, he told us that we needed a two-thirds majority.

At commencement, several of us expressed our "silent outrage" at the principal's simple/two-thirds shift. The boys on the committee wore Palm Beach suits and the girls wore white dresses with vertical colored stripes on the front. When Mr. Benner handed me my diploma, he smiled broadly and vigorously shook my hand. I guess he was thinking about two years ago, when he said to me, "Well, Butch, what do you think you'll be when you graduate, besides unemployed and twenty-two years of age?"

POST HIGH School

A few days after commencement, enlightened and encouraged by Bishop Ransom, I realized that I was dubious about attending college for fear that I would be unable to cope academically. Therefore, I enrolled in several extension courses at the University of Kansas and completed them within a few months.

Toward the end of June, my father told me that several church elders would like to meet with me. When I asked him what it was that they wished to talk about, he said that he did not know. Following the meeting with the elders, my father asked me what had taken place. I told him that they wanted me to accept a church-sponsored scholarship at a seminary in Illinois and become a Methodist minister. "Well," my father asked, "what did you tell them?" I thanked them for the opportunity and told them I had no more desire to become a Methodist minister than I did to become a big-city gangster." While my father respected my decision, he was not remotely pleased with the analogy I used in my response.

When my father had asked me in early May what I would like for a graduation gift, I told him I would like to drive to Evansville, Indiana, to visit Bobbie Knight. I had corresponded with her several times during high school and she encouraged me to visit in July.

Although Bobbie was working at her summer banking job during the day, we and several of her friends spent some memorable evenings visiting the Ohio River Locks, attending baseball games, visiting amusement parks, etc.

On the third morning of my visit, after Bobbie had gone to work, her mother tapped softly on my bedroom door and entered under the pretense of retrieving the iron and ironing board from the closet. I immediately recalled how long it had taken for me to help Miss Wilton find my Christmas gift over a year ago.

When I returned home, I told my father that we had enjoyed our visit a great deal, and Bobbie's mother seemed to enjoy my visit, too.

During the remainder of the summer, I attended an umpire's training session in Cincinnati and also interviewed with three large meatpacking companies relative to a career choice.

On August 1st, following prolonged labor and a difficult delivery, my sister Rachel became a mother for the first time when my niece, Linda Lou Ary, was born. The complications from the difficult birth caused my sister's death on the 22nd of August. I had already experienced the loss of step and half-siblings, but the date of the death of my first, full sibling would be cast in stone.

In October, the Almighty granted Grandpa Jim his long-sought request. Shortly after he had enjoyed his last glass of dandelion wine, finished his last pipe-full of Prince Albert smoking tobacco, and placed his false teeth in a glass of soda water, he retired to his bed and his eternal rest.

LOST Innocence

On June 2nd, one of my boyhood heroes, Lou Gehrig, the New York Yankee's first baseman, died at the age of thirty-seven. A few months later, the Yankees defeated the Brooklyn Dodgers in the World Series.

On June 22nd, Germany invaded the Soviet Union and quickly made massive inroads towards the country's major cities.

On October 30th, a German submarine sank the U. S. destroyer *Reuben James*, and the threat of our country going to war appeared to be on the horizon. When our father announced at our Thanksgiving family gathering that our stepmother was expecting a baby in early May, my sister Evelyn seemed to profile the community's dilemma of our large family with these words, "Dad, you are still confusing all of the people in the county. They can't figure out whether we are good Catholics or careless Protestants."

On the afternoon of December 7th, I was enjoying the movie *Buck Privates,* starring Abbot and Costello when the screen went black. The voice of John Daly, a leading national newscaster, came over the intercom with the news that the Japanese had launched a surprise attack on Pearl Harbor in Hawaii. Later in the day, I learned that the battleships *Arizona*, *California*, *Oklahoma*, and *Utah* had been sunk and several others heavily damaged. I also learned that three thousand Americans had been killed, and that Japan had also attacked the Philippines, Wake Island, and Guam.

The following day I listened attentively as President Roosevelt declared war upon Japan. In these few short hours, I concluded that I had lost my boyhood innocence and would be standing in the ranks of my fellow countrymen as Coach Blackburn had prophesied more than two years ago.

Brother Henry visited with me at Camp Lee, Virginia, shortly before we were sent to Europe.

A Covenant with God

The period between the Japanese attack on Pearl Harbor and my entry at the university represented an uneasy period of my young life. During this period, my sense of patriotism, similar to that of nearly all my friends, was at a feverish pitch. I attempted, unsuccessfully, to enlist in the Army, Navy, Marine Corps, and Coast Guard. In each case, I was denied entry because I was unable to pass the physical exam due to high blood pressure.

Early in my first semester at the university, while participating in football, I requested permission to join the ROTC-Reserve Officers' Training Corps. Shortly after applying for ROTC status, I was enrolled in the program without having to have taken a physical exam. A few months later, the ROTC program was given a quota to meet. I and several other members of the ROTC program had our names drawn from the corps' roster, and I reported to the reception center at Columbus, Ohio.

Following nearly two months at the reception center, I traveled by train to a military camp located near Richmond, Virginia. Here I completed my basic training, participated in and officiated athletics, and served over a year as a noncommissioned officer. During my basic training and cadre service, I set a new regimental obstacle course record, was awarded a position on the camp's all-star basketball team, and was a utility infielder on the baseball team.

In the spring of 1944, our baseball team, under the capable management of foul-mouthed, tobacco- chewing Luke Appling of the Chicago White Sox, played a Sunday double-header against the Washington Senators at College Park, Maryland. I was baffled by the knuckle balls of Johnny Niggling and Dutch Leonard. While riding back to camp on the bus, Luke put my big-league baseball ambitions into perspective with the following, cogent remark, "Whitey, you can run like a rabbit, field like a cat, and throw like an arrow, but you couldn't knock a sick whore off of a piss pot with a baseball bat." So much for my father's promised early retirement!

I was accepted into the Reserve Officers' Training Corps—ROTC—in September of 1942.

In August, 1944, our unit was relocated to Camp Kilmer, New Jersey, and we were equipped to depart for an unknown destination. Before the baseball season had ended, I was on "G" deck of the *Aquitania*, a British passenger ship that had been converted to a troop transport. After nearly three days on the Atlantic, I was informed somewhat jokingly by the ship's steward that if we were struck by a torpedo from a German U-boat, it would probably pass through this area of the ship. With a touch of salty humor, he implied we were lucky to be on "G" deck since "we wouldn't have to look for a lifeboat."

I remember asking the steward if this ship, the *Aquitania*, was a sister ship to the *Lusitania*, and he said that it was. Well, I guessed, I was paying attention in history class when our teacher showed us photographs of the *Lusitania's* sliding beneath the waves during World War I after it had been torpedoed by a German U-boat.

Later that day, while reclining on my bulkhead bunk, I made a covenant with God. I thanked him for all of the care-giving people and the good times in my life. I promised God that if he would safely steer me through this crisis in my life, that I would spend my short time on earth serving other people, especially youth.

Post Script

At this writing, more than three-score years have passed since my covenant with God to spare my life during two years of military service in war-torn Europe. To this day, I remain eternally grateful for his guardianship.

With the sands of Normandy Beach in my boots and the ghastly images of the Holocaust lingering in my mind, I returned to America in the spring of 1946 and entered Bowling Green State University (Ohio) on an athletic scholarship, pursuing a degree in public education.

During my sophomore year, I was introduced to meaningful study skills and the cultural arts by the most beautiful coed on campus—Janet Kiplinger. During our senior year, I wooed and won her hand in marriage. She became the mother of our three children—William Walter, Jennifer Gayle, and Curtice Kiplinger—and nurtured them to adulthood. Today they are worthy and productive citizens in the image of her guidance. Mere words are wanting to express my gratitude for her contribution to their lives. Following graduation, I began a forty-four-year career in public education—serving in Michigan, New York, Alaska, and Connecticut as a teacher, athletic coach, and administrator.

In the classroom, in the image of my mother and childhood teachers, I attempted to create and maintain a

My father and Sgt. Winston at the farm, January 1945.

"lived-in, learned-in, and loved-in" environment, and the children traditionally thrived on this positive relationship.

As an administrator, in the image of my father, I attempted to administer discipline affectionately by employing a 5-F approach: firm, forthright, fair, friendly, and when necessary, flexible.

Concurrently, in every position, I served on local, state, and national committees which focused on the welfare of the cornerstone of America—youth. I remain ever grateful that in some small way I was afforded an opportunity to guide, individually and collectively, their futures.

My father departed this life a year after I began my teaching career. I would like him to know that the small slaughterhouse he built over three-quarters of a century ago, and where much of my character formation took place at his elbow, is currently a large pork processing plant for a chain of restaurants that stretches from coast to coast—Bob Evans. "Dad, I daily thank you for your parental mentoring and hopefully, I have perpetuated your work ethic during my time on earth."

Further, I grope for adjectives to convey my appreciation to Rebecca Massey Cultice. For more than a quarter century, she has been my love, my wife, and my life. Professionally in a somewhat biased opinion, education in America has never known a more dedicated public servant.

In closing, as I approach my ninety-second year, I would like it known to all concerned, especially to the Almighty, that I did not close the door on my dedication to youth at sixty-five and then complain that I could not serve. No! I have served more than two and a half decades beyond that mark. With his providential care and guidance, I am looking forward to another decade of service in support of our covenant.

Left page: Henry, Wendell, Winston, & Lowell Cultice, spring of 1946.
Right page: Sgt. Wendell W. Cultice, Paris, France, 1946.

Glossary

B

bag—to shoot and kill an animal

Barley Corn—whiskey

barrow—castrated pig

blind pig—a place that sells intoxicants illegally

bloomer bootleg—an illegal whiskey concealed in a lady's bloomers

boar batteries—hog testicles

Boston butt—upper section of pork shoulder

bull burgers—hamburgers

bullin'—cow in heat

C

cackle berries—chicken eggs

canned gas—canned beans

cat's meow—to express approval

chatterbox—radio

chip-off-the-old-block—to display the characteristics of a parent

chitterlings (chittlin's)—hog intestines

Chittlin' walk—similar to a cake walk

chompers—teeth

circle jerk—several individuals masturbating simultaneously

cracklings—rendered pork fat and skin

cross bar hotel—local jail

cuffin' his carrot—masturbating

cut-a-cheese—flatulence

D

date bait—a very attractive girl

duds—clothing

E

eyes open—eggs cooked "sunny side up"

F

fly swatter soup—oxtail soup

force meat—any type of stuffed meat

fries—animal testicles

gauntlet—a double file of men facing each other and armed with clubs or other weapons with which to strike at an individual who is made to run between them

ginger & vinegar—possessed of energy and mischief

goose grease—hair oil

grain-of-salt—not to be taken seriously

Jimmy Henderson, riding; my three half-brothers, left to right: Russell, Roger, & Marlin.

G

gams—female legs

grass widow—husband not at home

ground hog—pork sausage

H

hairless dogs—wieners

high pockets—hog testicles

hiney fodder—toilet paper

homemade hair tonic—bootleg whiskey

hoodwink—to fool an individual

hoofer—an accomplished dancer

Hoosier cabinet—large kitchen cabinet manufactured in Indiana

Hoover buggy—an automobile drawn by a horse

horse apples—horse manure

horse sense—common sense

hot patootie—girl friend

hackleback—durable fabric of cotton, linen, or both

I

Indian bread—cornbread containing ground cracklings

J

jake—outhouse/toilet

jar vegetables—home-canned vegetables

jerk—the art of milking a cow

K

knacker—a buyer of worn-out, domestic animals

L

lickers—animal tongues

lights—animal lungs

loud food—beans, sauerkraut, etc.—causing flatulence

M

maws—hog stomachs

melts—animal pancreases

moniker—nickname

N

New York shoulder—whole pork shoulder

nature's wind—flatulence

O

offal—interior animal organs

oomph—attractive female body

P

packin'-her'puddin'—sexual intercourse

panhaus—cooked meat scraps (scrapple)

panther piss—after shave lotion

patted-in-the-face-with-a-spade—to be buried
perspiring puppies—wieners
pisser stew—kidney stew
pita—acronym for pain-in-the-ass
poontangin'—sexual intercourse

Q

queers—homosexuals
quinsy—sore throat

R

rabbit food—any leaf vegetable
rattlers—pork neck bones
redeye gravy—gravy made from smoked ham grease
Reuben—slang for a person who doesn't belong
Ripple—port wine
roast butt—roasted pork shoulder
Rocky Mountain oysters—animal testicles
rot gut—homemade whiskey

S

sauce—homemade whiskey
shaman—one who uses magic to cure the sick
shingles—toasted bread with jam or jelly
shit-on-a-shingle—dried beef gravy on toast
shuckin'-his-nubbin—the act of masturbating
slats—pork spare ribs
sliced butt—sliced pork shoulder
slick chick—very attractive female
S.L.O.P.—acronymn for some leftover pieces
slunk—unborn calf
slut—female dog
smart food—animal brains
smashed spuds—mashed potatoes
sod widow—husband dead
soppin's—any type of gravy
sow belly—fresh pork side meat
squirrel fever—a crush on a person
sticky stuff—syrup
strong meat—animal offal meat
stovin'—cooking and baking
suds—shaving cream
Sweet Lucie—port wine
swishers—ox tails
sugar breads—sweetbreads (thymus glands)
sundown sentence—a judicial order to be out of a given area by sundown

T

tad—a short period of time

tally whacker—penis

tankage—dried animal residue

T.B.—tired butt

tendergroin—beef or lamb testicles

tin lizzie—Model T Ford

three-cornered pants—diapers

thunder mug—portable toilet container

trotters—pig feet

Y

yard bird—chicken, duck, goose, guinea, turkey, etc.

In the spirit of Sadie Hawkins Week, I'm dressed as Daisy Mae's mother.

About the Author

In fulfilling a covenant he made with the Almighty on his way to war-torn Europe in 1944, Wendell W. Cultice has spent his adult life working with the cornerstone of America—youth. He spent more than five decades as a teacher and administrator in the Midwest and on both coasts. He is the author of more than a half-dozen books, and currently reads to preschoolers several times a week. A father of three and grandfather of three, he lives with his wife, Rebecca, in historic Greene County, Ohio.

Wendell W. Cultice